TRADITIONS OF VICTORIAN
WOMEN'S AUTOBIOGRAPHY

VICTORIAN LITERATURE AND CULTURE SERIES

Karen Chase, Jerome J. McGann, *and* Herbert Tucker, *Editors*

TRADITIONS OF VICTORIAN WOMEN'S AUTOBIOGRAPHY

The Poetics and Politics
of Life Writing

Linda H. Peterson

UNIVERSITY PRESS OF VIRGINIA
Charlottesville and London

The University Press of Virginia
© 1999 by the Rector and Visitors of the University of Virginia
All rights reserved
Printed in the United States of America

First published 1999

∞ The paper used in this publication meets the minimum requirements of the American National Standard for Information Sciences—Permanence of Paper for Printed Library Materials, ANSI Z39.48-1984.

Library of Congress Cataloging-in-Publication Data
    Peterson, Linda H.
        Traditions of Victorian women's autobiography : the poetics and politics of life writing / Linda H. Peterson.
            p.   cm. — (Victorian literature and culture series)
        Includes bibliographical references and index.
    ISBN 0-8139-1883-9 (cloth : alk. paper)
        1. English prose literature—Women authors—History and criticism. 2. Great Britain—History—Victoria, 1837–1901—Biography—History and criticism.   3. English prose literature—19th century—History and criticism.   4. Women and literature—Great Britain—History—19th century.   5. Autobiography—Political aspects—Great Britain. 6. Autobiography—Women authors.   I. Title.   II. Series.
    PR788.W65P47   1999
    828'.80809492072—dc21   99-19832
                                                                    CIP

For my mother and father

Contents

Preface

THIS STUDY OF Victorian women's life writing began with a question posed by a friend and colleague in the history department at Yale University. To my lament that Victorian women did not publish the classic, hermeneutic autobiographies that flourished among their male counterparts, he responded: What kind of autobiography *did* they write? Many kinds, as it turns out.

Victorian women's autobiography emerged at a point when the field of life writing was especially rich. Spiritual autobiography had consolidated itself as a form and was developing interesting variations in the heroic memoirs of pioneering missionary women and in probing intellectual analyses of Nonconformists, Anglicans, agnostics, and other religious thinkers. The *chroniques scandaleuses* of the eighteenth century were quietly disappearing or being transformed into the respectable artist's life (what William H. Epstein has called "life-course") of the professional woman.[1] The domestic memoir, a Victorian variation on the family histories of the seventeenth and early eighteenth centuries, flourished in a culture that celebrated the joys of home, family, and private life. Perhaps most important, Victorian women writers were experimenting with these forms in various combinations and permutations.

In recognition of such wide-ranging possibilities, I have titled this book *traditions* of women's autobiography, and in the first chapter I delineate the primary generic traditions as they were interpreted and reconstructed by nineteenth-century editors, critics, and readers. The word *traditions* is also meant to acknowledge the scholarly work of predecessors who have labored to discover, resuscitate, and analyze women's life writing from all periods, including Mary G. Mason in "The Other Voice" (1980), Estelle C. Jelinek in *The Tradition of Women's Autobiography* (1986), Sidonie Smith in *A Poetics of Women's Autobiography* (1987), Carolyn Heilbrun in *Writing a Woman's Life* (1988), and many others whose contributions are cited in the notes. If my choice of the plural *traditions* indicates a different perspective—in that I see not a singular, unified women's tradition but diverse, multiple possibilities available to Victorian autobiographers—I nonetheless acknowledge my debt to their groundbreaking scholarship.

My subtitle includes the more recent term *life writing,* in part to acknowledge the diversity of forms in the nineteenth century, in part to register the difficulty of writing solely about *autobiography,* even when autobiographies—professedly truthful records of a life, composed as single, retrospective works and told from a consistent temporal point of view—are my emphasis. As I have learned, women's auto/biography is often a hybrid genre, a combination of first-person narrative and editorial amplification or excision, and it makes better sense to explore the implications of this hybridity than to attempt generic divisions between self-authored and biographical accounts. Victorian women self-consciously drew on many genres of life writing—biography, diary, family history, domestic memoir, *Bildungsroman, Künstlerroman,* as well as classic spiritual autobiography—as they represented their experiences. The phrase "specular autobiography," used by Janice Carlisle to describe life writing that sees, comprehends, even creates the self by mirroring (often with distortions) the life of another, might be applied to virtually all the texts I discuss in this book.[2]

Poetics and *politics* are words plural in form but used with singular verbs. I certainly mean them to register a multiplicity of approaches to, intentions about, and public purposes for women's life writing. Their interconnection will, I trust, become clear as I tease out the relevance of the form(s) in which an individual woman chose to record her life and the political assumptions that underlay, sometimes explicitly motivated, her choice. Victorian women may have written about their private lives—their spiritual crises, their intellectual development, their domestic arrangements, their familial relations—but their accounts are very much public, too. In their self-conscious engagement with different forms and conventions of life writing, they enter important Victorian debates about the condition of women's lives—and much more.

Acknowledgments

IT GIVES ME GREAT pleasure to acknowledge the intellectual friendships and institutional occasions that have encouraged the writing of this book. In its early stages my colleagues in two NEH Institutes at the Yale Center for British Art—Duncan Robinson, Frank Turner, George Landow, Susan Casteras, Antony Wohl, and Patrick Brantlinger—and participants in the seminars listened to lectures that have become chapters I, II, and V; they offered suggestions for revision, added texts for consideration, even provided titles for parts of this work. In many important ways, these Institutes, the first held in 1989, the second in 1991, represent the "origins" of this book.

I am grateful to colleagues at home and afar who, over the years, have sustained my work by reading chapters, responding to conference papers, and corresponding (in e-mail and old-fashioned letters) about its arguments: Isobel Armstrong, Mary Ellen Gibson, Andrea Horner, Linda Hughes, Elisabeth Jay, Annabel Patterson, Joanne Shattock, Pat Spacks, Dale Trela, and Ruth Yeazell. My alphabetical listing of their names should not efface their individual acts of intellectual generosity.

Several major conferences, two on autobiography, one on women's poetry, and two on Margaret Oliphant, have sharpened the focus of my work and clarified its arguments. The first, organized by Robert Folkenflik at the University of California, Irvine, in 1991, produced an early version of chapter I; a second, organized by Gerhard Joseph and Anne Humpherys at the CUNY Graduate Center in 1993, forced its revision. The International Conference on Women's Poetry at Birkbeck College, University of London, in 1994, organized by Isobel Armstrong, Virginia Blain, and Laurel Brake, started my thinking about *Aurora Leigh* and its relation to auto/biographies of nineteenth-century poetesses, now reflected in chapter IV. Centenary conferences on Margaret Oliphant organized by Dale Trela at Roosevelt University, Chicago, and Elisabeth Jay at Westminster College, Oxford, in 1997, provided occasions for presenting parts of chapter V. I am grateful to these scholars who took time to organize conferences and to the publishers who subsequently brought out collections that included my work:

Stanford University Press for permission to use an expanded and revised version of "Institutionalizing Women's Autobiography," included in *The Culture of Autobiography* (1993), edited by Robert Folkenflik.

Macmillan Publishing Company for permission to use an expanded and revised version of "Rewriting *A History of the Lyre:* Letitia Landon, Elizabeth Barrett Browning, and the (Re)Construction of the Nineteenth-Century Woman Poet," included in *Women's Poetry, Nineteenth Century to the Present* (1998), edited by Isobel Armstrong and Virginia Blain.

Women's Writing for permission to use a version of "Margaret Oliphant's *Autobiography* as Professional Artist's Life," published in a special issue (1999) on Margaret Oliphant.

Institutions that have supported the writing of this book include the National Endowment for the Humanities with a fellowship in 1989–90; Yale University with sabbatical leaves in 1991 and 1997–98; and the following libraries and archives: Beinecke Rare Book and Manuscript Library, Sterling Memorial Library, the Rare Book and Reference Libraries of the Yale Center for British Art, and the Divinity School Library of Yale University; the British Library; the National Library of Scotland; the Harry Ransom Research Center and Library of the University of Texas, Austin; the University of Nottingham Library; the Public Record Offices of Cheshire and Shropshire, England; and the many libraries that support scholarly research through interlibrary loan. The timely interventions of librarians at these institutions—Margaret Powell and Susanne Roberts at Sterling, Anne-Marie Logan and Lori Misura at the British Art Center, and Vincent Giroud at Beinecke—deserve special mention, as does a generous but anonymous librarian who led me through the stacks of the British Library in search of a cache of nineteenth-century women's memoirs.

Finally, and foremost, my thanks to Fred Strebeigh, the best of friends and intellectual companions.

I

On the Victorian "Origins" of Women's Autobiography: Reconstructing the Traditions

WHAT IS WOMEN'S autobiography, and when did women autobiographers first become conscious of their life writing as a tradition? To write of the "origins" or of "traditions" of women's autobiography in England is to create, perhaps inevitably, a past that never was. We do not know what Englishwoman produced the first autobiography; what women's texts we have lost from the mid–seventeenth century, that moment which seems to mark the beginning of an unbroken English autobiographical tradition; or what texts we have lost—or lost sight of—from centuries before and after the seventeenth. Despite these lacunae, feminist scholarship since 1980 has attempted to reconstruct a tradition of women's autobiography. Beginning with Mary G. Mason's "Other Voice" (1980) and continuing with Estelle C. Jelinek's *Tradition of Women's Autobiography* (1986), Sidonie Smith's *Poetics of Women's Autobiography* (1987), Carolyn G. Heilbrun's *Writing a Woman's Life* (1988), and Leigh Gilmore's *Autobiographics: A Feminist Theory of Women's Self-Representation* (1994), the agenda has been to (re)discover a tradition of women's own.[1]

That agenda has included more specific goals: the revival of lost or forgotten women's texts, the posing of literary questions about gender and genre, the posing of more general questions about women's self-representation, whether it has always been different from men's or whether women's writings show certain fundamental, "human" patterns of development. This study shares these goals, but its starting point differs, as does its argument. As versions of literary history, critical studies of the 1980s and early 1990s made a common assumption: that women's autobiography has been, from its origins, a separate and distinct tradition, that it represents a genre or subgenre different from the autobiographical writing produced by men. In Jelinek's words, "contemporary women are writing out of and continuing to create a wholly different autobiographical tradition from that delineated in studies of male autobiography." [2]

That women's autobiography represents "a wholly different autobiographical tradition" has been a practical, even necessary critical assumption. Until 1980 major critical studies of autobiography excluded serious consideration of women's texts, and the fact of exclusion seemed to demand new approaches to, and new theories about, women's life writing. [3] Nonetheless, the argument about a separate (and singular) tradition of women's life writing is worth reexamining—not simply because, as I believe, it misrepresents a significant number of Victorian women's texts but because it involves a blindness about the writing of literary history, an unself-consciousness about what scholars do when they reconstruct a literary tradition. To oversimplify, critical studies of women's autobiography have tended to read women's texts as if gender were the hermeneutic key to authorial intention and textual production; they have assumed that the experience of gender determines the form of a woman's life writing or at least that it motivates a woman writer to seek a separate autobiographical tradition. [4] Other possibilities—that gender may not be the crucial factor in some autobiography, that other allegiances (religious, regional, political, or social) may be equally important, that some women autobiographers may deliberately avoid a female literary tradition, or that some women's accounts may self-consciously invoke multiple traditions—these possibilities have been underexplored. So, too, have possibilities that implicate editors and critics—and the positions from which they write—in the process of defining what constitutes "women's autobiography." The *desire* to define a women's tradition has, in other words, shaped the writing of literary history and practical criticism.

In some critical writing on autobiography, most notably Regenia Gagnier's *Subjectivities* (1991) and Laura Marcus's *Auto/biographical Discourses* (1994), this desire has been resisted and the diversity of autobiographical texts rather than the singularity of a women's tradition argued. Gagnier, for example, suggests that working-class women (and, for that matter, men) who attempted to comply with Victorian middle-class norms in their life writing failed to represent their experiences adequately and often forced themselves into subject positions of failure or disappointment; her work demonstrates the alternative forms of auto/biography that working-class women created, often collaborative rather than individualistic, and then exploited for political purposes. Marcus's study, although not concerned exclusively with women's life writing, suggests the diversity of nineteenth-century discourse about autobiographical genres and its evolution during the century; this diversity complicates our thinking about what constitutes women's auto/biography and underscores the importance of historicizing our critical analyses of women's texts.[5] Such scholarship points to the need for reconsidering the relation of gender and genre in Victorian autobiography, particularly as women writers negotiated the competing claims of gender, social class, politics, religion, family allegiance, and regional affiliation.

In this study, I reconsider Victorian women's autobiography not by presupposing the existence of a women's tradition but instead by asking about possible self-representational modes available to, acknowledged, or created by women writers. And I begin not by proposing an alternate version of literary history but by looking closely at early attempts to identify "women's autobiography" and by examining the assumptions that undergird them. For, as it turns out, modern literary critics are not the first to construct a tradition of women's autobiography. The effort to construct a literary past—that is, a tradition of English autobiographical writing that accounts for women's texts as well as men's—originates in the nineteenth century. The "origins" of women's autobiography are distinctly Victorian.

By 1797 an anonymous literary critic in the *Monthly Repository* had coined the term *autobiography* for a "new" genre, and by 1809 Robert Southey was using it confidently in an essay on the Portuguese poet Francisco Vieira in the *Quarterly Review*.[6] Within two decades, Victorian antiquarians, scholars, and critics were furiously resurrecting and publishing the texts we cite today when we write about the "emergence" or "origins" of women's autobiography: the *True Relation of the Birth, Breeding, and Life of Margaret Cavendish* (1814), the *Memoirs of Lady Fanshawe* (1829), *A Legacy, or Widow's Mite, Left by Alice Hayes* (1836), the *Autobiography of Mary, Countess of Warwick* (1848), *The Autobiography of Mrs. Alice Thornton*

(1875), *The Autobiography of Anne Lady Halkett* (1875), and numerous spiritual accounts written by Nonconformist women.[7] Indeed, except for the autobiography of Margaret Cavendish, Duchess of Newcastle, which first appeared as part of her *Natures Pictures Drawn by Fancies Pencil to the Life* (1656), these seminal women's texts would be lost to literary history were it not for the efforts of the Victorians.

The Victorians rescued and wrote about these autobiographies for reasons similar to our own: for their historical interest, for the social and historical information they contained, for their contribution to literary discussions of a "new" genre, for their relevance to their own lives. Above all, they wrote about these texts because they knew they were reclaiming a tradition, one that had been lost for nearly two centuries but that nonetheless impinged upon their lives—as they lived then, as they imagined women's lives might be.[8] Nineteenth-century efforts at reconstructing literary history can, I believe, illumine our own efforts at delineating traditions of autobiography, whether men's, women's, or both. Victorians' views can challenge or affirm our assumptions about women's life writing and its development, our claims that the masculine tradition of autobiography excludes or misrepresents women's lives; that women's self-representation assumes a form different from men's, one that is "relational" or "contextual" rather than "positional" or "linear"; or that the traditions of male and female autobiography developed separately—and, by implication, that critics do best to treat them separately.

This chapter examines three Victorian (re)constructions of autobiographical traditions: (1) a tradition of spiritual autobiography, embodied in the documents of *The Friends' Library* (1837–50), a collection that includes more than twenty accounts by Quaker women; (2) a tradition of family memoirs, represented not by a single collection but by the publications of various nineteenth-century antiquarian societies (1829–75); and (3) the women's texts, most of them artists' lives in the form of *chroniques scandaleuses,* chosen for Hunt and Clarke's ground-breaking *Autobiography* series (1826–33), the first known attempt to create a literary collection of autobiographical writing. These three reconstruct the most common, coherent traditions available to nineteenth-century women writers, though not the only possibilities. As we shall see, the question of "women's" autobiography has been vexed from its origins, with neither writers nor editors agreeing on the relation of gender and genre.

Women Writers and the Tradition of Spiritual Autobiography

Has women's autobiography been, from its origins, fundamentally different from men's? In her survey of "archetypal" women's autobiographies, Mary G. Mason argues this position categorically: "Nowhere in women's autobiographies do we find the patterns established by the two prototypical male autobiographers, Augustine and Rousseau." Augustine's use of a dramatic structure of conversion, where the "self is presented as the stage for a battle of opposing forces and where a climactic victory for one force—spirit defeating flesh—completes the drama of the self," is, according to Mason, essentially alien to women's self-conception; so, too, is Rousseau's "unfolding self-discovery where the characters and events are little more than aspects of the author's evolving consciousness."[9] Mason argues more emphatically than other critics, who suggest that women's autobiographies "merit separate treatment" or that current critical theories "are not applicable to women's life studies." But whether emphatic or moderate, such an argument assumes that gender determines generic production—and not, as the late Paul de Man proposed, that what the autobiographer does "is in fact governed by the technical demands of self-portraiture and thus determined, in all its aspects, by the resources of [the] medium."[10]

In fact, one of the earliest reconstructions of an autobiographical tradition suggests a view of self-portraiture quite different from Mason's and more compatible with de Man's; it used women's autobiographies to suggest that sex or gender was an almost negligible concern of (or influence on) life writing. Between 1837 and 1850, the Quaker historians William and Thomas Evans published a series of spiritual memoirs that included both men's and women's accounts. Their series, called *The Friends' Library,* was meant to preserve the seminal texts of Quakerism and, through its representative auto/biographies, set the standard for Quaker self-presentation in life and in print.[11] As the prospectus explained, "It is both our duty and our interest to be intimately conversant with [the early Friends'] writings; to imitate their piety and devotedness, and to strive to be imbued with that fervour and heavenly mindedness which so conspicuously marked their example." The editors assumed, as was generally true for spiritual autobiography, that subsequent writers would imitate these autobiographical models, exemplary as they were in their "heavenly mindedness." They seem to have assumed also that women's and men's texts were equally representative, equally based on seminal forms (such as George Fox's *Journal*) and thus equally imitable by subsequent writers.[12]

Quite apart from stated intentions, what the women's autobiographies in *The Friends' Library* demonstrate is that seventeenth-century women writers readily adopted the traditional model of spiritual autobiography. They treated their lives as a struggle between opposing forces. They delineated a pattern of spiritual progress from bondage in sin and spiritual darkness to enlightenment and victory over the world, flesh, and devil. Most important, they composed their lives without a sense that they were appropriating a masculine tradition or that their experiences were radically different from men's. These women's accounts belie the label of the Augustinian or Bunyanesque form as prototypically "masculine."[13] Quaker and other Nonconformist women participated early and directly in the writing of English spiritual autobiography and, by composing powerful personal accounts, helped shape its conventions.

When, for example, Elizabeth Stirredge wrote *Strength in Weakness Manifest* (1711), included in the second volume of the Evans collection as *The Life and Christian Testimony of That Faithful Servant of the Lord, Elizabeth Stirredge* (1838), she followed the general formula for spiritual autobiography, beginning with her earliest recollections of religious seriousness and her "dread and terror" in contemplating death. She continued at great length with her temptations to sin (the most serious being a hankering after "fine clothes"), her wanderings without spiritual guidance (like the children of Israel in the wilderness), her conviction of sin and conversion under Quaker preaching, and finally her persecutions for religious conscience. Formally, Stirredge's account differs little from the male autobiographies included in the same volume. *A Brief Account of the Life and Travels of Thomas Wilson* contains the same testimony to youthful "hungerings and thirstings," the same prolonged conviction under Quaker preaching, the same detailing of religious persecution and perseverance.[14] Equally for the male Wilson and the female Stirredge, the structure of autobiography results from a religious perspective on human experience, which views life as a journey or progress toward the eternal realm and which considers spiritual reality all-encompassing. Both their accounts rely heavily on prior Quaker documents of personal history and, as Richard T. Vann has shown, on the Puritan literary heritage that many Quakers drew upon as they remembered and inscribed their religious pasts.[15]

Within the autobiographical tradition constructed by *The Friends' Library,* variations in form reveal little correlation with gender. Both men and women report rebellious episodes (Elizabeth Ashbridge disobediently elopes at age fourteen, Joseph Pike confesses his delight in the company of "wild boys" so that he may digress on the importance of parental supervision). Both sexes incorporate dialogues that record serious clashes with worldly authority (Alice Hayes and Benjamin Bangs describe doctrinal disputes with Anglican priests, Thomas Wilson harangues the Baptists). Both men and women recount their journeys as Quaker ministers (Jane Hoskens subtitles her life *A Minister of the Gospel,* a claim possible for most women in the Evans collection, as Quakers encouraged the public testimony of both sexes).[16] Such formal homogeneity was encouraged within religious communities, where a similarity in the representation of experience gave assurance of genuine conversion. To adapt Joyce Quiring Erickson's formulation in discussing accounts by Methodist women, the religious self is "an intertextual self," consciously under construction by an individual, constantly under revision by the community.[17]

A stylistic homogeneity also marks the autobiographies of *The Friends' Library*—achieved in part by the stylistic practice of spiritual autobiographers, in part by the editorial policy of William and Thomas Evans. Quaker autobiographers, like other Protestant writers, relied heavily on the language of Scripture to recount their lives, the ideal being to merge the words of their text with the divinely inspired words of a biblical author. Thus Alice Hayes's multimetaphoric sentence—"Now was the refiner's fire very hot, in order to burn up the dross and the tin"— echoes the words of Malachi and Ezekiel to describe her trials under conviction of sin.[18] This stylistic practice was exacerbated (or improved, it depends on one's point of view) by an editorial decision to modernize and regularize the original documents. Because the Evanses felt that the early accounts were often "prolix and redundant," they made "a judicious selection and abridgment," thereby presenting the series "in a more attractive form, [its] intrinsic value enhanced."[19] Or so they claimed. While abridging, they also moderated extremes of style, thus eradicating many telling, individualistic features of style we today associate with autobiographical writing.

My point here is not to lament Quaker stylistics or editorial practice but rather to stress the virtually genderless writing in many early English autobiographies. The modern critical notion that women writers choose figurative language that derives from "female" experience does not hold.[20] In its first five volumes alone, *The Friends' Library* reproduces eight samples of women's autobiography, all of them showing writers who worked comfortably within what today is identified as a masculine form. If these women perceived the world differently from men, they did not register their perceptions in the shape or style of their spiritual accounts.

Nor was their gender registered in special thematic concerns. Modern autobiography studies tend to assume that women writers will show a special facility or predilection for domestic themes, for the exploration of matters relating to marriage, children, or housewifery. This assumption, complemented by modern psychological theories of women's "relational" approach to self-definition, often predisposes critics to foreground autobiographical episodes in which women writers touch on familial matters or domestic details.[21] Of course such details appear, but no more frequently in women's spiritual accounts than in men's.

If we compare Quaker autobiographers on the themes of marriage and the family, we discover that neither the male nor female autobiographer develops such themes, although occasionally they appear in the accounts of both. We know that Elizabeth Stirredge was married, for instance, because *The Friends' Library* prefaces her account with "testimonies" from acquaintances who refer to her husband, James. Stirredge herself gives no account of courtship or marriage; her husband appears incidentally (if effectually) in an episode about persecution, where the king's officers attempt to confiscate their personal goods and James protests with her against the action. Jane Hoskens refers to her marriage only in a subordinate clause, written to explain why she left the care of Quaker mentors in 1738; after this reference, she continues her narrative as if nothing special had occurred.[22] Another autobiographer, Mary Pennington, discusses her first and second marriages at some length, but primarily to testify to her long search for religious truth. With her first husband, Sir William Springett, she decides to reject Anglican modes of worship; with her second, Isaac Pennington, she weds "without ring" and resists the infant baptism of their children. So, too, for male autobiographers. Like Pennington, Joseph Pike gives some account of his marriage, but his interest lies in the "instruction and information" he can derive; after naming his wife and listing their fourteen children, he goes on to cite several paragraphs of scriptural texts that stress the importance of seeking God's light in marriage.[23] Because doctrinal and behavioral concerns dominate his and other autobiographers' retrospective glances, we discover little about their marital experience—unless it appears as evidence within a larger religious framework.

It may be only coincidental, then, that we read details of courtship in a man's autobiography, Benjamin Bangs's *Life and Convincement* (1757). Bangs's encounters with Mary Lowe, his future wife, occur as interstices between records of his journeys as a Quaker minister. "Although we had often met together before in our Journeys," he comments, "I never so much as mention'd, one Word of Courtship to her; though my Spirit was closely united in a divine Fellowship with her."[24] One does not question his silence, given the tendency of Quaker accounts to efface such moments. The repression of romance becomes even more complete in *The Friends' Library* version, where Bangs's reference to courtship disappears and his words to Mary Lowe become, in the Evanses' editing, simply an "impart[ation]" of his mind.[25] Perhaps the editors wished to lift Bangs's account to the same level of heavenly-mindedness that George Fox demanded in his teaching on marriage: "as it was in the beginning, before sin and defilement was."[26]

Whatever the editorial motive, it is coincidental, too, that we encounter details of domesticity in the life writing of Mary Pennington and Joseph Pike. Pennington describes, with obvious pleasure, her purchase and repair of a small house to replace The Grange, a family estate confiscated in an anti-Quaker pogrom. But her interest is not uniquely feminine. Joseph Pike writes a detailed description of Quaker clothing and furniture, more interesting as social history than any other single segment of Quaker autobiography I have read. He includes it, however, to illustrate his efforts at purifying the lifestyles of the Irish Friends among whom he lived, and thus we learn only by chance of the "fine veneered and garnished cases," the "swelling chimney-pieces, curiously twisted banners," and "large looking glasses with decorated frames" that graced the residences of such wealthy Quaker families as his.[27]

This tendency to efface details of romance or domesticity demonstrates the powerful operation of generic conventions on the spiritual autobiographer's self-understanding—whether the writer is male or female, whether we understand that operation to occur as the writer lives her life or converts it later into textual form. The spiritual autobiography, unlike the domestic memoir, does not particularly concern itself with marriage, the home, or the family. Its generic power asserts itself most peculiarly in the spiritual autobiographer's treatment of children, ultimately to the point of complicating linguistic signification. We might guess that women writers would devote more space to children and child rearing than men, that they would stress their maternal concerns even as they reported their travels in the ministry. Indeed, the best autobiographer in the Quaker tradition titles her account *A Legacy, or Widow's Mite, Left by Alice Hayes to Her Children and Others,* thereby assuming a maternal role as writer.[28] Hayes's rationale for composing a life story begins with her concern "for the encouragement of the young to faithfulness and continual trust and confidence in the Lord." But this concern is equally common among male autobiographers: Joseph Pike similarly writes "for the benefit and instruction of my children" and "for others also," while Joseph Oxley prefaces his journal with an address to his children, admonishing them "to follow me, in like manner, only in greater degrees of purity."[29] If we label Hayes's autobiographical stance "maternal," then the stance of Pike and Oxley must be maternal as well (or "parental" in that there is no recognizable distinction between the two sexes).

Labels aside, what perplexes the reader of Hayes's text is the indeterminacy of the word *children* in its title. Does Hayes refer to her own children or to spiritual offspring, including the reader, left to her care? Presumably both, for Hayes mentions that her first husband, Daniel Smith, was "an indulgent father to our children," but she also frames her text with prayers for "all the babes and lambs of God."[30] Yet in Elizabeth Stirredge's autobiography, the reader can never determine if the "children" are anything other than Quakers under spiritual guidance. When she warns "my dear children" of the "subtle devices" of "the enemy of your immortal soul," she may refer to either natural or spiritual offspring. When she later recounts her testimony to King Charles II, including a plea for the end "of persecuting and shedding the blood of my dear children," she refers to all Quakers. Within the text the referent is never fixed. Stirredge's "maternal" stance becomes a function of her writerly role. This stance demands—for male and female autobiographers alike— the nurturing of a spiritual community.[31]

In stressing the attention (or lack of it) that autobiographers in *The Friends' Library* give to domestic concerns, I do not mean to suggest an emotional deficit in Quaker marriages or families. Quite the contrary. It is clear from supplementary letters and testimonies, as well as from small remarks within the accounts themselves, that these autobiographers cared deeply about their spouses and children. Rather, the minimizing of domestic concerns in spiritual autobiography should challenge the critical assumption that gender is always the dominant force in life writing; it should lead us to ask whether theory or criticism of women's life writing proceeds most perceptively when it emphasizes sexual difference. One might, of course, explain the documents in the Evanses' collection—and the construction of the literary history they represent—in various ways. One might say that the women who wrote such accounts were exceptional or anomalous, or that gender was necessarily a secondary issue among radical English sects under persecution, or that spiritual accounts allow only limited views of human experience.[32] These interpretations— psychological, sociological, literary—have validity, but the existence of such a large body of women's documents should make us wary of categorical assertions about a distinctively gender-linked origin for women's autobiography. In the texts of *The Friends' Library,* which represent some of the earliest autobiographies in the English tradition, gender does not initially or primarily influence genre.

This is not to say that gender is irrelevant or that it leaves no mark on the accounts in the Evanses' collection. If only sporadically within this religious tradition, women autobiographers relate episodes in which gender assumes—or has the potential to assume—a dominant function. Indeed, if we were to ignore the editorial apparatus and reorganize the women's accounts so that they appeared in chronological sequence as a group of "feminine" texts (editorial policies contrary to the Evanses'), we might argue that gender becomes increasingly important, especially in the transition from seminal seventeenth-century texts to later eighteenth-century versions.

Let me illustrate this point about reorganization with an example from the earliest woman writer in *The Friends' Library*. Elizabeth Stirredge (b. 1634) lived before the Toleration Act of 1689, when Quakers were still persecuted for publicly meeting and preaching. In one episode she recounts, during which she faced bodily harm (the priest's son had bought a new sword, claiming "it was no more sin to kill a Quaker, than it was to kill a louse"), she laments that she failed to speak out against the rationalizations of cowardly Quakers who urged clandestine meetings. Wrestling with her conscience, she uses her sex as an excuse for silence: "They will not hear me, who am a contemptible instrument," she tells God. "And seeing they despise the service of women so much, make use of them that are more worthy." As Stirredge relates this episode, moreover, she notes that some women who did speak out were told by John Story, a prominent Quaker leader, to "go home about their business, and wash their dishes, and not go about to preach."[33]

When we read Stirredge's account today, we tend to interpret the episode as a woman's confrontation with patriarchal authority. What she faces, we might say, are obstacles to self-expression embodied in the male priest, his son, and John Story. But Stirredge interprets her experience differently. To her, the incident illustrates two principles fundamental to Quaker life and life writing: the necessity of public testimony and the authority of the individual conscience. Thus Stirredge embeds her narrative within an extended plea for loyalty to undiminished Quakerism (the same concern, we might recall, that motivates William and Thomas Evans to publish *The Friends' Library*). Three centuries later we may read the priest as a figure of patriarchy (as indeed he is), but Stirredge views him as an agent of darkness who would suppress religious light, the same view that characterizes "Augustinian" autobiography. We may recognize John Story also as a patriarchal oppressor, but Stirredge sets her confrontation with Story within the context of early Quaker debates over individual freedom versus group authority. In her interpretation Story represents the Quaker who in easy circumstances proclaims the right of individual conscience but under threat of persecution silences himself and the potentially dangerous witness of others. That Stirredge does not view

Story as an exclusively "male" opponent is clear from her handling of other male figures in the episode. Taking her side against Story are her husband and another male Friend, who in Stirredge's view represent spiritual integrity versus what she calls, in a high prophetic mode, "the broth of abominable things."[34]

Whether we accept Stirredge's self-interpretation or impose another upon it is a matter of critical choice—a choice between accepting the autobiographer's hermeneutic and giving priority to our own. Our choice affects the way we read women's life writing, the connections we find between women's texts and those of male contemporaries, and, most broadly, the autobiographical traditions we construct from the seventeenth to nineteenth centuries. If we accept Stirredge's interpretation, we will view the episode as conventional, as integral to a document meant to model Christian behavior in a hostile world. Similar episodes appear in the autobiographies of male Quakers. William Edmundson, who like Stirredge served as a minister in the 1670s and 1680s, also reports a confrontation with an Anglican priest in which he narrowly escapes imprisonment. Thomas Wilson, who traveled and preached a decade later, still faces a sheriff "with some officers" who challenge, "from whom had he his commission to preach?"[35] While these male autobiographers confront no ridicule because of their sex, they nonetheless must defend their right to speak. They struggle against obstacles to freedom of conscience, which, like Stirredge, they interpret as evil forces opposing divine truth. Early spiritual autobiographers tend, in sum, to produce self-writing rooted in an oppositional, Augustinian mode—whether they are male or female.

Within two generations, however, the relations between gender and genre noticeably shift. Whereas seventeenth-century women writers in *The Friends' Library* tend to efface matters of sex and gender, subordinating them to more pressing religious themes, their eighteenth-century successors alter the balance. The "women's speech" theme that appears almost accidentally in Stirredge becomes a discrete episode—and hence a more prominent issue—for autobiographers such as Elizabeth Ashbridge (1713–55), Jane Pearson (died c. 1775), and Sarah Morris (1704–75). Typical of these later writers, Morris notes that she became a minister only "in great mortification to her own will." The *self*-mortification signals a new emphasis. Instead of external obstacles in the form of priests or prisons, the barriers to expression are now represented as internal; instead of male figures who challenge the right to testify, these women writers describe their own embarrassment at the possibility of speech. Like Morris, Jane Pearson struggles long with a "natural timidity" that leads her to sit silent in meetings and inwardly declare, when she hears others speaking, "I will never do so." And when Elizabeth Ashbridge first hears a woman preacher at a Quaker meeting, she recoils. "I'm sure you're a fool," she thinks, "and if I ever turn Quaker, which will never be, I will not be a preacher." [36]

We can account for this shift by pointing to various historical changes. Most simply, the Toleration Act of 1689 removed the political obstacles to Quaker preaching and thus the most severe threats of persecution. Toleration meant that women could no longer represent the obstacles to self-expression as purely political, and so they came to represent (and feel) them as social and psychological. Not that earlier autobiographers acted without psychological or social restraints. The seventeenth-century Alice Hayes attended Quaker meetings in the face of ostracism by husband, in-laws, and neighbors (her mother-in-law claimed she would "undo" her husband, her father-in-law threatened to starve her into submission).[37] But Hayes as autobiographer seems convinced of her right to speak, whereas eighteenth-century Quaker women seem compelled to detail their psychological and social inhibitions. Perhaps, as some social historians have argued, women had in the interim lost their economic independence and status as well as their political motive; perhaps, as Nancy Armstrong has argued, "gender" as a determining category was in the process of being created, with all its formulations of "feminine" behavior.[38] Thus eighteenth-century women, even Quakers whose perspective was supposed to be fundamentally religious, show the marks of cultural change in their autobiographical writings. In their accounts, then, the reluctance to speak becomes conventional rather than occasional or coincidental. And with this shift in conventions comes a slight but noticeable shift in autobiographical form. Episodes such as those reported by Elizabeth Stirredge no longer appear late in the narratives as evidence of Christian perseverance, but emerge early as part of—often the basis of—an inner struggle toward conversion.

In suggesting historical explanations for a shift within this autobiographical tradition, I have been writing as if experience (social, economic, political) determined literary form. Perhaps this is inevitable in historical criticism. But we might consider also a more purely literary explanation for changes such as those represented in the women's texts of *The Friends' Library*. Rather than locate the source of change in political or social conditions, we might consider the position that these women autobiographers assumed as readers and writers, as interpreters and creators of literary texts. To them as readers, the scene of silencing produced a recognition, perhaps even a memory of a more dramatic tale to tell. To them as autobiographers, the predicament was as much one of relation to literary predecessors as it was of identification as readers. Quaker writers, male and female both, were expected to model their accounts on representative texts—that is, texts that were *typical* of Quaker religious experience but that also *properly represented* experience in literary form. Nevertheless, in order to justify publication, the writers needed to produce texts original as well as representative, special in the details of experience if not in spiritual meaning. This impulse to uniqueness or individuality contributes to change within an autobiographical tradition. As women writers repeated the conventional episodes of their predecessors, we might suppose that they wrought variations, gave different emphases, omitted or added certain features—thus altering the form and, inevitably, the focus of spiritual autobiography. Even if they had not intended variation, the very act of rewriting would have produced it, for, as Hillis Miller has argued in *Fiction and Repetition,* repeating—an episode, a trope, a theme—introduces difference into a literary text.[39]

What we find in *The Friends' Library,* then, is a complex and increasingly complicated relation between gender and genre. Gender functions almost negligibly in the earliest texts of this tradition; only later, when women writers begin to vary the episodes and metaphors of their predecessors and thus foreground gender-relevant matters, does the potential for a separate women's tradition develop. Not that it emerges fully in the case of spiritual autobiography. Even in the late eighteenth-century accounts included in *The Friends' Library,* the power of genre supersedes the possibilities of gender. In form, style, and theme, the women's spiritual autobiographies remain remarkably similar to those of their male counterparts.

These texts, especially in the homogenized arrangement of *The Friends' Library* or in the similarly ahistorical republications of spiritual autobiographies from various English religious traditions, provided a legacy for Victorian women who wished to join a universal or gender-less tradition of life writing.[40] If, unfortunately, women of many religious heritages had lost, during the eighteenth century, the habit of writing spiritual autobiography—and with it their place in a dominant hermeneutic tradition of English autobiography—the republication and editorial revival of historically important autobiographical texts made it possible for Victorian women to reclaim this legacy.[41] Some, such as Harriet Martineau and Frances Power Cobbe, chose to claim their place within a spiritual tradition as part of what we would now call a feminist agenda; they meant to minimize rather than give prominence to self-representational forms associated with gender. Others, such as Charlotte Elizabeth Tonna and Charlotte Brontë, preferred to link spiritual auto-biography with domestic memoir, the more highly feminized genre I discuss next. In any case, the use of spiritual autobiography by Victorian women writers became a polemical and political act, a choice signaling public intentions, not just private confessions.

Women Autobiographers and the Domestic Memoir

If *The Friends' Library* consolidated a form of autobiography that effaced or minimized matters of gender, a different editorial trend helped to authorize a form that was explicitly feminine. This trend involved the publication of archival material that came with no generic label but that increasingly came to be called "autobiography" by its editors. The form they reproduced was, in modern critical terms, the domestic (or family) memoir, a *res gestae* account rooted not in a conception of an individual self or a religious soul but in the autobiographer as recorder of communal history.[42]

As a form of English women's life writing, the domestic memoir originates in the seventeenth century, the earliest examples emerging contemporaneously with the earliest spiritual autobiographies (1654 for Anna Trapnel's *Legacy for Saints*, 1656 for the *True Relation of the Birth, Breeding, and Life of Margaret Cavendish*).[43] Early modern domestic memoirs placed great emphasis on social continuity and family service in national causes, thus revealing their essentially upper-class origins and modes of self-definition. Indeed, the use of the word *legacy* in the title of many spiritual autobiographies suggests that lower- and middle-class writers were consciously echoing their secular, aristocratic counterparts but offering a spiritual inheritance instead of a corruptible earthly one of status and wealth. While the two forms may be historically linked, they represent radically different ways of representing subjectivity. The spiritual autobiography focuses on the individual writer's spiritual progress or regress, whereas the memoir stresses the writer's place in an extended family unit and makes her (since most such writers were female) the repository of its significant accomplishments, more likely those of a husband or father than her own.

Ann, Lady Fanshawe's *Memoirs* (1829) delineates the typical pattern and its conventional features. Fanshawe's account originates in a desire to pass on her own and her family's history to her children. She addresses her words to her "most dear and only son," beginning not with memories of her childhood but instead with several paragraphs of Polonius-like advice (2–4) and a hagiographic character sketch of her late husband, the boy's father (4–9). She includes two long segments of genealogy, one tracing the paternal line (9–25), the other the maternal (25–32), both including details of the family estates, finances, and public honors. When the narrative proper gets under way, the *Memoirs* follows the career of Fanshawe's husband, who served as secretary of war to Charles II (then Prince of Wales), later as ambassador to Portugal and Spain.

Because Ann Fanshawe witnessed foreign court life in both its official pomp and its unofficial details, her account records many political events from a "feminine" perspective. She takes particular note, for instance, of the perquisites she received as ambassador's wife, right down to the large silver chocolate pot, twelve fine filigree cups, two large silver salvers, and twelve fine sarcenet napkins that the English merchants of Seville presented to her and her husband on their arrival from England (204). Because her account is also a domestic memorial, she narrates many intimate stories about her marriage, including her husband's tears on their first separation (45), her secret 4:00 A.M. visits while he is imprisoned in Whitehall (116–17), and even her assumption of cabin boy's garb so that she can fight by his side when pirates attack their ship (91–93). Had her *Memoirs* been addressed to her daughters, she might have included even more domestic incidents, perhaps detailing the education and home life of young women of her generation. In its structure,

Fanshawe's is a typical seventeenth-century domestic memoir: it ends when Sir Richard's life ends, Lady Fanshawe finding it within her power (or desire) only to describe his funeral and then her father's death before breaking off the narrative.

Despite the autobiographical elements of this and other such documents, and despite their early emergence in the history of life writing, the domestic memoir was not recognized as an autobiographical form until the nineteenth century. With the exception of Margaret Cavendish's *True Relation* (1656), all the well-known memoirs of seventeenth-century women, including Lady Fanshawe's, were privately kept within family archives and published only two centuries later by descendants or antiquarians. When published, the accounts increasingly came to include "autobiography" in the title or editorial preface, as the following chronological listing suggests: the *Life of Mrs. Lucy Hutchinson* (1806), *A Pairt of the Life of Lady Margaret Cunninghame* (1827), the *Memoirs of Lady Fanshawe* (1829), the *Autobiography of Mary Countess of Warwick* (1848), the *Autobiography of Mrs. Alice Thornton* (1873), the *Autobiography of Anne Lady Halkett* (1875). Even Cavendish's account, published during her lifetime in *Natures Pictures Drawn by Fancies Pencil to the Life,* was first issued as a separate text in 1814 by Sir Egerton Brydges, who in the preface attached the label "auto-biography" that has stayed with it ever since.

It is worth asking why these texts were first published and in such numbers in the nineteenth century and why they were then designated autobiography (rather then, say, history). A simple answer would be, of course, that the term *autobiography* did not become established until the Victorian era, along with rising interest in the genre; thus, not until the nineteenth century were these older texts likely to attract critical attention or fashionable terminology. A more complex answer would point to the cultural conditions—and contradictions—that authorized these texts as "women's" autobiography; it would include consideration of what critics and editors said about such texts, what they praised or blamed, what they sanctioned or omitted.

Nineteenth-century editors seem to have been unusually nervous about publishing women's private documents, yet they articulated the case for doing so and in the process authorized certain kinds of life writing as legitimately feminine. Charles Jackson, editor of Alice Thornton's autobiography, expresses a common rationale for making these private documents public when he states that such specimens, "hid among the archives of many of our ancient houses," deserve to be shared with the English nation; "from their intrinsic merit, [they] have a right to be considered *publici* as well as *privati juris*."[44] What does he mean by "intrinsic merit"? One criterion for merit was historical value. Like Charles Jackson, Lady Halkett's editor stresses "the value of the historical information which she actually imparts"; Lady Warwick's, the "great historical value" of such records of "the domestic occurrences of the period, soon after the restoration of Charles II." Similarly, the preface to Lady Fanshawe's *Memoirs* claims that, whether the work "be read for the historical information which it contains, or with no higher motive than for amusement," it will "more [than] amply gratify either object"; Lucy Hutchinson's editor praises the ability of the work to make the reader feel "a party in the transactions which are recounted."[45]

Amplifying these last two claims, both nineteenth-century editors and twentieth-century critics have added appeals to literary merit to those of historical value, praising the works as lively, imaginative examples of an evolving genre or arguing that they are "contributions to the early development of the English secular autobiography."[46] Despite the defensibility of these historical and aesthetic claims, the evidence for literary influence is dubious—at least as formulated by modern critics. Few (virtually none) of these women's memoirs were published before the nineteenth century, at which point the secular tradition of autobiography had already been shaped. We need an alternative explanation for the publication of these seventeenth-century women's accounts and the promotion of their nineteenth-century equivalents—a promotion that did subsequently influence one tradition of women's life writing.

These documents represent, I think, a literary manifestation of the doctrine of separate spheres—at best a form of commitment to the private and domestic, at worst a form of compensation for loss of the public, professional, and political. At best, women embraced the domestic memoir because they valued the private sphere, invested themselves in domesticity, and esteemed their roles in the home. When Margaret Oliphant began a series on autobiography for *Blackwood's Edinburgh Magazine,* for example, she rated the domestic memoir equal in value to public and professional history; indeed, she made it clear that she preferred the former. "The narrowest domestic record widens our experience of human nature, which, of all things involved, changes least from one generation to another," she wrote, going on to enumerate the pleasures of life

writing that ignores political events and chooses instead to record romantic and familial experience:

> *To see how little agitated is the race even when it is agitated most, to listen*
> *to a soft little love-strain singing itself to all the gentle echoes under the*
> *very horrors and fierce excitements of the French Revolution, and to*
> *know that the least misadventure of his son Tom was more important*
> *to a village chronicler than the tragic exit of "the martyr Charles" or*
> *the coming of "the hero William" are curious revelations; but they fill*
> *up—better even than those narratives of the back-stairs and records of*
> *all the underplots that influence a great event, to which the world is so*
> *much addicted—the full and catholic story of human life.*[47]

Oliphant's insistence on "the full and catholic story" represents a strong
defense of domestic life writing. Romantic, filial, and familial relations
gain value, great political events diminish in interest.

At worst, however, we might say that Victorian women turned to
domestic memoirs because they had lost their place in the public traditions of autobiography. They tended—one might say they were subtly
forced—to gravitate toward private, culturally sanctioned forms of life
writing because they were excluded from others. The memoir—domestic in its focus, relational in its mode of self-construction—allowed
women to write as mothers, daughters, and wives. It allowed them to
represent their lives in terms of "good" feminine plots. But it did not
allow them to develop—or disturb—the primary masculine traditions
of autobiography, the public, *res gestae* account of professional life or the
more introspective, developmental form of an intellectual career.

That there is a cultural link between the publication of seventeenth-
century family memoirs and the remarkable increase of nineteenth-
century domestic memoirs is suggested by the bibliographical records.
Whereas women wrote and published significant numbers of spiritual
autobiographies from the mid-seventeenth to early eighteenth century,
by the nineteenth such women autobiographers had virtually disappeared
from the public view.[48] Instead, women with religious inclinations turned
inward to spiritual diaries or outward to what William Matthews cate-
gorizes as autobiographies of "clergymen's wives," actually domestic
memoirs of life in a vicarage or on the mission field.[49] At the same time
in the secular arena, Victorian editors resurrected memoirs by diplomats'

and soldiers' wives such as Ann Fanshawe and Lucy Hutchinson and published dozens of their nineteenth-century equivalents, written by women
who accompanied their husbands to India, Egypt, the West Indies, or the
Far East, and who conceptualized their experiences under such titles as
Foreign Courts and Foreign Homes, Our Home in Cyprus, At Home in India,
and *Garden of Fidelity.*[50] So, too, in the memoirs of Anne Halkett and
Alice Thornton, the Victorians edited women's perspectives on the domestic disruptions of the Interregnum, just as they published books by
their own diplomats' and politicians' wives on domestic conditions during internal and colonial crises. And they published numerous memoirs
of what William Matthews calls simply "domestic and family life," accounts in which women recorded their memories and the social mores of
Victorian Britain.[51]

As social history, these memoirs preserve invaluable information
about attitudes, customs, and conditions in seventeeth- and nineteenth-
century England; in themselves, they represent important documents of
cultural history, evidence testifying to the flourishing Victorian cult of
domesticity. As an autobiographical mode, such memoirs provided Victorian women with a means of contributing to an increasingly popular
genre; while their male counterparts established the narrative structures
and interpretive modes of the classic *res gestae* and developmental forms,
women tried alternative structures and added a "feminine sensibility" to
the genre, "a deeper revelation of sentiments, more subjectivity and more
subtle self-analyses."[52] Because this sensibility and the nascent structures
were present in seventeenth-century women's texts, literary history—in
the form of archival documents and critical commentary on them—
seemed to validate the notion of a separate autobiographical sphere and
the development of a separate autobiographical tradition. After all, did
not the memoirs of their female predecessors represent the origins of
women's autobiography? Did not these original and originary texts add
historical weight to the enterprise of domestic life writing and give a
sense of tradition that Victorian women valued?[53]

As I have been arguing, origins are created, not found; traditions are
constructed, not discovered. The fact that the Victorians created—or,
rather, believed they had discovered—a generic link between seventeenth-century women's memoirs and those of their own era is the significant point. The texts they resuscitated did not, in fact, represent a

unified feminine tradition or a coherent genre. If we momentarily re-linquish their perspective, we can see that Lady Halkett's reads like a historical romance; Lady Cunninghame's, a legal deposition; Lady War-wick's, a spiritual confession but without the religious ecstasies or her-meneutic vagaries of sectarian practitioners. Alice Thornton's autobiog-raphy was compiled from four discrete books of record, its basic structure (so far as one can tell) suggesting a spiritual diary with meditations fol-lowing each entry.[54] Even within a single autobiography, we can find different modes of self-expression—as in Lady Cunninghame's, which uses a plain, factual style in the primary text but shifts to highly abstract, typological discourse in an extended letter to her husband.[55] Despite their diversity, Victorian readers treated these accounts as a generic unit, as part of the same women's tradition of life writing. And they gave the texts coherence by stressing a fundamental quality: a feminine mode of self-conception.

This mode I shall designate, following modern psychological theory and common practice in autobiography studies, as relational[a]. According to such theorists as Nancy Chodorow and Carol Gilligan, women's ways of conceiving the self are "relational"—that is, they focus on relation-ships with another person or group. In Chodorow's terms, "the basic feminine sense of self is connected to the world, the basic masculine sense of self is separate." Girls emerge from childhood "with a basis for 'em-pathy' built into their primary definition of self in a way that boys do not"; they "come to define and experience themselves as continuous with others; their experience of self contains more flexible and permeable ego boundaries." In contrast, boys have "engaged, and been required to engage, in a more emphatic individuation and a more defensive firming of experienced ego boundaries"; hence, their self-conceptions tend to be "positional" rather than "relational."[56] Nineteenth-century editors did not, of course, refer to modern psychological theory when they char-acterized seventeenth-century women's texts. But, judging from their editorial prefaces and critical reviews, we can recognize a comparable language for interpreting women's experience, whether as written or lived. For virtually every text, the critical commentary and rhetorical weight fall on the woman writer's accomplishments as daughter, wife, and mother.

Editors view these early women autobiographers—and believe

these women viewed themselves—in relational terms, in their connections with fathers and mothers, husbands and children. Ann Fanshawe's editor describes his authoress as "a beautiful example of female devotion" (xxxiv). Although he notes her "literary merits" (ix) and frequently remarks on the fascinating historical information she conveys, the self he conceives for his subject is that of wife and mother—as in his sequence "an accomplished and clever woman, the wife of one of the most faithful servants of Charles the First and Charles the Second" (vi–vii). His emphasis in analyzing the autobiography lies on Lady Fanshawe's feminine virtues, those "instances of conjugal devotion, of maternal excellence, and of enduring fortitude under calamities, which render her a bright example to posterity" (ix). Similarly, Alice Thornton's editor characterizes her book as "that of a true daughter, wife, and mother." Even as he acknowledges the "carelessness and weakness" of her husband, he praises Thornton for her quiet refusal to censure: "it is plain to see how devoted she was to her husband." Even better is her maternal devotion: "the true woman shines out when she speaks of her children" (xii). So, too, Margaret Cavendish's Victorian editor praises her devotion to the duke, though he qualifies her achievements as an author and laments her lack of "taste." This lack is less noticeable in her *True Relation,* he argues, because "it is all domestic, and this domestic painting is its charm." [57]

The emphasis on the relational mode of these domestic memoirs is not purely the work of the Victorian imagination; in many cases, it is grounded in the writers' own self-conceptions. Lucy Hutchinson composed her autobiography (a fragment, never finished) to accompany a massive biographical memorial, the *Memoirs of the Life of Colonel Hutchinson.* Margaret Cavendish, after multiple and contradictory attempts at self-definition, finally concludes her autobiography with an unadorned relational formula: "I was daughter to one Master Lucas of St. Johns, near Colchester, in Essex, second wife to the Lord Marquis of Newcastle; for my Lord having had two Wives, I might easily have been mistaken, especially if I should dye and my Lord Marry again" (310). And Alice Thornton recalls most of her experiences relationally—under such headings as "The mariage of Alice Wandesforde" or "A thanksgiving affter the delivery of my daughter" or "Of Mr. Thornton's affairs" or "Of my husband's sisters." It may even be true that Lady Halkett finds the conclusion to her account only when she accepts Sir James and comes to define herself as his wife; her account may trace a quest for relational (rather than individual) self-definition.

Certainly these seventeenth-century women understood themselves in relation to others. But what signify more—at least for the history of women's autobiography—are the rhetorical maneuvers by which nineteenth-century editors made relational definitions of self not only superior to but identical with literary merit. I have already referred to the most overt maneuver in the dismissal of Margaret Cavendish's "taste" and praise of her conjugal devotion. When Sir Egerton Brydges, one of her nineteenth-century editors, states that "her Grace wanted taste," that she "had not the talent of seizing that *selection* of circumstances," that she "knew not what to obtrude, and what to leave out," he refers to her literary productions generally. From this judgment, however, he excludes her *Life of William Cavendishe, Duke of Newcastle* and presumably her own pendant autobiography. These productions reveal her "great fault" less because they are "domestic."[58] Apparently Brydges means that the domestic writer cannot praise her husband too excessively, that the reader does not expect aesthetic balance anyway, that the evidence of feminine virtue is what really matters.

More subtly, Ann Fanshawe's editor attributes a woman's literary fame to domestic merit. Unlike Cavendish's editor, Fanshawe's praises the style, thought, and reliable historical sense of his authoress: "Celebrated as this country is for female talent and virtue, there is no one with whom Lady Fanshawe may not be compared and gain by the comparison." But as his link of "talent" and "virtue" hints and as his subsequent comments make explicit, the former depends on the latter; in order to achieve a lasting place in the literary canon, the woman writer must be "a bright example to posterity."[59]

This lesson is raised to the level of religious truth in the Reverend Julius Hutchinson's preface to his ancestor's auto/biography of herself and her husband. Hutchinson discusses the literary merit of the *Memoirs of the Life of Colonel Hutchinson* using traditional criteria—"the only ends for which any book can be reasonably published are to inform, to amuse, or to improve" (xxi)—and he argues that Lucy Hutchinson's work achieves all three. That these are objective criteria, acceptable in the male world of letters, he suggests by granting Lucy "the vigour of a masculine understanding." But he adds that she also possessed "the nice feeling and discrimination, the delicate touch of the pencil of a female." It would seem that this combination of masculine and feminine explains Lucy Hutchinson's unique contribution to historical writing: because she perceives personal habits and motives that underlie political actions, she can "account by common and easy causes for many of those actions and effects which others [male historians] have left unaccounted for." But this is not how Julius Hutchinson argues her case. In the final paragraph of his preface, after he has suggested that her auto/biography will please and instruct "every class of reader," he turns his attention to female readers specifically. "Ladies," he writes, "will feel that it carries with it all the interest of a novel, strengthened with the authenticity of real history"— a conventional enough remark. Then comes the decisive rhetorical turn: "They [ladies] will no doubt feel an additional satisfaction in learning, that though the author added to the erudition of the scholar, the research of the philosopher, the politician, and even the divine, the zeal and magnanimity of a patriot; yet she descended from all these elevations to perform, in the most exemplary manner, the functions of a wife, a mother, and mistress of a family."[60] In her descent from the heights, Lucy Hutchinson reenacts the *kenosis* of the Son of God, who in an act of self-humiliation emptied himself of divinity and took on the limits of humanity. So Lucy, in this model of feminine authorship, renounces the (male) joys of philosophy, divinity, and scholarship and limits herself to more lowly (female) roles. Lucy's reward is permanent fame—like Christ's reward for *kenosis,* his exaltation by God as "a name which is above every name" (Phil. 2:9). Had she aspired to literary fame by masculine means, she would, in the editor's schema, presumably have failed.

The critical responses and rhetorical choices of Victorian editors allow us to sense the immense pressure on women to make their life writing domestic, their self-conceptions relational. It is not so much that the editors of seventeenth-century texts had direct influence on autobiographers—although in the case of Margaret Oliphant, who reviewed three of these memoirs for *Blackwood's,* the influence may have been immediate.[61] Rather, Victorian editors express prevailing assumptions about proper modes for women's autobiography. One consequence was the rise of the domestic memoir, a form that flourished from the 1830s onward in privately printed and formally published works such as the anonymous *Memoirs of a Gentlewoman of the Old School* (1830), Mary Lisle's *Long, Long*

Ago: An Autobiography (1856), Rose Porter's *The Years That Are Told* (1870), Mary Kirby Gregg's *Leaflets from My Life: A Narrative Autobiography* (1887), and Janet Bathgate's *Aunt Janet's Legacy to Her Nieces: Recollections of Humble Life in Yarrow* (1897).[62] A more significant literary consequence was the incorporation of domestic patterns—plots of sisterhood, motherhood, conjugal life—into the auto/biography of virtually every major Victorian woman writer, even when such patterns caused disjunctions in narrative structure. From the spiritual autobiographies of Charlotte Elizabeth Tonna and Frances Power Cobbe, to the *Bildungsromane* of Charlotte Brontë, George Eliot, and Margaret Oliphant, to the professional life stories of Oliphant, Fanny Kemble, and Harriet Martineau, women writers felt the pressure of the domestic memoir even when their agenda was to avoid this tradition and reclaim another.

The relational mode of self-conception required—inevitably, it seemed—a relational narrative pattern. Such patterns, which I shall designate relational[b], diminished the autobiographer's authority over what Hayden White calls "emplotment," over self-interpretation through narrative construction.[63] Early writers of the domestic memoir found plots external to their lives and literary work: in the patterns of their husbands' lives; in the unpredictable actions of parents, brothers, children; in the larger course of British history. The structure of Ann Fanshawe's *Memoirs* is the plot of her husband's life, to which she attaches her personal reminiscences. Alice Thornton's plot is governed first by parents (including a mother who arranged Alice's marriage for her own and her sons' financial comfort); then it is shaped by a husband, by pregnancies and childbirths, ultimately by the Interregnum. Even Anne Halkett, who most successfully contrives a plot for her autobiography, depends on a relational[b] narrative; as Mary Beth Rose has suggested, Halkett construes marriage "as the destiny which the female hero struggles through romantic conflict to achieve."[64]

In the older critical terminology of autobiography studies, we would say that these women autobiographers did not invent "metaphors of the self," that they had "selves in hiding."[65] We might better say they did not conceive independent plots for themselves. The relational demands of domestic autobiography gave ready metaphors but took narrative inventiveness away from the writer—so dramatically that in most of the early texts I have been discussing, the account ends at the death of a husband or in an ellipsis, as if the writer could neither conclude nor proceed.

Victorian women who wrote within the domestic tradition inherited this problem of narrative authority. Sara Coleridge's *Memoirs* (1873), to cite one telling instance, begins with a plan to divide her history into logical narrative segments: "into childhood, earlier and later, youth earlier and later, wedded life, ditto, widowhood, ditto." Coleridge adds that she will "state the chief moral or reflection suggested by each—some maxim which it specifically illustrated, or truth which it exemplified, or warning which it suggested." [66] Yet, logical as her plan seems, she never gets beyond early childhood, beyond reminiscences of her poet-father and their literary circle. When she reaches the end of the first segment, she breaks off in mid-sentence: "On reviewing my earlier childhood, I find the predominant reflection . . ." (26). Coleridge neither interprets her experience nor narrates her life further; despite her considerable achievements as a writer and scholar, the relational aspects of the generic burden diminish her capacity for self-presentation.

Because domestic patterns seemed to limit women writers, some—like Harriet Martineau—worked within alternative autobiographical traditions. Martineau's impulse was to push beyond the limits of domesticity and compose a developmental autobiography applicable to both sexes. That impulse, if not her generic choice, was shared by many contemporaries. Whether they experimented with masculine modes of self-development or tested the limits of the feminine *Bildungsroman* or committed themselves to genderless autobiographical patterns or altered the domestic memoir to make it independent of external history and more responsive to the rhythms of private life, Victorian women writers worked to reclaim lost generic traditions, even as they developed their domestic inheritance.

From *Chroniques Scandaleuses* to Professional Artist's Life

By comparing the editorial work of *The Friends' Library* with the archival discoveries and publication of early modern domestic memoirs, we can sense the contradictions that Victorian women faced when they considered writing autobiography. The two traditions imply different ways of constructing the self: one minimally concerned with gender, the other highly gendered; one inner and psychological, the other social and domestic; one religious, the other secular. Women autobiographers might, of course, have aligned themselves with a tradition simply on the basis of the last difference, sacred versus secular. Yet even that choice was not necessarily clear-cut—as I suggest in chapter II, on Tonna's and Martineau's polemical uses of *both* traditions and in my discussion of the uneven mixture in Brontë's *Jane Eyre: An Autobiography.* Victorian women's autobiography drew on multiple traditions and embedded the contradictory impulses of those traditions within it. Such contradictions become even more striking when we add a third tradition of women's life writing, the *chroniques scandaleuses,* included in the Hunt and Clarke series *Autobiography: A Collection of the Most Instructive and Amusing Lives Ever Published, Written by the Parties Themselves,* as the primary example of women's life writing.

The scandalous memoir originates in the eighteenth century with fictional tales such as the "Memoirs of a Lady of Quality" in Smollett's *Peregrine Pickle* and the purportedly nonfictional accounts of such writers and actresses as Laetitia Pilkington (1748), Charlotte Charke (1755), George Anne Bellamy (1785), and Sophia Baddeley (1787).[67] One might, I think, just as appropriately designate this genre "masculine," as several of these autobiographies were actually ghost-written by such men as Alexander Bicknell, who made good money by "collecting" and "arranging" women's lives. But in the Hunt and Clarke collection, it is the woman autobiographer who produces the scandalous memoir.

Beginning in 1826, the publishers John Hunt and Cowden Clarke embarked on an autobiographical series—to my knowledge, the first of its kind, the first to capitalize on the newly named genre—which they presented as "a diversified study of the human character." Their "Advertisement" in the inaugural volume featured a list of forthcoming works classified not by mode or subgenre but by the writers' public roles: statesmen (Sully, Bubb Doddington), men of genius and literature (Edward Gibbon, David Hume, Jean-François Marmontel), religious enthusiasts (John Wesley, George Whitfield), artists (Benvenuto Cellini), dramatists and players (Colly Cibber, Carlo Goldoni), mystics and imposters (William Lilly, James Hardy Vaux).[68] Despite the wide range of lives projected, no women's names appear in the original list, an omission suggesting either the limited roles available to women or their general exclusion from autobiographical writing or both. Nonetheless, by the end of 1826 Hunt and Clarke decided to add samples of women's life writing, for volume VII reproduces the *Memoirs of Mrs. Robinson,* a well-known actress and writer, perhaps better known during her lifetime as mistress of the Prince of Wales, and *A Narrative of the Life of Mrs. Charlotte Charke,* the daughter of Colley Cibber, also known for her cross-dressing on stage and in real life.

It can scarcely be coincidental that Hunt and Clarke chose autobiographies of actresses to represent the female self. Historically, the emphasis on roles and role-playing marks what Ronald Paulson has identified as a major shift in literary metaphors during the eighteenth century. Rather than life as a pilgrimage, the major trope of spiritual autobiography, life had become theater, wherein the human participants willfully and provisionally assumed roles to maneuver their way through life's experiences.[69] The depiction of roles and role-playing in these actresses' lives thematizes the problematic relation between public appearance and private life and makes their accounts especially important to the series, which had proposed that autobiography, unlike biography, reveals the "truth" of the inner self—even despite a writer's attempt to show only "what he wishes to appear."[70] The choice of actresses' lives complicates, however, assumptions about the truth of an inner self. It does not occur to the editors that accepting the metaphor of roles might lead to self-annihilation rather than self-discovery; nor do they sense a disjunction between this metaphor and their belief that an autobiographer's core of self may be known, "what he really is."

The memoirs by Mary Robinson and Charlotte Charke complicate, moreover, editorial assumptions about gender and life writing, as evident in prefatory comments about autobiographical form. To the editors, the truth of self for women seems to mean the truth of biology. Whereas they imagine multiple roles for men—from scientist to litterateur, sycophant to statesman or saint—they imagine only a limited range for women. These are traditional roles defined by sex and gender: wife, mistress, mother, daughter. What the editors imagine and what the texts suggest are not fully congruent.

The first autobiography in volume VII, the *Memoirs of Mrs. Robinson,* adopts feminine roles so conventionally that it seems almost parodic. Its two main plot lines juxtapose the autobiographer's progress in one set of roles (daughter, mother) against her regress in the other (wife, mistress). The first plot traces the fall of a beautiful young woman from chastity to infidelity. As Mary Robinson looks back on her history, she sees a sensitive, talented girl—too soon left unprotected by her father (who heads for America with his paramour), too soon married to a dissembling London rake (who neglects her for his many mistresses), too readily exposed to the temptations of the stage (where male viewers accost her virtue), and too fondly charmed by the amorous supplications of a prince (who falls in love with "Perdita" and loses interest after she becomes his lover). This plot repeats the pattern of the *chroniques scandaleuses,* one that depends upon its writer's sex to titillate the reader and then evoke pity.[71] Mary Robinson refuses to complete this plot, breaking off just before she consummates her affair with the prince and leaving it to her daughter to complete the account posthumously and record her mother's sufferings.

The intervention of Mrs. Robinson's daughter as editor—indeed, as coauthor and corroborator of her mother's story—represents a characteristically Victorian modification of the memoir form. The daughter's appearance in the text also validates the second plot: that of Robinson as loving mother and faithful daughter. As autobiographer, Robinson superimposes this second plot on the less commendable course of her actions as a wife, explaining her marriage to Thomas Robinson as an act of filial obedience and her fidelity to him, even during the worst of his profligacies, as a commitment to her children and family. She insists that she consented to his marriage proposal only because "of being still permitted to reside with my mother"; she hints, too, of latent maternal impulses: "only three months before I became a wife, I had dressed a doll."[72] Shortly after her marriage, when she discovers his infidelities and indifference to her sexual honor, she describes her sole joy as the prospect of motherhood: "I divided my time betwixt reading, writing, and making a little wardrobe for my expected darling. I little regretted the busy scenes of life; I sighed not for public attention" (59–60). Recalling the birth of her daughter, she claims inadequacy as a writer: "I cannot describe the sensations of my soul at the moment when I pressed the little darling to my bosom, my maternal bosom; when I kissed its hands, its cheeks, its forehead, as it nestled closely to my heart, and seemed to claim that affection which has never failed to warm it" (64). Robinson is, of course, quite adequate to her rhetorical task—as her repetition of the word *bosom,* with its deflection away from amorous possibilities toward maternal function, suggests.

Throughout her autobiography Robinson makes many such deflections, disturbing the smooth narrative of the main plot with suggestions of an alternative reading. The most provocative occurs when Robinson treats her relations with Richard Sheridan, who contemporary gossip claimed was her lover.[73] She notes that Sheridan's attentions were "unremitting," but focuses on his concern for her dramatic success and her "domestic comforts." She then narrates the death of her second child, Sophia, an occasion on which Sheridan showed "a sympathetic sorrow which penetrated my soul" (86–87). Given Robinson's tendency to introduce the maternal whenever she wishes to avoid the amorous, one suspects that contemporary gossip about their liaison was right. But Robinson stresses the maternal here and throughout her account—through rhetorical excess, through abrupt interruptions of her narrative with baby stories, through episodes of motherly solicitude and filial piety. With the maternal plot that punctuates the *Memoirs,* Robinson counters—and thus hopes to redeem—her tale of a woman's fall.

Robinson's nineteenth-century editors seem to have approved these tactics, for while they admit "some little negative disingenuousness," they also suggest that the autobiography "show[s] the exposed situation of an unprotected beauty" and, unlike other "autobiography of this class," is not "dangerous" (v). That they judge the *Memoirs* to be without danger suggests, perhaps, their need to rationalize its risqué elements. Yet it also suggests a shrewd patriarchal sense that, whether scandalous or maternal, Robinson's autobiography is safe because it stays carefully within the known boundaries of feminine behavior. The shape of the *Memoirs* is determined by gender, by the social roles allotted to women, and by literary traditions identified as feminine. These roles stay under the protection of men, at least officially. Even when a woman is left socially "unprotected," as Mary Robinson was, she remains literarily enclosed within a safe autobiographical form.

Or almost safe. For within Robinson's *Memoirs,* conventional as they may seem, a third plot not apparently subject to restrictions of gender emerges (or threatens to break loose). This plot, the account of a

professional artist's career, also punctuates the narrative of Robinson's regress—although not as deliberately or coherently as the maternal. Mary
Robinson succeeded, as she reminds us, as an actress, poet, novelist, and
journalist, and her autobiography commemorates these artistic achievements. It demonstrates her verbal ability in the gothic word painting with
which it opens and in scenes of her dramatic recitations of poetry as a
child. As Robinson narrates the course of her marriage, she inserts details
of her artistic interests—of female friends who write novels (48–49), of
an actress she admires (54), of her first attempt at publication to avoid
imprisonment for debt (71), of the patronage of the Duchess of Devon-
shire (75–77), of her various dramatic roles (89–90). Although the two
other plots sometimes cannibalize these details—her dramatic career
leading to the role of Perdita in which she captivates the prince, her authorial career arising from financial concerns for her family—they resist
subordination to either erotic or domestic concerns.

Robinson may claim, for example, that she turned to poetry, then to
the theater to support herself and her daughter, but she never fully convinces us that maternal motives dominate her actions. We sense a real
pleasure when family finances make it necessary for her to venture into
print, just as we recognize her delight in costume and in public performance that earning a living as an actress allows.[74] Such conflicting motives
prepare generically for artists' autobiographies of the Victorian period,
which typically expand such artistic scenes in order to explore the relation between maternal and creative interests, to show them as complementary or to worry about them as contradictory. (If the scandalous plot
typically disappears from Victorian texts, the origins in scandal cannot be
fully effaced; women writers continue to fear the equation of writing for
money with selling the self.)

Robinson's accounts of her artistic experiences show her straining
between contradictory autobiographical modes. To cite a pivotal instance: when the playwright Richard Sheridan visits her at home to persuade her to appear at the Drury Lane Theatre, she gives this record of
their encounter:

> *I was then some months advanced in a state of domestic solicitude, and*
> *my health seemed in a precarious state, owing to my having too long*
> *devoted myself to the duties of a mother in nursing my eldest daughter*

> *Maria. It was in this lodging that, one morning, wholly unexpectedly, Mr Brereton made us a second visit, bringing with him a friend, whom he introduced on entering the drawing-room. This stranger was Mr Sheridan.*
>
> *I was overwhelmed with confusion: I know not why; but I felt a* (82)
> *sense of mortification when I observed that my appearance was carelessly* dishabillé, *and my mind as little prepared for what I guessed to be the motive of his visit. I however soon recovered my recollection, and the theatre was consequently the topic of discourse.*

Why was Robinson overwhelmed with confusion? We might dismiss her claim "I know not why" as duplicity, in that Robinson knows retrospectively that her "*dishabillé*" aroused Sheridan's desire and encouraged his quest as a lover. But the confusion is more complex. Then and years later, when Robinson wrote her autobiography, it was unclear what role she should assume, what self she should present: the devoted mother greeting a friendly visitor? the erotic object confronting a male viewer? the aspiring professional actress negotiating with a theater owner? Such confusions—representing different possible subject positions—punctuate the entire account, with Robinson alternating details of her dramatic career with comments about her infants' illnesses or her husband's infidelities or her filial relationships. As autobiographer, she seems caught between a (masculine) tradition of public self-presentation and a (feminine) tradition of private self-revelation, between the forms of classic "autobiography" or *res gestae* on the one hand and the "diary" or "domestic memoir" on the other.

Robinson's daughter Maria, who edited the *Memoirs* and added the biographical account of her mother's last years, suffers from no such ambivalence about auto/biographical modes. A Victorian editor before her time, Maria firmly links the plot of authorship with that of maternity. As Maria completes the *Memoirs,* she dates the "commencement of her [mother's] literary career" from 1788, the year they both returned to England from the Continent (130).[75] In 1788 Mrs. Robinson began not only to write but to nurse her daughter back to health: "Maternal solicitude for a beloved and only child now wholly engaged her attention: her assiduities were incessant and exemplary for the restoration of a being to whom she had given life, and to whom she was fondly devoted" (131).

In the daughter's revision, maternal devotion pays off in literary production—or perhaps literary production reactivates maternal conscience. As Maria puts it, "the silence of the sick-chamber prov[ed] favourable to the muse" (131). Whatever the case, in editing her mother's life, Maria Robinson effects what her mother's narrative only hints: she created a safe, culturally viable myth of female artistry by shifting the narrative focus from romantic to domestic love. Put another way, we might say that Maria foresaw the virtues of linking the artist's autobiography generically with the domestic memoir.

Even without her daughter's editorial intervention, Robinson shows little desire to escape feminine plots. Indeed, her tale of Meribah Lorrington, the governess who received a "masculine education" (20) and taught young Mary all she knew, haunts the *Memoirs* as a negative example of the woman who dares to imitate men's modes. Meribah takes to drink and ends up in the Chelsea workhouse—in Robinson's words, "almost naked" and "completely disfigured" (23). Disfiguration, represented by a marring of facial features and a lack of clothing, is Meribah's punishment for masculine aspiration. The nakedness, the stripping away of sartorial protection, recalls Robinson's obsession with feminine costume and her terror in its absence. We can read her numerous descriptions of dress, ridiculously frequent and detailed in the *Memoirs,* as defensive strategies to ward off the fate of Meribah, as expression of a fear that to be without feminine dress is to be without identity. Perhaps she also fears (what we suspect) that feminine identity may *be* a matter of dress. In any case, she fears patriarchal retribution for seeking to find out.

Mary Robinson's counterpart in volume VII, however, records a different story about a woman's assumption of masculine models. In a sense, we can read the *Narrative of the Life of Mrs. Charlotte Charke* as a version of Meribah Lorrington's tale writ large. Officially—that is, in the view of her eighteenth-century contemporaries, her nineteenth-century publishers, and many of her modern readers—Charke's life traces a course of failure in virtually every feminine role: wife, daughter, sister, even actress. Charke confesses that she married too young and foolishly, only to discover within "the first twelvemonth of her connubial estate" that her husband had an "insatiate fondness for a plurality of common wretches, that were to be had for half a crown." She also admits that she damaged her career as a London actress by quarreling with the manager of the

Haymarket Theatre, and then behaving capriciously after he agreed to take her back. That Charke failed in the role of daughter is demonstrated by the *Life* itself, which she published in an attempt to regain the affection of her father, Colley Cibber. Charke never explains why Cibber disowned her; she refers only to her "mad pranks," to the "most notorious" gossip of her enemies, and to the machinations of her eldest sister, a "Goneril" who "deprive[s] her of a birthright."[76] In these repeated examples of failure, Charke reenacts what Patricia Meyer Spacks has identified as the most pervasive of eighteenth-century feminine plots: that of woman as victim, as sufferer of marital, filial, or social wrong.[77]

The editorial apparatus surrounding Charke's text urges us to read this plot as dominating its author's life. In the Hunt and Clarke series, the editors introduce Charlotte as a creature more "whimsical, wild, heartless, and unprincipled" than her brother; they characterize her tale as one of those "weeds" that "may spring up spontaneously . . . in the hot-bed of corrupt civilization" (v–vi). Lest this warning seem too gentle for the errant (female) reader, they conclude Charke's life with a biographical sequel that narrates the known facts of her history from 1755, when she published her *Life,* to 1759, the year of her death. The sequel reports the visit of a bookseller to "a wretched thatched hovel" near the New River Head, "where it was usual at that time for the scavengers to deposit the sweepings of the streets" (165). Surrounded by refuse and attended only by a "squalid handmaid," Charke makes her final appearance sitting

> on a broken chair under the mantle-piece, by a fire merely sufficient to
> put us in mind of starving. At our author's feet, on the flounce of her
> dirty petticoat, reclined a dog, almost a skeleton, who saluted us with a
> snarl. . . . A magpie was perched on the top rail of her chair, and on her   (166)
> lap was placed a pair of mutilated bellows—the pipe was gone. These
> were used as a succedaneum for a writing desk, on which lay her hopes
> and treasure, the manuscript of her novel.

Whether we feel sympathy or only (as the editors recommend) "surprise," this sequel suggests we interpret Charke's fate as a self-victimization—her misfortunes being "altogether of her own creating" (167). The addendum duly punishes her for feminine transgressions and masculine aspirations. Her writerly instruments have been taken away; her treasured manuscript is sold for ten guineas. Whether she has been physically punished for assuming male costume we cannot tell—except that the "squalid handmaid" who lives with her is ambiguously gendered, identified as a woman only by "a blue apron, indicating, what was otherwise doubtful, that it was a female." The sequel remains silent about Charke's appearance.

Despite this effort to make Charke's autobiography conform to a recognizable feminine pattern, we can see that the reader's responses have been manipulated by editorial intervention. Hunt and Clarke added sequels to all the lives that lacked them, advertising that they would include "brief introductions, and compendious sequels carrying on the narrative to the death of each writer." If we compare the original 1755 edition of Charke's *Life* with their version of 1827, we find no final episode of degradation in the original. Rather, in the original conclusion Charke reaffirms her confidence in the eventual restoration of fatherly affection and declares her "design to pass in the Catalogue of Authors," promising her readers that she "will endeavour to produce something now and then to make them laugh."[78] This note of good humor carries over to the dedication—written when the autobiography was complete but printed as its preface—which Charke addresses to herself, "your real friend." The self-dedication might be taken as evidence of the author's pathetic isolation, of her lack of other friends. But it might also be read as a brilliant commentary on the autobiographical act itself. Autobiography demands, as Charke implies, an act of self-performance. If the autobiographer writes to herself as well as to others, she may or may not persuade the others, but she will through "prudence" and "reflection" come finally to know herself: "for once to call you, FRIEND," as Charke says affirmatively, "a name I never as yet have known you by."[79] This is self-acceptance, not self-victimization.

What I am suggesting is that nineteenth-century editors taught readers to view Charlotte Charke's *Life* through the lens of gender, and they incorporated her text into a tradition of feminine life writing by misrepresenting its form.[80] Editors imposed a conventional shape upon the text and made it conformable to their sense of an errant femininity, even though the work resists, formally and thematically, such conformity. Why should they have done so?

The motives lie in the danger of Charke's autobiographical approach. Charke claims a universal application for her history: "I have, I think, taken care . . . that every person who reads my volume may bear a part in some circumstance or other in the perusal, as there is nothing inserted but what may daily happen to every mortal breathing" (10). This claim to universal human experience is conventional in early English autobiography, its corollary being the readerly habit of searching a biographical text for personal applications of its episodes or morals. Universal applicability is precisely what Hunt and Clarke wish to deny Charke's *Life,* however. To them the text is "curious," marked by the "extreme singularity" of the "pursuits and tendencies" of its author; it traces the career of a "reckless and anomalous individual"; Charke is a *"lusus naturae* of the moral world" (v–vi). At issue is whether or not Charke, a woman writer, and an errant one at that, may legitimately claim to represent *human* experience. Given the contrast with Robinson's autobiography (the two texts appear in the same volume), we might surmise that the editors refuse to allow this possibility, instead choosing to present Charke as a wayward female who is thus anomalous. Despite their attempt in the sequel to normalize her account, the editors seem to recognize a fundamental and irremediable deviation from normal human patterns. And thus they deny Charke access to—even deny the existence of—universal human experience or life writing.

Read apart from its editorial apparatus, Charke's *Life* challenges the notion of gender-specific autobiography. Much of her text focuses on acts of cross-dressing, both social and dramatic, and thus asserts by example that autobiographical writing can be androgynous, if not genderless. During her lifetime Charke made her reputation as a transvestite actress; she began her career with successes in female roles (Lucy in *George Barnwell,* Arabella in *The Fair Quaker,* Thalia in *Triumph of Love and Honour*), but soon shifted to male parts (Lord Place in *Pasquin,* Roderigo in *Othello,* George in *George Barnwell,* and, her most famous, MacHeath in *The Beggar's Opera*).[81] About the same time she assumed men's parts in the theater, she took to men's clothing in real life. She claims she did so "for some substantial reasons" (56), the telling of which she "beg[s] to be excused, as it concerns no mortal now living but myself" (161). All we can deduce from her autobiography is that the "substantial" reasons are partly amorous, partly financial; they are intimately connected with a man she privately "marries" and whose death deprives her "of every hope and means of a support" (55).

Yet we should not exaggerate the financial motives, for several episodes in the *Life* make it clear that money cannot fully explain Charke's preference for appearing *en cavalier*, as she calls it (56). Her autobiography begins, for example, with an episode of cross-dressing meant to reveal the natural bent of her personality: as a child of four, Charlotte dresses up in periwig and hat, waistcoat and sword, hoping to be taken for "the perfect representative of my sire" (13). As an adolescent, she takes up riding and shooting, "coming home laden with feathered spoil" and imagining herself "equal to the best fowler or marksman in the universe" (19–20); she also sets herself up as a physician (23–26), works as the family gardener (26–28), defends the house against robbery (29–30), even takes to horse trading (31–32). As an adult, now in male costume, she courts a wealthy young orphan (64–69), becomes valet to Lord Anglesea (82–83), takes up as a higgler "in breeches" (84), serves as a waiter in a public house (95–100), and travels as a strolling actor for nine years under the assumed name of "Mr. Brown," all the while keeping company with a "Mrs. Brown." As this list of episodes suggests, Charlotte Charke was a lifelong cross-dresser, perhaps a transvestite.[82] She does not use these terms or analyze her sexual behavior, but she does emphasize her masculine preferences throughout the autobiography.

Hunt and Clarke never name Charke's transvestism; instead, they refer to her besetting sin as "vagabondism" (v).[83] This inability to name Charke's sexual activities may represent the same sort of prudery that moved their contemporary Thomas Bowdler to publish an expurgated Shakespeare. But "vagabondism," euphemistic as it sounds, nevertheless describes Charke's cultural and literary predicament. By acting and writing as a man, she is guilty of its root meaning (Latin *vagari*), of wandering, erring, straying from the prescribed feminine path. This (mis)labeling allows the editors to categorize Charke's social crime and justify the sequel of her shame.

More important, it helps to obscure what was of greater danger than Charke's sexual deviance: her literary cross-dressing. In the *Narrative of the Life of Mrs. Charlotte Charke,* Charke assumes the stance of a masculine autobiographer, explicitly rejecting conventional feminine roles and trying out alternatives. The danger is not simply that she scorns feminine pursuits, claiming that she had little acquaintance "with that necessary utensil . . . of a young lady's education, called a needle," but adding that she understood French well before young ladies were traditionally employed in "ornamenting a piece of canvas with beasts, birds, and the alphabet" (12). Nor is there real danger in the scandalous content of the *Life,* in Charke's recital of the male roles she assumed; in the end, she admits failure or frustration in many of these guises. The danger of Charke's autobiography lies in the mode itself. This is the mode that Mason terms "Rousseauian" and claims that no women autobiographer has ever adopted. Rousseau's mode in the *Confessions*—"an unfolding self-discovery where characters and events are little more than aspects of the author's evolving consciousness"—stands, according to Mason, in marked contrast to the relational mode of women's self-writing, which recognizes the "real presence" of other consciousnesses and grounds identity "through relation to the chosen other." [84] Whether we name the mode after Rousseau or call it pre-Romantic or late picaresque or gender it as masculine, the point seems to be that male autobiographers move *through* experience, taking from it and others what they choose, whereas women autobiographers live *within* contexts, being shaped by others who share the space. [85] As one heroine of modern fiction puts it, "men [are] supposed to be able to go out and take on all kinds of experiences and shuck off what they [don't] want and come back proud," whereas everyone assumes that "being female ma[kes] you damageable" and "a certain amount of carefulness and solemn fuss and self-protection [are] called for." [86]

If we place Charlotte Charke within these dichotomies, it must be with Rousseau and men and taking on all kinds of experiences. Despite her many references to husband, child, lovers, sisters, brother, mother, and even father, she does not define her identity through such relationships. Even her appeals for fatherly affection, which motivate the publication of her *Life,* do not dominate its formal or thematic organization. As Lynne Friedl has pointed out, "the text in fact provides an unusual example in this period of a woman whose sense of self is defined primarily in relation not to her familial status (wife, mother, spinster, daughter) but to her occupational status." [87] Narratively, Charke arranges her autobiography as a movement through various (feminine and masculine) roles in a search for her (true) self.

Charke must have understood the danger that her life narrative posed. Although she admits it to be "the product of a female pen," she does not plead feminine inadequacy or excuse its faults on that account; instead, she asks that her narrative be given "the common chance of a criminal, at least to be properly examined, before it is condemned" (9). Her choice of criminality as a trope for her life writing marks a fine sensitivity to the literary and cultural codes she transgresses. She uses a female pen, but she writes in a masculine mode, in a forbidden autobiographical discourse.

Charke's trope of criminality recurs at other key moments in her autobiography. She does not express guilt when her husband dies in Jamaica or when she escapes her creditors or enters into an illicit sexual liaison. But when she reports the gossip told about her relationship with her father, she sounds guilty and uneasy. Gossip had it that Charke, in the guise of a highwayman, attacked her father in Epping Forest, drew a pistol, and "threatened to blow his brains out that moment if he did not deliver" (70); a more humorous rumor claimed that, while she was engaged as a fishmonger, she "stept most audaciously up to him" and slapped a large flounder "full in his face" (85). Such gossip sends Charke into "an agonizing rage" from which she cannot recover "for a month" (70). The intensity of her response and her incapacitation suggest that she is being provoked on a point about which she feels much pain. Yet she will not reveal the origin of her pain; nor will she confess why her family has disowned her.

One biographer claims that Colley Cibber disowned Charlotte when she dared to play his famous role of Sir Fopling Flutter.[88] Equally provocative was her appearance as Lord Place, who in *Pasquin* satirizes Cibber as poet laureate:

> *Second Voter. I am a devilish lover of sack.*
> *Lord Place. Sack, you say? Odso, you shall be poet laureat.*
> *Second Voter. Poet! No, my lord, I am no poet, I can't make verses.*
> *Lord Place. No matter for that—you'll be able to make odes.*
> *Second Voter. Odes, my lord. What are those?*
> *Lord Place. Faith, sir, I can't tell what they are; but I know you may be qualified for the place without being a poet.*[89]

Yet, beyond these instances, we might assume that the unnamed and unnameable origin of Charke's pain is her transvestism or, in a larger sense, her unfulfilled desire for a masculine identity and patriarchal privileges.

From her childish theft of her father's clothes to her successful career as a male actress to her various stints in men's jobs to her life in breeches with Mrs. Brown, Charke usurped forms that patriarchy had reserved for itself.

And she usurps again in writing autobiography. For it was her father who wrote the first English autobiography of an actor and author, *An Apology for the Life of Mr. Colley Cibber, Comedian* (1739), later published as the inaugural volume of Hunt and Clarke's series (1826). To Cibber, Charlotte's *Life* must have seemed an unfilial challenge to and a travesty of his authority—both a literary travesty (Charlotte's self-dedication, for example, mocks the effusive rhetoric of her father's dedication "To a Certain Gentleman") and a social travesty (Charlotte's public flaunting of her masculine career mocks the gender codes, so fundamental to Cibber's drama, that keep women in skirts and men in breeches). Even the woodcut Charke used as frontispiece in her 1756 edition must have embarrassed the father who engendered her. Dressed in female garb, Charke exposes two powerful forearms and turns a decidedly masculine face to her audience.

That we should, in the twentieth century, read the *Narrative of the Life of Mrs. Charlotte Charke* as a criminal text is to mistake it, however, and to accept the restrictive view of gender and genre that limits her nineteenth-century editors. It is also to miss the subtler implications of her own use of criminality as a trope for life writing. For if Charke asks that her autobiography be treated as a criminal, it is with a sense that, before the law, all are equal. Justice should be done to a writer's performance whatever the sex, whatever the literary mode: "should it be found guilty of nonsense and inconsistencies, I must consequently resign it to its deserved punishment" (9).

There is good reason now to move beyond the critical practice of identifying feminine, relational modes with "women's autobiography" and to adopt a more expansive approach to what women, as autobiographers, have produced. As Shirley Neuman has argued, "the question with which the poetics of autobiography has yet to come to terms" is the multiplicity of selves in any single autobiography, the relation between individual identity and group identification in women's life writing; for, thus far, "the different poetics we have elaborated are vastly reductive before the experiences of autobiographers." [90] The multiple traditions of autobiography that Victorian women inherited opened up the possibility of complex identities, multifaceted self-representations. Some Victorian women followed in the way of spiritual autobiographers such as Hayes and Ashbridge, with their theological sophistication and political commitment. Others wrote domestic memoirs and, like Mary Robinson, linked maternity and domesticity to literary authorship. Even Charlotte Charke had a few literary followers—perhaps not in the picaresque mode that led her from acting to higgling "in breeches" to fishmongering to hack writing, but in the determination with which she tried out different autobiographical modes in representing and recording her life.[91]

II

The Polemics of Piety:
Charlotte Elizabeth Tonna's
Personal Recollections, Harriet
Martineau's *Autobiography,* and
the Ideological Uses of
Spiritual Autobiography

IN MODERN LITERARY criticism and cultural history, Charlotte Eliza-beth Tonna (1790–1846) and Harriet Martineau (1802–76) have come to represent a middle-class subjectivity and literary domesticity typical of early Victorian women writers.[1] On the face of it, this similar categori-zation makes sense. Both women were born into middle-class homes in provincial Norwich; both grew up in families with sophisticated literary and musical tastes and with active interests in local cultural life; both, in large part because of childhood deafness, turned to literature for intel-lectual and psychological solace; both became writers out of personal de-sire combined with a commitment to the public good; both employ, in Shelagh Hunter's apt phrase, a "poetics of moralism."[2] Yet despite their many similarities, as autobiographers Tonna and Martineau represent quite different responses to the traditions of spiritual autobiography and domestic memoir that they engage. Indeed, so different are the effects of their autobiographical accounts, so antithetical their treatment of com-mon conventions of life writing, that they represent different forms of female subjectivity, different responses to Victorian domestic ideology, and different approaches to women's authorship.

This chapter delineates the formal features and ideological functions of Tonna's *Personal Recollections* (1841) and Martineau's *Autobiography*

(1877). In so doing, it suggests that we can best understand their differences as autobiographers, perhaps even as women writers, not by referring solely to their gender or class but by placing their accounts within the regional, religious, and political contexts from which they emerged and to which they respond.

Charlotte Elizabeth Tonna wrote her autobiography to avoid, as many subsequent women writers did, the possibility of misrepresentation. Acknowledging that an author, even a quiet woman whom "it has pleased God to bring . . . before the world," becomes "in some sense public property," she sought to suppress posthumous literary gossip and biographical speculation and to avoid a literary treatment of herself as "the heroine of some strange romance."[3] Tonna's resistance to being miscast as a romantic heroine represents a lifelong Evangelical bias against fiction and the Romantic imagination, which she believed were "inimical to rational pursuits, and opposed to spiritual-mindedness" (7). But it also represents Tonna's calculated decision to control the genre—the shape, the content, the significant details, the social and political import—in which her life and work would be presented to her reading public.

Charlotte Elizabeth Browne Phelan Tonna had pursued a literary career to support herself after her separation from (perhaps desertion by) her first husband, Captain George Phelan. She had adopted the pen name Charlotte Elizabeth to avoid his legal claim to her literary profits. After Phelan's death, she had married the considerably younger Lewis Hippolytus Joseph Tonna, a minor Evangelical writer who was, like herself, a proponent of what is now called Zionism. Such details were the stuff of the *chroniques scandaleuses,* the autobiographical genre often chosen by women authors who took up literary careers out of financial necessity. Tonna wished to avoid that genre, its gossipy tone as well as its rationale for professional work, and construct another kind of life story, through which she would influence more positively her female readers and successors. The genre she chose was spiritual autobiography, but blended with domestic memoir.

Given this intention, Tonna begins her *Personal Recollections* with chapters on home and family life. With simple titles like "Childhood," "Youth," and "Early Days," character sketches of father, grandmother, and brother, and details of life in provincial Norwich, these chapters resemble many other Victorian domestic memoirs. More overtly than such memoirs, Tonna's celebrates the virtues of the "rural English HOME" in which she grew up and on which she considers English prosperity and political freedom to be founded (37). Unlike most domestic memoirists, however, Tonna does not make marriage pivotal in her narrative; instead, she places a classic Protestant conversion experience at the center of her account, presenting it as "the commencement of all that deserves to be called life" (103). Tonna makes conversion seem the natural climax of a domestic sequence, and her autobiography creates a strong if implicit narrative link between family life and religious experience. Orthodox religion depends upon—naturally results from, Tonna implies—a solid Victorian home life.[4]

Although she uses domestic scenes to establish the origins of her religious orthodoxy, Tonna was not, in fact, converted as a child in her parents' home. She became an Evangelical Christian during the early years of her marriage, while living alone on her husband's Irish estate. Her emotional condition during those married years—"a restless, unsatisfied, unhappy feeling, that seemed in quest of some unknown good" (103), followed by "the resolution of being a perfect devotee in religion" (119) and then "a full conviction of my own past sinfulness and present helplessness" (122)—led her to read the Bible, the Anglican liturgy, and what few religious books she could get hold of in rural Ireland. This intense reading, especially of the New Testament Gospels and a spiritual memoir for which she gives no title, produced her conversion, as it had produced the conversions of so many of her autobiographical predecessors.[5]

It also produced a desire to write. Mary Jean Corbett has noted that Tonna's career as a writer began almost immediately after her conversion.[6] While living alone, studying her Bible to obtain "a view of the whole scheme of redemption" (134), she received a parcel of religious materials published by the Dublin Tract Society:

> *With equal wonder and delight I opened one of them, a simple, spiritual little production; and the next that I took up was an inducement to distribute tracts among the poor. From this I learned that some excellent people were engaged in a work quite new to me; and, with a sigh, I* (135) *wished I had the means of contributing to their funds. Presently the thought flashed upon me, 'Since I cannot give them money, may I not write something to be useful in the same way?'*

What might seem to be merely a chronological coincidence—undergoing a conversion, receiving the tracts, desiring to write—becomes, in Tonna's narrative, a causal connection. This connection between conversion and authorship is crucial to Tonna's revision of the genre of spiritual autobiography. Just as male autobiographers had traditionally followed their accounts of conversion with calls to the ministry,[7] so Tonna records her call to didactic writing. The conventional pattern of spiritual autobiography, transformed to fit a woman's circumstances, provides the divine and literary authority she seeks.

If the narrative Tonna constructs is less explicit in its causality than it might be, it is perhaps because Victorian women seldom received divine calls to authorship. Tonna admits that she wrote her first tract in an all-night fit of inspiration, and only the next morning received a letter requesting a writerly contribution to the Dublin Tract Society. "I saw in it a gracious acceptance of my free-will offering at His hands to whom it had been prayerfully dedicated" (136), she adds, without explicitly interpreting the experience as a sanction of female authorship. Yet if Tonna's narration is tentative, it is perhaps also because she knows other causalities might be invoked: those linking domestic and spiritual crises, professional authorship and financial need.

It is possible, for example, to read the *Personal Recollections,* especially the pivotal fifth and sixth chapters, as the autobiography of a woman brought to religion by marital malaise. Tonna's silence about her marriage and her substitution of a conversion experience for the more conventional scenes of romance, courtship, and marriage suggest such an interpretation. It is also possible to read the *Personal Recollections* as the autobiography of a woman brought to authorship by means of intellectual boredom, cultural discomfort, and financial distress. Chapter V, which begins with the description of Tonna's "restless, unsatisfied, unhappy" state, includes not only the account of her conversion but also an account of life in Ireland. Tonna admits her extreme resistance to moving to Ireland, her husband's home, though she attributes her attitude to an ignorant misunderstanding of Irish people and culture. Nonetheless, her "restless, unsatisfied, unhappy feeling" might describe as well her response to married life as her spiritual condition. The chapter abounds in hints of uneasiness: she feels it "a sort of degradation to have an Irish name" (105), the name she has acquired through marriage; when she travels to Dublin, she thinks nostalgically of her dead father and characterizes herself as a "poor girl," now "with none to guide, none to guard, none to speak a cheering word" (105); once in Ireland, she feels "ashamed" of the treatment of tenants on her husband's estate (119) and secludes herself within the house and garden; and when she alludes to the lawsuit that was the original cause of her husband's removal to Ireland, she calls it "a property not worth litigating" (135).

Such details—domestic, social, ethnic, financial—betray a distaste for the marriage into which she has entered. Yet Tonna links such details to her spiritual condition or, more obtusely, refuses to consider their hermeneutic implications—that is, the details either serve as evidence of her "conviction of sin" or remain narrative dead ends, unexplored and uninterpreted. What results is an autobiography that creates spiritual authority for Tonna's literary productions while it simultaneously represses other generic and hermeneutic possibilities.

The literary authority that Tonna gains by her rhetorical maneuvers has been well analyzed by such critics as Mary Jean Corbett and Valerie Sanders, who emphasize the woman writer newly invested with power for "producing and reproducing the ideologies that structure Victorian culture."[8] This new authority deserves the emphasis it has received, for it represents a significant phase in the history of women's authorship. Tonna gains credibility for her literary work by aligning it with women's domestic (cultural) work. But Tonna's narrative repressions deserve greater attention for what they reveal about the history of women's autobiography and the modes of self-interpretation possible at this early moment in the tradition. Autobiographies like the *Personal Recollections* make possible a transition for the woman writer away from the *chroniques scandaleuses* and toward more respectable forms of self-representation. What they repress, inevitably, are other literary possibilities.

In order to link spiritual autobiography with the domestic memoir, Tonna must deny two such possibilities: (1) that domestic life may give rise to spiritual and theological crises, that domestic memoir does not necessarily contribute to the orthodox form of spiritual autobiography that Tonna's life seeks to illustrate; and (2) that authorship may arise from economic rather than religious motives, that an alternative form of the artist's autobiography, deriving from the *chroniques scandaleuses,* may be analytically superior to spiritual atuobiography as an explanatory genre for the woman writer.

I have already suggested that Tonna's emotional state may have

resulted from a marital rather than a purely religious crisis. (Modern biographers have speculated, for example, that her husband was not only
insane but also physically violent.) Tonna simply refuses to consider her
marital difficulties, invoking the standard Victorian principle of speaking
ill of no person: "I have carefully abstained from any particulars respect-
ing myself that could either cast a reproach on the dead or give pain to
the living" (116). Later, in telling the circumstances of her return to England, where she lived for two years in her brother's household, she even
more emphatically refuses to explain her domestic affairs: "Many, and
sharp, and bitter were the trials left unrecorded here; and shame be to the
hand that shall ever dare to lift up the veil that tender charity would cast
over what was God's doing, let the instruments be what and who they
may" (230–31). Her formulation turns domestic difficulties—a marital
estrangement and presumably her husband's "incipient madness"—into
spiritual trials, making them the metaphorical "stroke of the rod" or "the
bitter cup" (231) that each Christian must undergo in the quest for spiritual perfection. But does not her injunction against "lift[ing] up the veil"
betray an anxiety about undesirable personal revelations, about unspeakable "personal recollections," about possible unsolicited or unflattering
biographical portraits that Tonna wishes to prevent?

One suspects that Tonna fears the discrediting of her domestic character, on which her literary authority depends. The *Personal Recollections*
are silent on key questions: whether Captain Tonna deserted his wife or
she chose to separate from him, whether his personal and professional
failures led to their marital crisis or her domestic inadequacies caused
them, whether her conversion to Evangelical Christianity exacerbated
the difficulties of their marriage or smoothed them over.[9] The answers to
such questions would lead readers to conclude for themselves whether
Charlotte Elizabeth was a model of Christian femininity or whether her
domestic experiences discredit her spiritual and literary authority. Earlier
women autobiographers tended to specify their domestic guilt or innocence: Charke discusses her husband's penchant for Covent Garden pros-
titutes, Robinson her husband's sexual and financial profligacies and later
the Prince of Wales's desertion. Tonna, of course, implies her innocence
and her commitment to "domestic love" (234)—not by discussing her
husband but by detailing her happy childhood, by describing the domestic tranquillity and her literary productivity while she lives with her

brother at Sandhurst, and by emphasizing her ability to "mother" and educate a foster child, the deaf-mute Jack Britt, whom she adopts while in Ireland and later takes to England. Yet she does not allow her autobiography to become an apologia for her domestic innocence.

Instead, Tonna produces a version of spiritual autobiography that uses scenes of domestic life to establish her normality, even superiority, but that also represses other possible relations of religion and domesticity. The result is a curious, uneasy mixture of genres. On the one hand, by blending domestic memoir with spiritual autobiography, Tonna endorses generically—and helps to create—the Evangelical equation of religious and domestic faith that dominated English culture until mid-century. On the other hand, by keeping certain elements of spiritual autobiography distinct from domesticity—by treating conversion, for example, as an essentially theological matter and by limiting certain chapters to doctrinal issues that the Christian autobiographer must work out in the course of her salvation—Tonna's account reveals the difficulties in that cultural equation. Not all domestic happiness links to spiritual progress; not all spiritual progress results from or leads to domestic health. The narrative lapses suggest the preferability, at least for some women writers, of working within a "purer" form of spiritual autobiography. And, although it would have horrified her to think so, Tonna's account prepares for the ultimate undoing of the cultural equation by late Victorian women writers such as Annie Besant, whose *Autobiography* critiques the union of patriarchal religion and Victorian domesticity that Tonna so fondly endorses.[10]

In the *Personal Recollections,* Tonna's primary agenda is to associate, positively and productively, domestic and spiritual work. Like other Evangelical women writers, Tonna assumes her writing to be an extension of domestic labor. Yet this association leads Tonna into another narrative repression. Throughout her account she avoids or obscures the economic aspects of authorship, insisting simply that she did not write for financial profit. (Nor, she implies, should any good Christian woman. She leaves it ambiguous whether a good Christian man might write for profit, but her view of female literary production as an extension of domestic work makes it impossible for her to consider her own financial motivations.) The absence of detail about Tonna's literary work—not only a silence about her earnings but also a reticence about many of her major publications, including her social-problem novels and her editorship of the *Christian Lady's Magazine*—has frustrated many feminist scholars, who chalk it up to either modesty or neurosis.[11] But Tonna's silence is the inevitable result of domesticating literary work and choosing the spiritual autobiography as her primary representational mode.

When Tonna speaks of writing, it is as a "literary avocation" (221) or, in biblical terms, as a "free-will offering" (136). The amateurism implied by "avocation" is deliberate, a refusal of professional status consonant with her belief that her writing should be of a "homely simplicity," fully intelligible to a five-year-old (179).[12] The use of "free-will offering" reinforces Tonna's conception of women's writing not as a required task but as one of many possible forms of Christian service.[13] Such allusions are expanded narratively by episodes in which Tonna resists the allure of professional secular authorship with its profit motive. The most difficult temptation occurs when she has separated from her husband, who, it seems, leaves her to provide for herself but attempts to claim her literary profits. She is invited to contribute tales anonymously to a magazine, "as moral as I pleased, but with no direct mention of religion" (237); she is also asked, by a dear friend, to rewrite a novel that has failed to sell. Although both offers are lucrative and although she desperately needs money, she decides against them, quoting Satan's temptation of Jesus in the wilderness: "All these things will I give thee, if thou wilt fall down and worship me" (241, Matt. 4:9).

In Tonna's account, it is the fame and financial reward of professional careers that women writers must resist. These potential "sins" replace the temptations to religious apostasy or moral backsliding more conventionally found in spiritual autobiography. It would be easy to ridicule Tonna's rhetoric or deconstruct her rationale for authorship, offering instead a more sophisticated explanation based on the economic facts of the Victorian literary marketplace or middle-class codes of social behavior. Yet Tonna's insistence on her writing as a "sacred" rather than "secular" task permitted her to become a writer, even as it gained respectability for other women whose literary productions were on the "secular" side of the dichotomy.

Tonna must make awkward narrative substitutions, however, in order to maintain her integrity as a "sacred" writer, one whose work is an extension and example of divinely sanctioned female labor. I have already noted that she gives little account of her twelve-year editorship of the *Christian Lady's Magazine* and virtually none of her major literary works: *The System* (1827), *Combination* (1832), or *Helen Fleetwood: A Tale of the Factories* (1841). But the most awkward, if also most essential, substitution appears in chapter XIV, "Employment," in which Tonna discusses work not in any professional or economic sense but as the spiritual labor every Christian should undertake for the harvest of souls. "Employment" begins with a call to discipleship and Christian work:

> *How is it that Christians so often complain they can find nothing to do for their Master? To hear some of them bemoaning their unprofitableness, we might conclude that the harvest indeed is small, and the labourers many. So many servants out of employment is a bad sign; and to obviate the difficulty complained of, I purpose showing you two or three ways in which those who are so inclined may bestir themselves for the good of others.*   (308)

Examples of Tonna's Christian labor follow—examples that include conducting Scripture lessons for working-class children, establishing a Protestant mission in the parish of St. Giles, and helping male politicians to work against Popery and other religious heresies. Tonna's examples of "employment" embody the Tennysonian principle that a woman's "hands are quicker unto good," a principle, as Mary Jean Corbett has observed, that Victorian women often replicate in the final sections of their religious autobiographies in their emphasis on "the work of the ministry." [14] In the final chapters of her *Personal Recollections* Tonna presents herself not as a famous literary figure but as a good Christian woman who labors for the Kingdom of God.

These final chapters also include a broader if perhaps less evident aim: they seek to establish a feminine tradition of authorship with Hannah More as its luminary figure and Tonna as the pivotal figure of the next generation. In the decade before the *Personal Recollections,* More had been the subject of two hagiographic biographies—William Roberts's *Memoirs of the Life and Correspondence of Hannah More* (1834) and Thomas Taylor's *Memoir of Mrs. Hannah More* (1838)—and, even as the *Personal Recollections* were being revised and posthumously reissued, of a third,

Helen C. Knight's *A New Memoir of Hannah More; Or, Life in Hall and Cottage* (1851). Roberts's biography, like those that followed, is "a saint's life, an account of how Hannah More turned her back on the world of the great and the gay and its vanities to become a humble but useful instrument of the Lord"; as such, it established the model for how a woman might become "a professional writer without sacrificing her respectability." [15] I suggest that Tonna drew on key features of these biographies, explicitly aligning herself and her work with Hannah More.

Tonna discusses More at two pivotal moments in the *Personal Recollections,* in both instances to draw parallels between their lives and their literary work. In recalling her first meeting with More at Clifton in 1825, she describes More's interest in her work with "deaf and dumb children" (223) and More's displacement from her home through "domestic treachery" (226); Tonna also gives a character sketch of "the aged saint" (224) and a reassessment of her work. [16] The character sketch is conventional, but the reassessment is not. Whereas contemporaries had praised More for "her schools, her charities, her letters, her devotional and educational publications, and all of these deserve the full celebrity that they have attained" (223), Tonna selects the "Cheap Repository Tracts" as the chief of More's attainments: "I thought more of her 'Cheap Repository Tracts' than of all her other works combined" (224). The judgment indirectly confers praise on Tonna as well, since her chief literary work at that period was the "Dublin Tracts."

Beyond self-praise lies an agenda for female authorship and autobiography. What Tonna stresses in her assessment of More's *work*—and thus what she establishes as the criteria for meritorious female authorship—are its didactic purpose, its stylistic simplicity, and its freedom from writerly pretension or pride. These were virtues More had herself extolled. In the *Strictures on the Modern System of Female Education* (1799), More had stressed the importance of women's influence and defined the role of woman as moral teacher, with power "to raise the depressed tone of public morals, and to awaken the drowsy spirit of religious principle." [17] In the *Strictures,* More had also inveighed against young women who took up the pen "with a pretension to sentiment," writing in high-flown, vacuous styles, producing "an elegy on a sick linnet, or a sonnet on a dead lap-dog," yet unfortunately receiving the praise of "fond and flattering friends." [18] The Hannah More whom Tonna describes is quite the feminine ideal—an author devoted to the public good, but without a trace of vanity: "If I could have discovered, which I could not, a single trait of consciousness that she was a distinguished being, exalted into eminence by public acclaim, I must have conceived her to be dwelling upon this branch of her many privileges, that she had been a Deborah when many a Barak shrunk from the post of honour, and skulked behind a woman" (224). Tonna presents More, in other words, not as the popular young dramatist and friend of Garrick, or as a distinguished member of the *Bas Bleu* circle, but as a woman writer who has devoted herself to instructing and encouraging English people of all classes, without glorying in the role of literary leadership she has been given.

What Tonna stresses about More's *life*—and this emphasis represents, in Tonna's view, the primary motive for all women's life writing—is More's behavior in affliction. During the period of "domestic treachery," which Tonna alludes to but does not describe specifically, More had endured the theft and dishonesty of her servants, all the while maintaining that it was God's will she should be so mistreated. Tonna reads More's behavior as an example to others less famous or fortunate, who may wrongly believe that the eminent escape affliction. According to Tonna, More demonstrates the heuristics of affliction: "God's children find that it is good for themselves that they should be afflicted; but they do not always remember how good it is for the church that they should be so" (226). Given this interpretation of More's life, Tonna can transform the domestic afflictions of her own, potentially embarrassing and far from exemplary, into a model for readers of her autobiography. Consonant with her depiction of authorship as a form of sacred service, the episodes of domestic affliction—More's and her own—become occasions for women writers to display ideal feminine character, their piety, patience, and endurance.

At stake for Tonna was the establishment of a tradition of female authorship and autobiography, in what might be characterized as a movement away from Mary Robinson toward Hannah More, or a movement away from the *chroniques scandaleuses* toward the domestic memoir, or a shift in focus from public, professional spectacle to private, domestic character. In the transition what got lost was the integrity of spiritual autobiography as a genre devoted to religious questions, to theological or philosophical models of self-interpretation, and to intellectual concerns equally and universally relevant to men and women. These concerns would motivate Harriet Martineau's very different approach to autobiography in the generation after Tonna's *Personal Recollections.*

What Tonna revered and found self-authorizing, Harriet Martineau questioned and found professionally problematic. Martineau's *Autobiography* responds in form and specific details to Tonna's autobiographical tactics, not the least of which was Tonna's elevation of Hannah More to the head of a feminine literary tradition. For Martineau, More had also been a seminal figure, but a less mythical, more troubling one. I begin with Martineau's very different treatment of More as a means of introducing the different polemical purposes of her *Autobiography* as it, like Tonna's *Personal Recollections,* negotiates the conventions of spiritual autobiography and domestic memoir. I then turn, in an order that approximates the divisions of volume 1, to Martineau's oppositional treatment of birthplace and home life, to her social-scientific (anti-Evangelical) discussion of illness and childhood trials, and to her separate if concurrent narratives of spiritual growth and professional progress.

Martineau's first professional publication in the *Monthly Repository,* "Female Writers of Practical Divinity," had discussed Hannah More (November 1822), and continued (December 1822) with More, Anna Laetitia Barbauld, and Elizabeth Smith.[19] Martineau had analyzed their work for its spiritual benefits but also, one infers, for the literary models they provided; as Valerie Pichanick suggests, she "identified with these women, and saw herself as their likely successor."[20] Indeed, at the beginning of the *Monthly Repository* series, Martineau justified her choice of subject "as doing justice to those whose names are before the public, and as exciting the emulation of those of their sex who are capable of imitating such bright examples."[21] As a young writer, Martineau clearly imagined herself as "capable." Her mentor, the Reverend Lant Carpenter, under whose spell she had fallen in late adolescence, had held up More as a worthy figure to emulate: "If any female writer should [hereafter] come forward to the public, possessing the clearness, simplicity, correctness, and well-stored understanding of an Edgeworth, the brilliant yet chaste imagination and 'devotional taste' of a Barbauld, and the energy and high-toned moral principle of a More, divested of bigotry, and founded upon genuine Christian theology, in the scale of utility she will probably stand unrivalled among her contemporaries." [22]

Despite her initial emulation, Martineau soon recognized the limitations of More's religious and literary practice and for most of her career chose a different professional model. By the time Martineau wrote her third article for the *Monthly Repository,* "On Female Education" (1823), she was implicitly criticizing More's educational theory, disagreeing with More's assumptions that women were intellectually inferior to men and more likely, if educated, to become vain about their learning.[23] By 1832, when Martineau embarked on her immensely successful *Illustrations of Political Economy,* she was interpreting her literary career as being without a female precedent. To Lord Brougham's praise for that series she responded, "I feel too deeply to express very plainly the gratification that it is to a solitary authoress, who has had no pioneer in her literary path but steadfastness of purpose, to find her exertions approved by yourself." [24] And by the 1850s, when she translated Comte's *Positive Philosophy* and composed her *Autobiography,* she was charting a course of influence and development quite distinct from—indeed, in opposition to—the Evangelical, feminine model of More and Tonna.

It is true that Martineau's emphasis on her solitariness, on the absence of pioneering women, belies the literary connections of her didactic writing with More's "Cheap Repository Tracts" and Tonna's "Dublin Tracts," both of which attempted to convey social and political principles (not just religious sentiments) to a popular audience and both of which established literary precedents for industrial fiction such as Martineau's own *The Rioters* (1827), *The Turn-out* (1827), and *A Manchester Strike* (1832).[25] Martineau ignores, too, the common tradition of social protest literature in which both she and Tonna participated—although, in this instance, the younger Martineau's industrial novels preceded the elder Tonna's more famous *Helen Fleetwood* (1839–40).[26] Martineau's denial of influence also contradicts much current literary and cultural history, including Leonore Davidoff and Catherine Hall's important *Family Fortunes: Men and Women of the English Middle Class, 1780–1850* and Mary Jean Corbett's *Representing Femininity,* which consider Martineau within the tradition of More and Tonna and connect her views with the "domestic ideology" of the rising middle class. For Davidoff and Hall, Martineau is chief among those early Victorian writers who "celebrate domesticity."[27]

Despite these literary connections, I want to take seriously Martineau's statement that she had "no pioneer in her literary path," and thus delineate her intention in the *Autobiography* to construct a model for female selfhood and authorship different from those imagined by More and Tonna. This self-construction depends on a reformulation of the spiritual autobiography and a relatively slight use of the domestic memoir. Although there are traces of domestic memoir in the *Autobiography,* the presence of this homely genre—and the topos of domesticity—do not necessarily make Martineau a compatriot of other women writers who adopt the memoir form or discuss domestic matters. Domesticity is, rather, a common concern for many early Victorian autobiographers, male and female alike, and what matters is not *whether* but *how* they engage the conventions of the memoir within their autobiographical accounts. In the first half of the century there were multiple domestic ideologies, multiple middle classes, and multiple autobiographers from those classes, whose responses to domesticity are inflected by their different religious, political, social, and regional affiliations and whose views are registered through their particular negotiations of generic possibilities.

Both Tonna and Martineau came, for instance, from Norwich, a provincial town known in the early nineteenth century for its active literary and artistic life.[28] Tonna and Martineau affiliated, however, with different religious, social, and political groups: Tonna was Anglican and Tory, her father an Oxford-educated Anglican clergyman, her family connected socially with members of the gentry; Martineau was Unitarian and radical, her family solidly bourgeois, its male members distinguished as surgeons and textile manufacturers. The two young women grew up in different parts of the town, Tonna in the Cathedral close and outlying village of Bawburgh, Martineau in the commercial district near the family business—geographical facts reinforced by the illustrations to their autobiographies, Tonna's of Norwich Cathedral, Martineau's of her solidly bourgeois home (see figures 1 and 2). To adapt Susan Morgan's words, "place matters."[29] These different affiliations and locations influ-

Figure 1. Norwich Cathedral. Frontispiece to Charlotte Elizabeth's *Personal Recollections,* 4th ed. (London: Seeleys, 1854). Courtesy of Yale University Library.

ence the treatment of birthplace and home in their autobiographical accounts, as well as the models of authorship that emerge from them.

In Tonna's *Personal Recollections,* to grow up in Norwich is to imbibe the principles of English Protestantism, as if from the very air, water, and soil of East Anglia. Tonna begins her narrative this way:

Figure 2. House in which Harriet Martineau was born. Frontispiece to Harriet Martineau's *Autobiography*, vol. 1 (London: Smith, Elder, 1877). Courtesy of Yale University Library.

> *To commence the task [of writing autobiography], in which I earnestly implore the Father of all mercies, and Teacher of all truth to guide me, to guard me from mis-statement, to preserve me from self-seeking, and to overrule it to the glory of His great name.—I must remind you that my birth-place was Norwich. . . . Many years have elapsed since I last*

beheld it, . . . [b]ut I cannot forget the early impression produced on my
mind by the peculiarities of the place; nor must they be omitted here.
The sphere in which it is my dearest privilege to labour in the cause of
Protestantism; and sometimes, when God has blessed my poor efforts to
the deliverance of some captive out of the chains of Popish delusion, I
have recalled the fact of being born just opposite the dark old gateway of
that strong building where the glorious martyrs of Mary's day [Bloody
Mary, the popish queen] were imprisoned.

(5–6)

In this opening passage Tonna adapts two conventions of autobiography:
the invocation of God's guidance in the matter of truth telling (as in
Augustine's *Confessions*) and the re-creation of the birthplace as an influential site not only of physical health but of moral integrity (as in Wordsworth's *Prelude*). In Tonna's account the two are linked. For her, to grow
up in Norwich is to grow up Evangelical and to grow up truthful: after
all, the Protestant martyrs died for the cause of truth, and those martyrs,
she tells us, were her childhood heroes.

Martineau responds to this formula, implicitly critiquing Tonna's
depiction of Norwich as historical and native site. Although Martineau
does not include Tonna among the literary figures she discusses in the
Autobiography, perhaps because she never met her, perhaps because she
considered Tonna's work subliterary, Martineau certainly knew of and
about her fellow Norwichian. In 1844 Tonna had denounced Martineau
in a pamphlet, *Mesmerism: A Letter to Miss Martineau,* which characterized
mesmerism as "a branch of sorcery" and a form of "Satanic power"; she
begged Martineau to give up "this devilish device." [30] When Tonna died
in 1846, Martineau commented in a letter to Fanny Wedgwood, "So
poor 'Charlotte Eliz.' is dead. How amazed she will be yonder at finding
that she could be mistaken; and that there were things visible to others
beyond what she saw! I trust she will be happier there." [31] It is usually said
that Martineau composed her *Autobiography* in the 1850s after learning of
a fatal heart disease. It may be equally true that she began her *Autobiography* in the 1840s, shortly after reading Tonna's *Personal Recollections.* [32]
Tonna had linked their common birthplace to religious truth, but the
truth to which Tonna's account leads is an Evangelical Protestantism that
Martineau, as a scientific Comtean, considered "fictitious."

Tonna's claim to Norwich as a locus of truth includes a political castigation of her fellow citizens that Martineau, as a radical, was even less likely to countenance. In the chapter "Early Days," Tonna describes the religious and political situation in Norwich as one of deep divisiveness and apocalyptic evil:

(45)

> *Antichrist bestrode our city, firmly planting there his two cloven hoofs*
> *of Popery and Socinianism. Many of our leading men belonged to these*
> *two systems, the former, the Jeringhams, Petres, &c. making up in*
> *wealth and private influence for what our then Protestant constitution*
> *withheld of political power, and the latter mingling its bad leaven in*
> *every part of the mass, sending to parliament one of the most active*
> *of its communion, to represent the ancient city.*

Tonna names the Catholic families who constitute half of Antichrist; she does not name the Socinians[33]—a common epithet for Unitarians—who stirred the working classes to unrest and sent a radical M.P. to London. Although not a Martineau, that Socinian M.P. was certainly a friend and political ally of the family.[34] By 1855, Martineau may have been out of sympathy with the Unitarians, whose beliefs she considered a halfway house on her journey from "fictitious" theology to "positivistic" science, but she was still proud of her religious and political origins. Unitarianism, she felt, had set her on the path to the higher stages of Necessarian and Comtean truth.

Martineau's allegiances contribute to her different account of Norwich life. Her descriptions of Unitarian radicals and their patriotism during the Napoleonic era quietly counter Tonna's fanatical, apocalyptic rhetoric. In the section "Juvenile Politics" (1 : 78 – 82), Martineau records her mother's sympathy with the royal family during the French Revolution, her own refusal to satirize the Prince Regent or other members of the English royal family, and the general atmosphere of patriotism during the Napoleonic Wars—all in contrast to Tonna's vision of disloyal Socinians serving an Antichrist with "cloven hoofs."[35]

More generally, the opening scenes of Martineau's *Autobiography* oppose the literary maneuvers of women autobiographers like Tonna, particularly in their relentless domesticizing of religious and intellectual issues. Unlike Tonna, who recounts childhood anecdotes in order to inculcate the tenets of Evangelicalism and the sacred virtues of the English home, Martineau begins with her earliest memories, "infantine impressions" (1:9) that reveal not only the bent of an individual personality but a lifelong interest in observing "the growth of a human mind" (1:52).[36] The subtitles Martineau chooses for the opening section (Period I)—"Ill health and terrors. Fragments of recollections. Early piety. Early politics. Early social morals. Love of money and management of it. Sewing."—implicitly insist that the female subject is not simply a domestic creature but fully a human being whose bodily, mental, religious, political, social, and economic circumstances contribute to her self-development and self-construction. Tonna's *Personal Recollections* include, of course, incidents that might have been classified under some of those heads, but whereas Martineau discusses "ill health" or "social morals" to understand her infantine need for the solaces of religion, Tonna treats illness as moral failure or evidence of domestic sin.

Both Tonna and Martineau suffered from severe childhood illnesses, in Tonna's case deafness and temporary blindness at the age of six, in Martineau's increasing deafness that became permanent by the age of sixteen. In Tonna's autobiography, illness becomes a punishment for female pride in precocious learning: she had begun studying French with an uncle whom she adored and, "stimulated to extraordinary efforts," she overstudied "starting from repose at the earliest break of dawn and strain[ing] [her] sleepy eyes over the page" until she became blind (11). Whatever the medical validity of this interpretation, Tonna is certain about its autobiographical significance. She interprets her blindness as a providential intervention in a misguided girl's life and as an occasion for relearning the importance of the domestic sphere: "It checked my inordinate desire for mere acquirements, which I believe to be a bad tendency, particularly in the female; while it threw me more upon my own resources, such as they were, and gave me a keen relish for the highly intellectual conversation that always prevailed in our home" (11).

In contrast, Martineau scrupulously avoids treating illness as an indication of divine providence or punishment and introduces domestic relations primarily to articulate the difficulties that handicapped children face. In response to her incipient deafness, her family "insisted that it was all my own fault,—that I was so absent,—that I never cared to attend to anything that was said,—that I ought to listen this way, or that, or the other; and even (while my heart was breaking) they told me that 'none are so deaf as those that won't hear'" (1:76). Thus in Martineau's account the domestic sphere becomes the site of pain, not a refuge from it. More important, deafness becomes an occasion for applying the Necessarian philosophy of cause and effect—that is, for exploring the possible causes of illness and its effects on religious sensibility or intellectual progress. Martineau acknowledges the immediate benefit of religious faith in affliction ("I doubt whether I could have got through without it" [1:12]). She probes the more subtle effects of deafness on mental development ("In such a case as mine, the usual evil . . . is that the sufferer is inquisitive,—*will* know everything that is said, and becomes a bore to all the world" [1:73]). She interprets her deafness as a pivotal moment in her self-development ("It showed me that I must take my case into my own hands. . . . Instead of drifting helplessly as hitherto, I gathered myself up for a gallant breasting of my destiny" [1:76]). Yet illness does not reinforce feminine domesticity; rather, it contributes to (or possibly hinders) development in various spheres of experience.

On a larger scale, these writers' treatments of "social morals" align spiritual autobiography and domestic memoir in oppositional ways. Both Tonna and Martineau recount incidents of prevarication, both involving parents and servants, both producing moral uneasiness. For Tonna a key incident involves lying to protect a servant, thus betraying her father's trust, and then willingly accepting the whipping her father inflicts, while her brother begs for mercy: "I wished every stroke had been a stab; I wept because the pain was not great enough; and I loved my father at that moment better than even I, who almost idolized him, had ever loved him before" (20). Quite understandably, modern critics interpret this incident psychologically as an instance of masochism, but Tonna treats it moralistically, almost allegorically, to reinforce Evangelical domestic ideology.[37] "The holy Father and the earthly Father are one," wrote another Evangelical daughter,[38] a view with which Tonna concurs, adding the earthly brother as a counterpart to the divine Son: "It is sweet to know we have a Brother indeed, who always pleads, and never pleads in vain for the offending child; a Father whose chastisements are not withheld, but administered in a tender love; judgment being his strange work, and mercy that wherein he delights, and the peaceable fruits of righteousness the end of his correction" (20–21). As elsewhere in Tonna's account, spiritual progress results from domestic education; domesticity reinforces religiosity.

For Martineau social morals can never so simply be understood. Moral and religious scruples frequently conflict with middle-class domestic decorum. In a minor episode, for example, Martineau recalls that her parents often asked her to convey "insulting messages to the maids, to 'bid them not be so like cart-horses overhead,' and the like" (1:24). Such incidents reveal the tensions between religious teaching ("on the one hand, it was a fearful sin to alter a message") and social morals ("on the other, it was impossible to give such an one as that: so I used to linger and delay to the last moment, and then deliver something civil, with all imaginable sheepishness"). For Martineau domestic codes frequently inhibit spiritual progress; religious principles (such as truth telling and passive obedience) conflict with social and political understanding; parental authority undermines individual growth.[39] These tensions repeatedly surface in the *Autobiography,* making it an unlikely vehicle for conventional Victorian "domestic ideology" and certainly not an unqualified celebration of domestic life.[40]

I would argue, in fact, that no intentional alignment of spiritual confession and domestic memoir occurs in the *Autobiography.* Martineau invokes an older, purer form of spiritual autobiography that focuses on theological crisis and spiritual growth, even as she recalls the domestic trials of such women writers as Alice Hayes and Elizabeth Stirredge, who rebelled against social expectations in pursuit of religious truth. Martineau also invokes the more modern, masculine autobiographer's privilege of focusing primarily on personal development and intellectual progress, as in John Stuart Mill's "A Crisis in My Mental History," with its conflict between Utilitarian doctrine and Wordsworthian poetry, or in John Henry Newman's *Apologia,* with its intricate reconstruction of his theological dilemmas in the 1830s and 1840s, before he converted to Roman Catholicism.

In the first volume of the *Autobiography* Martineau only minimally acknowledges the domestic memoir, which in its classic form begins by grounding the female subject in a network of familial relations. Martineau's treatment of this convention reveals her deviation from, not acquiescence in, conventional Victorian relational subjectivity and domestic ideology. In her "Introduction," written after most of volume 1 had been completed, Martineau presents an account of her "descent and parentage":

On occasion of the Revocation of the Edict of Nantes in 1688, a surgeon of the name of Martineau, and a family of the name of Pierre, crossed the Channel, and settled with other Huguenot refugees, in England. My ancestor married a young lady of the Pierre family, and settled in Norwich, where his descendents afforded a succession of surgeons up to my own day. . . . My grandfather, who was one of the honourable series, died at the age of forty-two, of a fever caught among his poor patients. He left a large family, of whom my father was the youngest. When established as a Norwich manufacturer, my father married Elizabeth Rankin, the eldest daughter of a sugar-refiner at Newcastle upon Tyne. My father and mother had eight children, of whom I was the sixth: and I was born on the 12th of June, 1802.

(1:7–8)

This introduction helps to establish Martineau's heritage of religious and political dissent, middle-class values, and regional affiliation, but not to project a relational sense of the self. Although it recalls such memoirs as Lady Halkett's and Lady Fanshawe's, the narrative that follows does not, like theirs, trace the lives of male family members and their achievements, but rather delineates Martineau's own intellectual and professional growth. The features of her ancestors that she enumerates become, in Necessarian terms, the antecedents that affect the development of her life.

That development Martineau interprets within a Comtean framework of human progress: from an early religious or "fictitious" stage (1802–19) through what she calls a "metaphysical fog" (1819–39) to a final stage of scientific or "positivistic" understanding (1839–55). In her translation and abridgment of Auguste Comte's *Positive Philosophy* (1853), Martineau explained individual development as a specific version of general, human progress: "The progress of the individual mind is not only an illustration, but an indirect evidence of that of the general mind. The point of departure of the individual and of the race being the same, the phases of the mind of a man correspond to the epochs of the mind of the race. Now, each of us is aware, if he looks back upon his own history, that he was a theologian in his childhood, a metaphysician in his youth, and a natural philosopher in his manhood."[41] These Comtean phases become Martineau's hermeneutic substitute for the biblical typology of orthodox spiritual autobiographers and her alternative to the domestic model of other women autobiographers.

Using Comtean philosophy, Martineau views her early morbid religiosity simply as a natural phase of human development, specifically as the effect of childhood difficulties. A sick and delicate child, she was sent to convalesce in a farmhouse near Norwich, where her nurse was "a Methodist or melancholy Calvinist of some sort" (1:12). Under such influence, she became intensely religious: "I came home the absurdest little preacher of my years (between two and three) that ever was. I used to nod my head emphatically, and say 'Never ky for tyfles:' 'Dooty fust, and pleasure afterwards,' and so forth. . . . The religion was of a bad sort enough, as might be expected from the urgency of my needs; but I doubt whether I could have gotten through without it" (1:12). Her religiosity continued throughout adolescence, perhaps even intensified during a long visit to Bristol, where she came under the influence of the Unitarian minister and educator Lant Carpenter. Then his "devout and devoted Catechumen" (1:95), Martineau now, as retrospective autobiographer and with Comtean enlightenment, recognizes the ambiguous effects of his teaching: "He made me desperately superstitious,—living wholly in and for religion, and fiercely fanatical about it . . . ,—with his instructions burnt in, as it were, upon my heart and conscience, and with an abominable spiritual rigidity and a truly respectable force of conscience curiously mingled together" (1:95–96). "Superstitious" is a Comtean designation for the religious phase in human development, and in this passage Martineau's judgment against religion is severe.

In other passages, however, the Comtean paradigm allows Martineau to analyze, even good-naturedly accept her childhood sensibility— even as she finally admits, after criticizing Carpenter's influence, that "fanaticism was a stage which I should probably have had to pass through at any rate" (1:96). More important, Comteanism allows Martineau to distinguish intellectual and moral progress from a gendered domesticity and to insist that women's development follows the same pattern delineated for men. Unlike Tonna's lessons about overreaching young women, Martineau's incidents of religious experience are relevant to both male and female readers, interpreted as they are within a universal Comtean narrative of human existence.

Martineau's crisis in her religious history thus becomes one equally possible for a male or female subject. When she was eleven years old, she stumbled on the theological debate over free will and foreknowledge, "how, if God foreknew every thing, we could be blamed or rewarded for our conduct, which was thus absolutely settled for us beforehand" (1:44). She asked her older brother for an answer, and perhaps because he had none, he told her "that this was a thing which I could not understand at present, nor for a long time to come" (1:44). It is tempting to interpret this incident as a classic female encounter with patriarchal authority (as I once did). Her brother Thomas's response sounds uncannily like those patriarchal thinkers, including Hannah More, who believed that the female mind was fit for "practical divinity" but ill suited to sophisticated hermeneutics or systematic theology, that females were prone to superficial questions but incapable of "that deep and patient thinking which goes to the bottom of a subject."[42]

Martineau does not make gender a pivotal factor in this episode, however. Although she insists it was only logical that "if I could feel the difficulty, I had a right to the solution" (1:44), she does not blame Thomas for superciliousness, and in her discovery of "the Necessarian solution" (1:109), she credits another brother, James, with providing timely advice. The Necessarian doctrine she eventually embraces—that the universe operates according to fixed general laws, that a special Providence neither interferes with those laws nor intervenes in human affairs, that human "will" must be understood in terms of the antecedent causes that have shaped it—operates regardless of sex. (That social perceptions of masculinity and femininity contribute to such causes is a point Martineau does not raise.) Martineau's account of religious progress insists that it is an intellectual, not a domestic matter: "all the best minds I know are among the Necessarians;—all indeed which are qualified to discuss the subject at all" (1:110). Domesticity is largely excluded from this section of the *Autobiography,* which traces the evolution of Martineau's religious beliefs.[43]

As Martineau describes the resolution of her spiritual crisis, she draws on the traditional language of spiritual autobiography—noting that "a new light spread through [her] mind," that she "was like a new creature in the strength of a sound conviction" (1:110), and that, "with the last link of my chain snapped," she became "a free rover on the broad, bright breezy common of the universe" (1:116). Yet if she momentarily employs traditional language in tracing her spiritual growth, she does not, as does Tonna, make the link common in spiritual autobiography between conversion and vocation. Instead, Martineau simply ends by sketching out the "gradations" through which she passed from "faith" to "a matter of speculation, of spiritual convenience, and of intellectual and moral taste" until to her Christianity "decline[d] to the rank of a mere fact in the history of mankind" (1:116). Authorship becomes the subject of separate and distinct sections of the *Autobiography* that trace her professional career.

When Martineau turns to her development as a writer, she even more rigorously avoids precedents that locate authorship within the feminine or domestic sphere, and repeatedly alludes to masculine models that identify her work as public and professional. From infancy Martineau showed a propensity for making books—as we learn from her childish attempt to assemble a book of maxims (1:12) and her adolescent project of collecting "scripture instructions under the heads of the virtues and vices" (1:35). These episodes mark young Harriet as a child gifted from birth, reminiscent of young John Ruskin writing abstracts of Sunday sermons or Felicia Hemans reciting long passages of Shakespeare to her astonished family. Her account of learning to write nonetheless introduces what will become a recurring pattern in the *Autobiography:* that of a female subject entering a masculine domain.

As Martineau tells it, at the age of eleven she was sent with her sister Rachel to a boy's grammar school where among the traditionally masculine subjects, including Latin and mathematics, she took lessons in composition:

> *Mr. Perry [the headmaster] prided himself, I believe, on his process of composition being exceedingly methodical; and he enjoyed above every thing initiating us into the mystery. . . . There was the Proposition, to begin with: then the Reason, and the Rule; then the Example, ancient and modern; then the confirmation; and finally, the Conclusion. This may be a curious method, . . . but it was a capital way of introducing some order into the chaos of girls' thoughts.*

(1:63–64)

That Martineau viewed her knowledge of composition as a masculine achievement is evident from her comment about introducing order into "the chaos of girls' thoughts" and from her comment in *Household Education* that the method she learned was "approved and practised" by her "master and many others."[44] She went on to study Hugh Blair's *Lectures on Rhetoric,* a likely source of Perry's method, and every other "book or process which could improve my literary skill,—really as if I had foreseen how I was to spend my life" (1 : 102–3). Knowing composition—that is, not only knowing how to organize ideas but also feeling competent in a masculine domain—influenced Martineau's decision to become a writer and to take on such nonfeminine subjects as political economy, social policy, and Comtean positivism. In 1834, after her success with the *Illustrations of Political Economy,* and again when she wrote the *Autobiography,* she praised her schoolmaster for his seminal influence, "probably the cause of my mind being turned so decidedly in that direction" (1 : 65).

The method of composition that Martineau learned was standard in English grammar schools and universities and thus a standard part of male intellectual development. When Martineau describes her composing process, she consistently links it to male writing, setting it off against female scribbling. She contrasts her production of serious nonfiction with the more feminine work of novelists such as Maria Edgeworth. Edgeworth's method—"scribbling first, then submitting her manuscript to her father, and copying and altering many times over"—Martineau dismisses as a waste of time, causing loss of "distinctness and precision" (1 : 121). Her own method—rigorously organizing and outlining first, then writing without revision—she associates with a male writer, William Cobbett: "I was delighted when, long afterwards, I met with Cobbett's advice;— to know first what you want to say, and then say it in the first words that occur to you. The excellence of Cobbett's style, and the manifest falling off of Maria Edgeworth's after her father's death (so frankly avowed by herself) were strong confirmations of my own experience" (1 : 122).

No doubt this judgment overrates Cobbett and underrates Edgeworth; today, theorists of composition would validate Edgeworth's process-oriented approach over Cobbett's "think it–say it" method. No doubt, too, Martineau was reluctant to associate herself with Edgeworth after the outrageous attack in the *Quarterly Review,* which ended by recommending that Martineau "burn all the little books she has as yet written" and "study the works of a lady" (Maria Edgeworth) who, "with immeasurably greater abilities in every way, was her predecessor in the line she considers so wholly original." [45] Whatever the motivation, underlying Martineau's description of her method of composition is a professional need to dissociate herself from female amateurs and a feminine tradition of fiction, and to align herself with male writers and a masculine tradition of serious thought and labor.

As Martineau describes her entry into public authorship, she under-scores this distinction between amateurism and professionalism, feminine work and masculine labor, the "needle" and the "pen." She wrote her first articles for the *Monthly Repository* after her brother James left for college and advised her "to take refuge" in "a new pursuit" (1:118)—that is, she wrote in an attempt to remain intellectually active and equal. When the articles appeared in print, her eldest brother, Henry, praised her literary efforts and sanctioned a career as a *professional* author. She describes the incident as an almost priestly laying on of hands: "He then laid his hand on my shoulder, and said gravely (calling me 'dear' for the first time) 'Now, dear, leave it to other women to make shirts and darn stockings; and do you devote yourself to this.' . . . That evening made me an authoress" (1:120). Henry articulates a distinction that Martineau observes throughout the *Autobiography:* that professional work is different from, not an extension of, domestic responsibility; that the female author must leave her needle and the domestic circle behind in order to take up the pen. This is masculine wisdom, and, initially, female family members resist it. Martineau's mother dismisses her daughter's first job offer, "to remain in town, and undertake proof-correcting and other literary drudgery," sending "peremptory orders to go home" and serve as a domestic companion (1:148–49). Later, when Martineau circulated a prospectus for her forthcoming tales on political economy, a cousin and her husband enclosed two sovereigns with a letter, "recommending rather a family subscription which might eke out my earnings by my needle" (1:168). That Martineau resisted domestic sentiment and viewed her literary career as an entry into a masculine profession we can sense from a letter she wrote to her mother in July 1832, when she left Norwich for London permanently: "I fully expect that both you and I shall occasionally feel as if I did not discharge a daughter's duty, but we shall both remind ourselves that I am now as much a citizen of the world as any professional *son* of yours could be" (3:91).

Martineau's decision to become "a professional son" is repeatedly legitimated in the *Autobiography* by a series of male mentors and compatriots: by W. J. Fox, who encourages her contributions to the *Monthly Repository* and under whose "literary discipline" she thrives (1:145); by the secretary of the Unitarian Association, who praises her rhetorical ability and announces that she has won all three prizes in an essay competition (1:155–56); by her brother Henry, whom she consults about the

Illustrations of Political Economy and who, when she debates going to London to seek out publishers, says "oracularly 'Go'" (1 : 164); by her "oldest surviving uncle," who consults with his sons and pays the printer's bill for the series (1 : 173); and by Richard Hanbury Gurney, the M.P. for Norwich, who promises his support lest the series fail (1 : 177). Not that Martineau underestimates the value of familial support. She notes with special pleasure that her sister Rachel appeared to witness her award in the Unitarian essay competition, and she thanks her mother for "domestic support" during the writing of the political economy series. But with each encouragement from a male mentor, Martineau finds validation for her departure from the domestic sphere and her choice of authorship as a profession. "I had now found that I could write," she states after winning the Unitarian prizes, "and I might rationally believe that authorship was my legitimate career" (1 : 156). Personal judgment is publicly confirmed with the success of her political economy tales: "Authorship has never been with me a matter of choice. I have not done it for amusement, or for money, or for fame, or for any reason but because I could not help it" (1 : 188).

What results from this treatment of her career is an autobiography more public and professional than any before Anthony Trollope's *Autobiography* (1883) or George Sala's *Life and Adventures* (1895). Like these literary men, Martineau provides details of her financial earnings, of contract negotiations with publishers, of techniques for research and composition, of meetings with the literary and political elite, and especially of her independent life in London, later in the house she built with her earnings at the Knoll, Ambleside, in the Lake District. Even more than Trollope, in whose *Autobiography* economic and editorial details dominate, Martineau narrates her rise to professional success. Her *Autobiography* is not a blueprint for all good women to follow, as Tonna intended her *Personal Recollections* to be, but a practical, revelatory account of how to succeed with "no pioneer in [one's] literary path," only "steadfastness of purpose."

The *Autobiography* also gives a definitive response to the conventional wisdom that women writers could not enter the professional realm without having their heads turned by fame and flattery. In "Of Female Education," Martineau had confronted the claim that "girls who take to scribble" do so to gratify their "natural vanity"—a claim made by Han-

nah More in her treatise on female education.[46] In the professionally ori-
ented sections of volume 1, Martineau disproves the cultural assumption
of "vanity so universally ascribed to the sex"[47] by recounting anecdote
after anecdote in which male authors prove themselves more prone to
flattery and literary puffery than female writers. Martineau shows William Taylor, a writer from Norwich, where Martineau grew up, suc-
cumbing to the vice—"he was completely spoiled by the flatteries of
shallow men, pedantic women, and conceited lads" (1 : 298)—whereas
the more eminent Anna Laetitia Barbauld behaves with unaffected decorum, sitting in the Martineau parlor for "a long morning chat," "holding skeins of silk for my mother to wind," "the stamp of superiority on
all she said" (1 : 302). In examples drawn from the London literati, many
a man more famous than Taylor turns vanity's fool. Lord Brougham lets
himself be flattered by silly women, to whom he talks nonsense; Lord
Jeffrey "flirt[s] with clever women, in long succession"; Bulwer-Lytton
sits "on a sofa, sparkling and languishing among a set of female votaries";
Edwin Landseer enters a room "curled and cravatted, and glancing round
in anxiety about his reception" so as to "make a woman wonder where
among her own sex she could find more palpable vanity"; Richard
Whewell appears "grasping at praise for universal learning" and "liking
female adoration"; and so on for fifty anecdotal pages on the vanity of
male authors and artists. "I had heard all my life of the vanity of women
as a subject of pity to men," Martineau comments, "but when I went to
London, lo! I saw vanity in high places which was never transcended by
that of women in their lowlier rank" (1 : 350).

The effect of the professional sections of the *Autobiography* is to represent, with all its defects, a literary "fraternity" (1 : 434), one that includes
both men and women, both susceptible to the temptations of literary
lionism, the men perhaps more so than the women. In any case, all are
fascinated by professional details of authorship, all willing to swap stories
about methods of composition or negotiations with publishers or even
quality of handwriting. And with these professional details Martineau
closes volume 1 of her *Autobiography.* "I have met with almost every variety of method among living authors," Martineau writes at the end of
this volume, "and almost every variety of view as to the seriousness of
their vocation. But I believe the whole fraternity are convinced that
the act of authorship is the most laborious effort that men have to make"

(1:435). It is clear that by 1834, the last year covered in the volume, Martineau considered herself one of that "fraternity," one of those men willing to make the laborious effort.

What, then, of the domestic tradition within which literary and cultural historians have frequently placed Martineau? At certain points in the *Autobiography* Martineau seems to relish domesticity, and certain sections—especially those describing life at home in Ambleside (Period VI, parts i, ii, and ix)—resemble, if not invoke, the domestic memoir. The most frequently cited passage in the *Autobiography* on the topic of domesticity reads:

(2:225)

> *No true woman, married or single,* can *be happy without some sort of domestic life;—without having somebody's happiness dependent on her; and my own ideal of an innocent and happy life was a house of my own among poor improvable neighbours, with young servants whom I might train and attach to myself; with pure air, a garden, leisure, solitude at command, and freedom to work in peace and quietness.*

The most frequently cited anecdotes about Martineau's domesticity recall her skill in needlework. To Henry Reeve, a distant cousin and editor of the *Edinburgh Review,* she wrote:

> *I heard your grandmother Taylor extolled (by her son Edward) as a darner of stockings who could not be rivalled in the next generation: but I don't know that I shd not have ventured to compete with her, if I had been driven to it. Few women of my time (amateurs) have done so much sewing as I, & with so much satisfaction.*[48]

In the *Autobiography,* as Martineau describes her midlife retirement to the Knoll, Ambleside, she admits to having "a thoroughly womanish love of needle-work,—yes even ('I own the soft impeachment') of wool-work" (2:414).

Comments like these acknowledge, if not celebrate, traditional aspects of women's domestic life. But in context they also, I think, help us analyze Martineau's problematic relation to dominant Victorian ideologies of domesticity and decipher her awareness of—and ultimate opposition to—autobiographical self-constructions that locate the female subject essentially within the domestic sphere. Consider, for example, Martineau's comment on needlework. For Martineau the author, needlework was an amateur activity, something she did in her leisure time or on her sickbed to produce gifts and charitable donations, whereas writing was a professional occupation. In the letter to Henry Reeve, she parenthetically marks herself as an "amateur" (that is, as a woman who does not earn her living with her needle), whereas in the 1832 letter to her mother, she underscores her status as a "professional son" (that is, as a writer who earns her living by the pen). In emphasizing the amateurism of her domestic skills, she thus rejects Victorian attempts to reinterpret housewifery as a "professional" skill and female homemakers as "professionals" within the domestic realm.

Taking this common tack, the American Catherine Beecher, whom Martineau had met during her tour of the United States, advocated better education for women as future wives and mothers in her *Treatise on Domestic Economy* (1842). Beecher opposed, however, other forms of female professionalism or public activity, stating that "in civil and political concerns, her interests [are to] be intrusted to the other sex."[49] In contrast, Martineau in *Household Education* (1849) treats the domestic sphere as a site for both male and female work, with little boys doing carpentry and lock repairs at their workbenches and little girls making beds, laying the tablecloth, washing up crockery, baking bread, preserving fruit, and ironing.[50] Martineau also treats the domestic realm as a site for parental (not just maternal) influence, with fathers and mothers both inculcating such moral qualities as courage, patience, love, veneration, and truthfulness.[51] In Martineau's ideology, domestic work is what all family members contribute to the home; professional work is what people do to earn money—usually away from the home, apart from domestic responsibilities.[52]

If Martineau does not advocate the nineteenth-century feminist attempt to professionalize domestic work, neither does she accept the more basic ideology of separate spheres that underwrites it, with the man laboring in the professional, economic realm and the woman exerting her moral influence at home. As Valerie Pichanick has persuasively argued, Martineau throughout her life "opposed female acquiescence to the limits which had been set on women's social role and political position."[53] In

"Political Non-Existence of Women," in *Society in America,* Martineau characterizes the doctrine of separate spheres as a man-made invention:

> *The truth is, that while there is much said about "the sphere of woman," two widely different notions are entertained of what is meant by the phrase. The narrow, and, to the ruling party, the more convenient notion is that sphere appointed by men, and bounded by their ideas of propriety;—a notion from which any and every woman may fairly dissent. The broad and true conception is of the sphere appointed by God, and bounded by the powers which he has bestowed. This commands the assent of man and woman; and only the question of powers remains to be proved.*[54]

In this passage, as elsewhere, Martineau dismisses separate spheres as a patriarchal construction, one approved and enforced by "the ruling party," not a natural or divinely ordained social structure. For her, a true conception of a person's "sphere" derives from an understanding of God-given powers, which every man or woman has not only the right but the duty to "prove" (meaning "to test, to establish the validity of") in his or her life.

Although Martineau became increasingly articulate on women's right to exercise their powers, this is essentially the position she held throughout her adult professional life. In her earliest contributions to the *Monthly Repository,* written in 1822 at the age of nineteen, she had been willing to use the rhetoric of separate spheres to argue for female education: "If they [women] are called to be wives, a sensible mind is an essential qualification for the domestic character; if they remain single, liberal pursuits are absolutely necessary to preserve them from the faults so generally attributed to that state."[55] But by the 1830s, once she had established herself as a professional writer, she abandoned this rhetoric. In *Society in America* (1837) she argued for women's legal and political rights. In *Household Education* (1849) she argued that girls ought to have unrestricted access to all branches of knowledge, that "everything possible should be done to improve the quality of the mind of every human being," that "every human being is to be made as perfect as possible."[56] In the *Autobiography* (1855), which she thought of as a final, deathbed publication, she restated her position: "Let [women] be educated,—let their powers be cultivated to the extent for which the means are already provided, and all that is wanted or ought to be desired will follow of course. Whatever a woman proves herself able to do, society will be thankful to see her do,—just as if she were a man" (1:401). That she, an established expert on political economy, could not vote, she thought "an absurdity, seeing that I have for a long course of years influenced public affairs to an extent not professed or attempted by many men" (1:402).

Martineau's rejection of women's domesticity (versus man's publicity) appears more emphatic in the "Memorials" to the *Autobiography* edited by Maria Weston Chapman. In the chapter "Fame," Chapman quotes the poetry of their contemporary, "the finely endowed Felicia Hemans," to illustrate what her friend Martineau rejected:

> Brought alone by gifts beyond all price,
> The trusting heart's repose, the paradise
> Of home, with all its loves, doth fate allow
> The crown of glory unto woman's brow.

According to Chapman, what's true for the goose is true for the gander— and vice versa: "the same, as far as it is true, is equally so of illustrious persons of both sexes; as the lives of so many great men show, notwithstanding the public opinion of these centuries; which, favouring the notion that it is man's exclusive privilege to do great things, has hindered woman in doing them by abundance of morbid statements like the above" (3:93–94). Victorian morbidity about domestic life—its unhealthy, sickening effect on women—is what the *Autobiography* means to counter, and in the chapter "Fame" Chapman is proud to cite evidence from François Guizot, minister of public instruction in France, to prove that women like Martineau might enter the public realm and substantially affect legislation "otherwise than through some clever man" (3:82).

What, then, of Martineau's expressed need to participate in domestic life? Like most Victorians, Martineau believed that the home should be both a repository of moral integrity and a source of physical and emotional well-being. The moral function of domestic life occupies much of Martineau's attention in *Household Education,* especially in the chapters grouped as "Care of the Powers," which concern the development of such abstract moral qualities as hope, courage, patience, truthfulness, and veneration.[57] In the *Autobiography* she addresses this moral function less explicitly, but treats in great detail the dangers of the public sphere, "the dangers and moral penalties of literary life in London" (1:224), as illustrated in the section "Literary Lionism" (1:271–97), which depicts the moral foibles of prominent literary and artistic men who live too much in the limelight. More positively, Martineau praises such writers as Dickens (still happily married at the time), whose work "can never permanently fail" because it is grounded in domestic values: "Every indication seems to show that the man himself [Dickens] is rising. He is a virtuous and happy family man, in the first place. His glowing and generous heart is kept steady by the best domestic influences; and we may fairly hope now that he will fulfil the natural purpose of his life, and stand by literature to the last" (2:379). Little did she know of Dickens's private life!

Although Martineau was interested in the moral uses of domesticity, it was the second function of domesticity—its restoration of physical and psychological well-being—that she found more crucial personally. With her chronic ill health and the difficulties her deafness caused in London society, domestic solitude (and solicitude) became essential. To the American William Ware she wrote after her American tour: "on coming back, I find so much more difficulty in society from this cause [deafness] than before, that I rather think I shall go out less than I did,— for my sake and others."[58] Volume 2 of the *Autobiography* abounds in complaints of the fatigue she suffered when socially active. It is arguable that her decision to move to rural Ambleside after she regained her health in 1845, rather than return to London society, was motivated not by an abstract or essentially feminine desire for domesticity, or by a belief in the moral virtues of domestic life, but by the real physical and emotional strain that her deafness caused.[59]

Her decision to move to Ambleside seems to have been motivated also by a third, unstated function of domesticity: its proof that a writer had achieved the status of author and was now fully professional. By the 1840s Victorian myths of authorship had evolved to include not only Romantic scenes of genius and superior literary taste but also evidence of the writer's ability to support a domestic establishment, complete with wife, children, and servants. In *David Copperfield* (1849–50), the novel Martineau praised even as she praised Dickens himself, the young author-hero proves himself not only by publishing "a good many trifling pieces" and earning an income of four figures, literary work that Dickens only sketchily describes, but also by marrying the right woman and mastering his domestic establishment.[60] Later in the century, in George Gissing's *New Grub Street* (1891), Edwin Reardon fails as an author and descends to the level of hack writer when—or because (the causality is uncertain)— he gives up his domestic establishment and allows his wife, Amy, to return to her mother's house. Embodying the same Victorian myth, Martineau's *Autobiography* recounts a successful rise to professional authorship, including scenes of the author's domestic independence and management.

When Martineau asserts that "no true woman, married or single, *can* be happy without some sort of domestic life" (2:225), we should recall, then, the context in which she makes this statement. It occurs as she describes a house-hunting trip in the Lake District, the trip that ultimately produces her permanent home, the Knoll. Martineau prefaces that trip with a statement about her attainment of emotional and professional maturity—"like the Swedish summer, which bursts out of a long winter with the briefest interval of spring" (2:205). She follows it with a discussion of the economic advantages of buying rather than renting— "that £20 was the interest of £500; and that for £500 I could build myself a cottage after my own heart" (2:225)—and with the sanction of two prominent authors, Wordsworth and Arnold, who point out the advantages of the land she proposes to buy. Moreover, Martineau's statement about the need for "domestic life" is surrounded by other comments that suggest her desire to create and *manage* a domestic establishment, not just live within one (which she had done, after all, in Norwich and London). She envisions "domestic life" in terms of having "poor improvable neighbours" and companions whose happiness is "dependent on her" and especially in terms of enjoying "solitude at command" and "freedom to work in peace and quiet" (2:225). This is the domesticity of a professional woman writer, one who proudly notes that sales of *Eastern Life* allowed her to pay off the mortgage (2:296).[61]

Yet even as Martineau creates a domestic life of her own and proves her professional status, she reinvents domesticity to counter the ideology of separate spheres. The domestic scenes she depicts in volume 2 of the *Autobiography* are explicitly antipatriarchal and nonheterosexual.[62] The two-story house she designs equalizes the private quarters by putting all the bedrooms on the same floor—her own, along with rooms for her nieces, guests, and female servants. Within the house, the community she creates is largely a community of women, and it acts as a family unit. On the day the women take possession of the house, for instance, they celebrate together: "The first night (April 7th, 1846) when we made our beds, stirred up the fires, and locked the doors, and had some serious talk, as members of a new household, will never be forgotten, for its sweetness and solemnity, by my maids or myself" (2:256). What troubles Martineau most in the final section of the *Autobiography* is the threat to this achieved domesticity: the loss of a beloved niece or servant to marriage (the patriarchal alternative), to emigration (the colonial or capitalistic demand), or to death (the inevitable end). Such losses threaten the breakup of "my little household"; they cause "domestic griefs" (2:407).

By reproducing the myth of the professional author and creating a nonpatriarchal form of domesticity, Martineau attempts to undo what Mary Poovey has called "the ideological work of gender." In Victorian domestic ideology, the woman at home played an essential role in confirming middle-class male identity, especially the identity of the male writer, whose social status was otherwise ambiguous. Martineau rejects common Victorian gender dichotomies—but, I must admit, only by maintaining class distinctions. Victorian women, as Poovey also notes, played an essential role in disguising the class exploitation essential to middle-class domesticity: "Paradoxically, the identity and economic well-being of the middle-class man depended on reinforcing the very class differences that the middle-class housewife (and the rhetoric of individualism) seemed to overcome." [63] If Martineau successfully invades the sphere of male professionalism and demonstrates that a woman writer can earn her keep, design and build her own house, manage a construction crew as well as her domestic servants, conduct an experimental farm, and generally improve "the appearance and the economy of my little estate" (2:342), she does so at a cost. Doing all this depends on having "poor improvable neighbours"—that is, on substituting class for gender. However much Martineau might want to help the less fortunate or efface certain class distinctions within her own home, her *Autobiography* reveals the dilemmas of achieving and depicting professional status. She can prove her authorial status, in life or literary form, only by surrounding herself with others of a status different from her own.

Thus the inclusion of domestic scenes reveals a certain generic intractability fundamental to the Victorian domestic memoir. While Martineau may exploit its conventions to counter dominant assumptions about gender, to argue against an ideology of separate spheres, she cannot do so without reinscribing class as a defining feature. The seventeenth-century women who wrote as domestic memoirists were typically aristocrats, women who recorded their family's heritage and public achievements for the sake of posterity; if these memoirists lacked gender status, they possessed the authority of class. The nineteenth-century Martineau was a radical, nonaristocratic to the core. Yet her (re)introduction of features of the domestic memoir into an otherwise spiritual and professional account suggests the difficulty of mixing forms. Martineau (re)turns to the authority of class as she gives up dichotomies of gender.

Martineau succeeds more fully with another feature of the domestic memoir: the "Memorials" added by Maria Weston Chapman in 1877 as the third volume of the *Autobiography*. As she follows the Victorian custom of asking a woman, usually a friend or relative, to edit her account and supply omitted biographical details, Martineau invokes the community of women she only partially managed to create in her Ambleside home. Chapman, her editor, was an abolitionist whom Martineau had met during her tour of America and admired as a model of female heroism: her "aspect meant by nature to be soft and winning only, but . . . so vivified by courage, and so strengthened by upright conviction, as to appear the very embodiment of heroism" (2:28). The choice of Chapman as editor testifies to an intellectual and spiritual—rather than merely domestic—community of women that Martineau wished to create and sustain. It testifies to a desire that her *Autobiography* be more than a (masculine) account of religious progress and professional achievement. It reintroduces domesticity for the sake of the intellectual and political progress of women. And, in its emphasis on female heroism, it hints at other possibilities in women's life writing that emerge more fully in *Jane Eyre* and the female missionary memoirs discussed in the next chapter.

III

"The Feelings and Claims of Little People": Heroic Missionary Memoirs, Domestic(ated) Spiritual Autobiography, and *Jane Eyre: An Autobiography*

WHEN CHARLOTTE BRONTË read Harriet Martineau's *Household Education* (1849), she was astonished by the autobiographical passages that seemed so uncannily to recount her own childhood experiences. She told Martineau that "it was like meeting her own fetch,—so precisely were the fears and miseries there described the same as her own, told or not told in 'Jane Eyre.'"[1] Similarly, when Martineau read *Jane Eyre,* she recognized the correspondences between her early life and that of Brontë's heroine: "I was taxed with the authorship [of *Jane Eyre*] by more than one personal friend, and charged by others, and even by relatives, with knowing the author, and having supplied some of the facts of the first volume from my own childhood."[2] I cite these comments not so much to recall the common misery of Victorian girls, which their adult autobiographies often sought to describe, explain, and meliorate, but rather to identify the common project in which both Martineau and Brontë were engaged—that of life writing, that wide-ranging and widely influential Victorian attempt to represent and thereby revise female subjectivity. Although Brontë wrote fiction, Martineau nonfiction, both understood their work to participate in a Victorian tradition of autobiography, as Brontë's subtitle, *An Autobiography,* and the allusion to her misery "told or not told" suggest and as Martineau's comment on "having supplied some of the facts" reiterates.[3]

Fictional versions of autobiography such as *Jane Eyre* intersected with and influenced the nonfictional traditions of Victorian women's life writing that are the primary subject of this book, and in this chapter I explore several such intersections: the use of spiritual autobiography in the first half of Brontë's novel to raise questions about modes of self-interpretation, about women's authority in biblical and other hermeneutics; the influence of missionary journals and memoirs in the second half to consider competing versions of "woman's mission"; and the implications of Brontë's domestication of both the spiritual autobiography and missionary memoir in what Deirdre David has described as Jane's decision, in the final scenes of the novel, to "rehabilitate the colonizer" rather than "convert the colonized."[4] Although I do not finally concur with David's proposition that the novel gives Jane "the most powerful form of female agency available to a woman of her social class and experience" (85), I do nonetheless suggest that *Jane Eyre: An Autobiography* participates in a mid-Victorian debate about what the "most powerful form" of agency and autobiography might be. Brontë does not engage quite so openly as Tonna or Martineau in what I have called the "polemics of piety," but like their accounts, *Jane Eyre* uses spiritual autobiography to initiate claims about women's rights and responsibilities.

Brontë's position in that debate put her at odds, ultimately, with Martineau. When these two women read each other's work in the late 1840s, they emphasized the similarity of their experience and the coincidence of their autobiography and fiction. By the mid-1850s, however, they were disagreeing about the appropriate form of women's life writing, whether in "fiction" or "reality." In an unsigned review, Martineau criticized Brontë's second autobiographical novel, *Villette,* for its obsession with romantic love: "All the female characters, in all their thoughts and lives, are full of one thing, or are regarded by the reader in the light of that one thought—love. It begins with the child of six years old, at the opening—a charming picture—and it closes with it at the last page." Martineau argued that in "real life" there were other "substantial, heartfelt interests for women of all ages, and under ordinary circumstances, quite apart from love."[5] Later, in an obituary written for the *Daily News,* Martineau expanded her criticism to include the whole of Brontë's oeuvre, even as she softened her judgment by acknowledging the positive social effects of Brontë's writing:

> *Though passion occupies too prominent a place in her pictures of life,*
> *though women have to complain that she represents love as the whole*
> *and sole concern of their lives, . . . it is a true social blessing that we*
> *have had a female writer who has discountenanced sentimentalism*
> *and feeble egotism with such practical force. . . . Her heroines love too*
> *readily, too vehemently, and sometimes after a fashion which their fe-*
> *male readers may resent; but they do their duty through everything,*
> *and are healthy in action, however morbid in passion.*[6]

Brontë responded—to the review, obviously, not the obituary—in a letter that somewhat evaded Martineau's point: "I know what *love* is as I
understand it; and if man or woman should be ashamed of feeling such
love, then there is nothing right, noble, faithful, truthful, unselfish in this
earth."[7] In effect, the issue that split these two writers and ended their
warm friendship was the appropriate form of women's life writing: Is love
to shape women's autobiography or something more "healthy in action"?
Is women's life writing to focus on the romantic and domestic or expand
its concerns beyond the heart and home? Even as Martineau posthumously acknowledged the worthiness of Brontë's intention, she objected
to the implicit—sometimes explicit—misrepresentation of women's experience, the falseness and false influence of Brontë's novels as examples
of women's autobiography.

    Modern critics who read this exchange tend to defend Brontë and
discount Martineau's criticism—as in Helene Moglen's remark that Martineau "mistook Charlotte Brontë" and responded with "an obuseness
born of militancy."[8] Yet Martineau's commentary is anything but obtuse:
she perceived that Brontë placed erotic desire at the center of her fiction
and shaped her heroines' lives in the (generic) terms of romance and domestic memoir. Martineau wanted women's lives to be conceived in
other terms, those of the spiritual autobiography and professional memoir. Indeed, Martineau's criticism anticipates a perplexity that has sur-
faced repeatedly in modern commentary on *Jane Eyre:* the oddity of a
heroine who does her moral duty while experiencing a "morbid" romantic passion, the disjunction between a fiction preoccupied with domestic romance and the rhetoric of spiritual autobiography that Brontë
at crucial moments employs. The Brontë-Martineau debate anticipates
the divided responses of modern critics to the novel's deployment of the
narrative and language of spiritual autobiography.

Critics have long recognized that *Jane Eyre* invokes the genre of spiritual autobiography. Jane Millgate (1969), Jerome Beaty (1977, 1996), Thomas Vargish (1985), and Barry Qualls (1982) all emphasize the providentialist element of the novel and its adaptation of religious autobiography and allegory.[9] In their classic feminist reading, "Plain Jane's Progress," Sandra Gilbert and Susan Gubar treat the novel as a pilgrimage toward "wholeness," a borrowing of the "mythic quest-plot" from Bunyan's *Pilgrim's Progress* and, more generally, from religious autobiography for the purposes of a "rebellious feminism." In Brontë's secularized version of the spiritual quest, they argue, a female protagonist "struggles from the imprisonment of her childhood toward an almost unthinkable goal of mature freedom." And, following Gilbert and Gubar, a dominant strain of feminist criticism, one that emphasizes the positive, revisionary elements of *Jane Eyre,* has developed a reading of the novel that traces Jane's movement from an immature hermeneutics based on the fairy tale and fantasy to a more mature hermeneutics derived from classic spiritual autobiography.[10]

Other critics, however, have puzzled over the disjunctions and contradictions within Jane's "secularized" spiritual autobiography—the "uneven developments," to borrow Mary Poovey's phrase, that result when a religious form reappears in romantic fiction. Barbara Hardy noticed one disjunction in 1964 when she pointed out that Jane invokes the religious precepts of Helen Burns in order to break away from Rochester but that we do not see "the process of her religious education and faith": "the divine law which she invokes in the crisis has not been associated with either her feelings or her reason." Extending this observation, Robert James Merrett exposed the "radical incongruity" of Jane's religious language and actions, her troublesome appropriation of "sacramental and religious principles in the interest of her sentiments." Most subtly, Peter Allen Dale has traced the tensions between the religious and romantic structures of the novel—the religious structure that demands and anticipates Jane's final confession of faith, which is strangely withheld, and the romantic structure that is substituted in its stead.[11] This second group of critics suggests the difficulty of reading *Jane Eyre* as a spiritual autobiography, the tensions that develop when theology mixes with domesticity, the complexity of the process we refer to as "secularization."[12]

These tensions become most severe, I believe, when Jane Eyre encounters a new form of autobiography that became popular in the

1820s, '30s, and '40s: the heroic female missionary memoir. Unlike the traditional form of spiritual autobiography that Jane generalizes and domesticizes in the first half of the novel, this more historically specific and urgent form demands a course of action: as St. John Rivers puts it, "He [God] opens to you a noble career" (360).[13] By introducing this newly popular form into her novel, Brontë raises the question of "woman's mission" and enters, albeit obliquely, a mid-century debate about the direction of women's life writing.

When Jane Eyre begins her autobiography, she reveals a child who has experiences that cry out for interpretation but who lacks a comprehensive hermeneutic or narrative framework in which to understand them. Jane is an autobiographer manqué, and her early engagements with autobiographical modes reveal their inadequacies, not their interpretive power. "Why was I always suffering, always browbeaten, always accused, for ever condemned?" the young protagonist wonders (12), even as the adult narrator explains, "Children can feel, but they cannot analyse their feelings" (19). Repeatedly in the opening chapters, Brontë shows Jane trying to "analyse," trying to use her reading as a guide to understanding, experimenting with different interpretive strategies and narrative patterns—from imaginative escape into the bleak landscapes of Bewick's *History of British Birds* (6), to historical analogy with the emperors and slaves of Goldsmith's *History of Rome* (8), to sympathetic response with Bessie's ballad of the "poor orphan child" (18). In each case, Jane finds a literary, historical, or natural point of comparison; but it is only that—a *point,* not a framework or system that can give coherence to her life. We know that Jane grows as a reader and interpreter during the early chapters of the novel—she tells us, for instance, that she found "a vein of interest deeper" in such books as *Gulliver's Travels* "than what I found in fairy tales" (17)—but as a child, she is still finding her way as autobiographer.

The interpretive system that might give coherence to Jane's life— biblical typology, the system of finding in the Bible parallels to or patterns in one's own life, a system that so many Victorian spiritual autobiographers used successfully—does not work for Jane, at least not in the first volume of the novel.[14] Why should biblical typology fail? When Jane first encounters this hermeneutics, it is rigid and repressive, made so by its institutionalization. The Reverend Brocklehurst uses typology, first in his meeting with Jane at Gateshead and then at his charity school, Lowood, to exercise his power and prevent independent thought (and possible rebellion) among his pupils. When he asks Jane if she reads her Bible, she gives multiple examples of passages she has read and enjoyed—"Revelations, and the book of Daniel, and Genesis and Samuel, and a little bit of Exodus, and some parts of Kings and Chronicles, and Job and Jonah" (28). In any of these scriptural books Jane might have found parallels with her own experience, but Brocklehurst chooses instead a part of the Bible she does not mention and does not like: the Psalms. The effect is to deny what knowledge and authority she may have and to substitute a biblical source she finds neither "interesting" nor relevant. She cannot engage spiritual autobiography at this point because Brocklehurst, in his repressive Evangelical mode, will not allow her the interpretive freedom necessary to do so. One burden of *Jane Eyre* as autobiography is to give its protagonist such freedom and to remake the typological mode so that it can illumine her experience.

The opening scene at Lowood School makes explicit Jane's disability—or, rather, Brocklehurst's institutionally sanctioned disabling of Jane. The inscription on the stone tablet that marks the school, "LOWOOD INSTITUTION. This portion was rebuilt A.D. ———, by Naomi Brocklehurst," includes a scriptural passage: "Let your light so shine before men that they may see your good works and glorify your Father which is in heaven. St. Matt. v. 16." Jane finds the tablet incomprehensible:

> *I read these words over and over again: I felt that an explanation belonged to them, and was unable fully to penetrate their import. I was still pondering the signification of "Institution," and endeavouring to make out a connection between the first words and the verse of Scripture, when the sound of a cough close behind me, made me turn my head.* (42)

The tablet assumes a complex connection between the institution, its founder, and the verse of Scripture. It assumes that the building of the institution fulfills the scriptural injunction; that the founder has duly applied a biblical model and performed a good work; that others should recognize this personal application of Scripture and reinforce it by praising God. This is a standard use of biblical typology. To the reader, however, as to young Jane, an orphan newly committed to the Brocklehurst institution, the connection between "the first words" and "the verse of

Scripture" seems less evident. What precedes the episode of the tablet—
a description of the wretched living conditions and penurious rations that
the Brocklehursts supply—undermines any interpretation of their actions as "good works."

So, too, does Brocklehurst's subsequent use of typology. To him,
Lowood Institution is "the troubled pool of Bethesda," where "the Jews
of old sent their diseased" (58, alluding to John 5:2–9). Although he
means to stress the positive, redemptive function of the school, his analogy characterizes orphans as "diseased," a comparison that suggests he
views poor young females like Jane as organically tainted. His extended
commentary reveals that he discriminates against the girls because of their
class and gender. His discrimination takes the form of refusing to allow
their *self*-interpretation; he insists on his hermeneutic authority as a
middle-class man and clergyman.

Modern critics sometimes argue that Helen Burns provides the lesson Jane needs to resist Brocklehurst and to recast her experiences in
terms of Christian heroism.[15] Helen does indeed offer Jane an alternative
religious mode—not only in the Christian stoicism of Johnson's *Rasselas*
but in what Jane calls "this doctrine of endurance" (48). Helen views
human life as "burdened with faults in this world" (51) and anticipates an
afterlife when "we shall put them off in putting off our corruptible bodies" (51); she counsels Jane to bear what fate requires (48), to "observe
what Christ says, and how he acts" (50), and to look forward to "Eternity
a rest—a mighty home" (51).[16] This traditionally passive, almost quiet-
istic position—one that sees earthly life as a passage to the celestial
realm—appeals to Jane. Yet although she later draws upon Helen's advice, most notably when Brocklehurst calls her a liar and sets her upon "a
pedestal of infamy" (58), Brontë does not endorse Helen's philosophy or
hermeneutics. As Jane points out, Helen's approach is not the alternative
it seems to be. If the passive and virtuous always submit, then the powerful and wicked will continue to "have it all their own way" (50). Helen's
approach, in other words, is not antithetical to but complementary of and
collaborative with Brocklehurst's aggressive, patriarchal hermeneutics.
Jane's mental rebellion at this stage anticipates the more radical independence she will later declare.

Of course, no reader would mistake Brocklehurst for an exemplary
interpreter of Scripture: his oppressive application of biblical models to
the lives of others and his failure to apply them equally to his own life

betray the inadequacy of his practice. Not all Victorian readers, however, accepted Jane Eyre as an exemplary Christian or female autobiographer. Contemporaries questioned her rebellious rhetoric and the revolutionary thrust of her religious and social ideologies. In the most hostile of reviews, Elizabeth Rigby, later Lady Eastlake, called "the autobiography of Jane Eyre" "pre-eminently an anti-Christian composition":

> *There is throughout it a murmuring against the comforts of the rich and against the privations of the poor, which,* as far as each individual is concerned, *is a murmuring against God's appointment—there is a proud and perpetual assertion of the rights of man, for which we find no authority either in God's word or in God's providence—there is that pervading tone of ungodly discontent which is at once the most prominent and the most subtle evil which the law and the pulpit, which all civilized society in fact has at the present day to contend with.*[17] *(Emphasis mine.)*

As the italicized phrase suggests, behind the revolutionary views that Rigby found objectionable lay a questionable autobiographical mode. This mode allowed an individual to differentiate herself and her experiences from general classes of humanity (such as "the poor"). It asserted an individual's right to interpret her life and experiences against the authority of religion ("the pulpit") or the state ("the law"). And, as Rigby's allusion to evils of "the present day" must have suggested in 1848, it participated in a growing democratization of autobiography as a genre, a trend evident in real and fictional autobiographies that represented the lives of women and working-class characters: in fiction, *Alton Locke, Tailor and Poet: An Autobiography* (1850), *Rose Douglas: Or, The Autobiography of a Minister's Daughter* (1851); in nonfiction, Samuel Bamford's *Passages in the Life of a Radical* (1844), Mary Ann Ashford's *Life of a Licensed Victualler's Daughter* (1844), *The Autobiography of Rose Allen* (1847), Alexander Somerville's *Autobiography of a Working Man* (1848), James Dawson Burns's *Autobiography of a Beggar Boy* (1855), and dozens of other working-class accounts now collected in John Burnett's *Annals of Labour*.[18] The mode of *Jane Eyre,* in Rigby's terms, "violated every code human and divine abroad, and fostered Chartism and rebellion at home"; even to Margaret Oliphant, a more sympathetic critic, it represented "a wild declaration of the 'Rights of Woman.'"[19]

Given Jane Eyre's traditional use of spiritual language at the end of volume 1, as she leaves Lowood and moves on to Thornfield, we might wonder why Rigby and critics of her ilk were not appeased. During her Lowood years Jane seems to adopt a Christian perspective—not Brocklehurst's or Helen Burn's, but something akin to Miss Temple's moderate providentialism. When Jane arrives at Thornfield, she offers up a prayer of thanksgiving: "The impulse of gratitude swelled my heart, and I knelt down at the bedside, and offered up thanks where thanks were due; not forgetting, ere I rose, to implore aid on my further path" (85). Mrs. Fairfax subsequently confirms Jane's good works and "the choice Providence led me to make" (107). The language is sincere, if conventional. Yet, as Rigby no doubt discerned, such providentialist moments scarcely motivate the narrative; Christian paradigms lack generative power in volume 2. Indeed, it is the repetitiveness, the uniformity of Jane's life, and the desire for "change, stimulus," even "a new servitude" (74), that motivate her departure from Lowood and initiate new modes of autobiography—modes that are antithetical to or incompatible with spiritual autobiography.

Gilbert and Gubar read Jane's departure from Lowood as a "pilgrimage toward selfhood" and her experiences at Thornfield as "emblematic" episodes "symptomatic of difficulties Everywoman in a patriarchal society must meet and overcome"—that is, like many other critics, including Thomas Vargish and Barry Qualls, they read volume 2 as a spiritual allegory, a secularized version of traditional religious autobiography.[20] Yet the genres that Brontë invokes in volume 2, as Jerome Beaty has so forcefully demonstrated, are not spiritual autobiography or allegory but the gothic tale and domestic romance. I suggest that the inability of spiritual autobiography to generate narrative for its female protagonist posed a problem for Brontë—a problem that she "solved" by introducing gothic and domestic romance, a solution that then served to highlight the incompatibilities of the genres she wished to yoke.[21] Despite the ease with which we refer to "moral gothic," or Jane as a "secular pilgrim,"[22] the two terms of these couplings are set at odds in volume 2 of *Jane Eyre*.

At Thornfield, the gothic mode initially shapes, dominates, and explains Jane's experience.[23] In the lanes around the house she conjures up visions of the Gytrash and meets a mysterious stranger; in the attic she happens upon a dark secret and hears "the slow ha! ha!" of a mysterious woman; and in the bedrooms she discovers strange fires, discerns unexplained footsteps, and witnesses unspeakable acts of violence. This invasion of the gothic signals male interpretive power and loss of female freedom. It supports Rochester's view of events rather than Jane's control of her life and life story; it threatens the autobiographical independence that Jane seemed to have achieved at the end of volume 1. For example, after Jane saves Rochester from the mysterious being who sets fire to his bed, whose "demonic laugh" Jane hears at "the very key-hole of [her] chamber-door" (130), Rochester refuses to discuss this gothic incident, leaving Jane "absolutely dumfounded" (136). Again, after the episode in which Bertha Mason rends Jane's wedding veil, Rochester insists that Jane has merely had a nightmare, that her female visitor is just "the creature of an over-stimulated brain" (250). Jane presses for a realistic, commonsensical explanation, but Rochester, determined to marry and possess her, insists that she accept his gothic version of the events.

If the gothic presents a challenge to Jane as interpreter, it only temporarily dispossesses her of control over her life and life story. Once Jane discovers the identity of Bertha Mason, the gothic mode loses its hold (as does Rochester, its primary user). The other genre dominant in volume 2, however, the domestic romance, presents a different kind of threat, one seen as hostile to Jane's spiritual progress if not to her narrative freedom. Whereas the gothic poses the generic issue as a contest between interpreters, Rochester's gothic versus Jane's realism, the romance poses the issue as a contest between autobiographical modes for women, the domestic versus the religious or spiritual.

As Jane describes her growing love for Rochester, she guiltily admits that he "was becoming to me my whole world; and more than the world: almost my hope of heaven" (241). Rochester and religion stand in opposition: "He stood between me and every thought of religion, as an eclipse intervenes between man and the broad sun. I could not, in those days, see God for his creature" (241). And Jane's troubled dreams—of "a shore, sweet as the hills of Beulah" (133)—suggest that Brontë understands the incompatibility of spiritual autobiography as such and a domesticized version in which marriage and an edenic home life substitute for a celestial Beulah, the promised land after the exile (Isa. 62:4). Jane's understanding of her domestic inclinations places romance outside of—indeed, in antithesis to—her spiritual pilgrimage, the genres here refusing to meld.

In the literary predecessors to *Jane Eyre,* the genres did not meld either. Nineteenth-century conduct literature and domestic fiction did not assume that a young woman would use biblical models to understand her romantic experience. When Hannah More wrote *Coelebs in Search of a Wife* (1808), she assumed that the man would do the searching for a wife and that he would apply religious principles in his choice, but not that he would consider his marital quest to be a version of a spiritual exodus.[24] When Mary Martha Sherwood wrote *Caroline Mordaunt* (1835), a governess tale that instructs young women about suitable relations with employers, a tale that influenced the plot of *Jane Eyre,* she devoted all but one of her fourteen chapters to issues of governessing and only a few paragraphs to the marriage of her heroine—and these not as the closure to a spiritual autobiography.[25]

At the end of Sherwood's novel, when Caroline Mordaunt's cousin "trace[s] the hand of God in all that had befallen" (298), the providentialist aesthetic he invokes applies only to governessing; there is no assumption that biblical types apply to courtship and romance. Caroline "interprets" her marriage only in order to analyze her future husband's character ("he was pious and humble, and possessed all that natural courtesy which originates from piety and humility") and to assure herself that "our religious principles agreed" (303). In Sherwood, there is no assumption that spiritual pilgrimages find their end in a husband and marriage.

In *Jane Eyre,* however, Brontë introduces a new hermeneutics to women's autobiography, a hermeneutics of the domestic realm. Paradoxically, what she poses first as a threat to Jane's spiritual state is finally affirmed as a valid autobiographical enterprise. In volume 3 the novel domesticates spiritual autobiography, making it compatible with romance. How and why does this happen? I want to propose two explanations, one descriptive in that it traces the changing uses of religious language in volume 3, the other generic and ideological in that it analyzes the contest between Jane's domesticized version of spiritual autobiography and St. John's alternative spiritual form, the female missionary memoir.

Domestication begins at the point of romantic crisis—the point at which Jane discovers Rochester's wife and resolves not to become his bigamous spouse or mistress. Until this point, the language of Providence has been minimized, only occasionally irrupting into Jane's thoughts. It reenters as Jane retrospectively notes that she has "trusted well in Providence, and believed that events were working together for good" (246). When she determines to leave Thornfield, she tells Rochester, who appeals to her in the language and logic of love, that he must "do as I do: trust in God. . . . Believe in Heaven. Hope to meet there again." (278). That is, she shifts her rhetoric (and thus their relation) from romantic love to spiritual pilgrimage.

As gothic is displaced and romance disrupted, the novel reinvents Jane's crisis as a moral one. Brontë transforms what in spiritual autobiography would traditionally have been a religious or theological crisis into romantic and domestic temptation. As she moves from theological matters to sexual morality, she translates the exodus pattern of spiritual autobiography from religious to romantic quest, making the episode of the Egyptian bondage into a threat of sexual bondage.[26] As Jane describes her forlorn state after the disruption of her wedding, she speaks in language that draws on Exodus 12:29–30: "My hopes were all dead— struck with a subtle doom, such as in one night, fell on all the first-born in the land of Egypt" (260). It is not hope of heaven or the promised land to which Jane refers, but hope of love and blissful married life with Rochester. Jane's false Eden has been shattered.

This combination—or conflation—of religious and romantic crisis comes to dominate fictionalized women's autobiography after *Jane Eyre,* whether in George Eliot's *Mill on the Floss,* where Maggie Tulliver finds opportunity to apply Thomas a Kempis's *Imitation of Christ* to a romantic dilemma, or in William White Hale's *Clara Hopgood* and *Catharine Furze,* where the heroines' spiritual crises are framed as romantic and marital choices.[27] (Indeed, Hale's fictional autobiographies offer a fair measure for comparing male versus female versions of Victorian spiritual autobiography: whereas the *Autobiography of Mark Rutherford* focuses on a theological crisis, as did Newman's more famous *Apologia pro Vita Sua,* Hale's two women's autobiographies shift the emphasis to moral crises in love and marriage.) *Jane Eyre* sets the pattern when the heroine leaves Thornfield, the site of moral testing, to begin a period of wandering in the wilderness.

That wandering literalizes the Exodus in that Jane, once escaped from Thornfield, trudges aimlessly on a northern English moor. It also re-allegorizes the Exodus, as Bunyan had done in *The Pilgrim's Progress.*

Jane puts her trust in Providence—"Sure was I of His efficiency to save what He had made" (285)—and, after days without food or rest, eventually finds a home at Marsh End with the Rivers family. But Brontë does not simply repeat the exodus pattern common in spiritual autobiography. Whereas a spiritual autobiographer might have completed her account with her work as an English schoolteacher ("a village schoolmistress, free and honest, in a breezy mountain nook in the healthy heart of England," 316) or as the missionary wife of St. John Rivers, or whereas a secular autobiographer such as Martineau might have ended with the discovery of vocation, Brontë makes spiritual satisfaction dependent on the integration of the romantic desires traditionally excluded from (or repressed by) spiritual autobiography. Brontë's autobiography insists on integrating those nightly dreams that Jane admits to having after her day's work: "dreams where, amidst unusual scenes, charged with adventure, with agitating risk and romantic chance, I still again and again met Mr. Rochester, always at some exciting crisis" (323).

The immediate threat to this integration comes from St. John Rivers, who forces Jane to consider another possible mode of spiritual autobiography. Jane is to find her destiny, her spiritual fulfillment, through marriage to him and a life of evangelism and good works in India. Rivers insists that Jane wants "employment" (351), that God has opened the possibility of "a noble career" (360), that her destiny lies not at home in England but abroad. When she refuses his proposal, he claims that she has forsaken "the Christian's cross and the angel's crown" (370). Generically, we might say, St. John poses a threat to Jane's desired amalgam of the romantic and biblical, in effect claiming that they need not (or cannot) be mixed. His threat includes the possibility of new careers—and hence new life writing—for women.

When St. John Rivers proposes that Jane accept his offer of marriage and missionary work in India, he is in effect proposing that Jane model her life on a new kind of women's autobiography that emerged in the 1820s, '30s, and '40s: the life story of the heroic female missionary. British missionary efforts in India did not officially begin until 1813, when the East India Company was forced to lift its ban on missionaries in its territories and the first bishop of Calcutta, Thomas Middleton, was appointed by the Anglican Church; but even before the ban was lifted, various British and American religious organizations began sending their representatives to establish posts in Calcutta, Bombay, Madras, and smaller settlements upriver.[28] Until the 1830s only male missionaries were officially sent to India and other parts of Asia, the task and the territory being considered too harsh for women (but not, ironically, for missionaries' wives). By 1835, however, single women were being interviewed and approved for service by the Society for Promoting Female Education in China, India and the East, a branch of the Church Missionary Society, and various sectarian groups were appointing both single and married women to go to India with missionary families and husbands—largely, it seems, because of the extraordinary successes of a small core of women, including Ann Hasseltine Judson, Sarah Hall Boardman, and Margaret Wilson, who had gone unofficially to India and whose lives and work were widely publicized in memoirs of the 1830s and 1840s.[29]

That St. John Rivers (and Brontë) knew of such memoirs seems evident from his suggestion that Jane become "a conductress of Indian schools" (the role that Boardman and Wilson made famous) and from the language of his marriage proposal (details of which echo those of Judson's and Boardman's courtships).[30] Margaret Wilson was a Scotswoman famous for establishing the Bombay School for Destitute Girls in the 1830s; her namesake, another Mrs. Wilson, did similar educational work in Calcutta, where new recruits of the Female Education Society were often sent for initial service.[31] Ann Judson, an American-born missionary, was noted for pioneering work in Burma and for her eloquent pleas on behalf of female education in the East.[32] Sarah Boardman (later Judson) founded schools in Burma, where, under British rule, the government made appropriations throughout the provinces for a network of schools "to be conducted on the plan of Mrs. Boardman's schools at Tavoy."[33] The journals and memoirs of these female missionaries suggest that St. John Rivers's proposal is neither demeaning nor disrespectful but, in terms of efforts to improve female education and expand careers for British and American women, represents an "advanced" position.

Virtually every account written by and about women missionaries in India stresses the importance of female education. When the Female Education Society was founded in 1834, one of its first resolutions was to include *India* in its name: "it was resolved that India, whose females stand equally in need of elevation by Christian Education, with the additional claim of being subjects of Britain, be included in the objects of this society, which shall be designated 'The Society for Promoting Female Education in India, China, & the adjacent countries."[34] The language of "elevation" by means of education became a standard feature of female missionary memoirs, sometimes with descriptions of "female degradation" or "female wretchedness" used to explain the subject's commitment to educational work, sometimes with a more general discussion of the high "station assigned to female character" in Christian nations versus the "appalling and gloomy contrast" of women in Eastern countries as motivation for her decision to enter the missionary field.[35] When Ann Judson appealed to her countrywomen to support female education in the East, she stressed the utter lack of education for girls in Bengal and Hindostan:

> *At the age of two or three years, [females] are married by their parents to children of their own rank in society. On these occasions all the parade and splendor possible are exhibited; they are then conducted to their fathers' abode, not to be educated, not to prepare for the performance of duties incumbent upon wives and mothers, but to drag out the usual period allotted, in listless idleness, in mental torpor.[36]*

The woman missionary viewed her educational efforts in India as improving women's lives and raising Eastern women to "the standard of moral and intellectual excellence" attained in Christian nations—goals, if not language, endorsed by British missions throughout the nineteenth and twentieth centuries.[37]

Nineteenth-century women missionaries also viewed their work as promoting the cause of—and improving career opportunities for—Western women, a secondary effect they readily and unequivocally discussed. Modern historians of British missions have noted, for example, the opportunities for women doctors in India, China, and Japan late in the nineteenth century, when medical practices at home were denied them.[38] As early as the 1830s, British women recognized the possibility of careers in India that would have been difficult to pursue at home. Virtually as soon as the first missionary memoirs were published, they pointed out this beneficial effect. In reviewing the *Memoir of Mrs. Judson*, Margaret Wilson, then a missionary in Bombay, observed: "[This species of biography] introduces us to individuals, formed by nature for a sub-

ordinate sphere of action, and deprived, in a great measure, of those powerful motives to exertion which the eager pursuit of knowledge, a love of
honourable distinction, and the expectation of reward, impart to their
possessors."[39] Despite the rhetoric of separate spheres, what Wilson implies—that her fellow missionaries found opportunity for heroic action
and honorable distinction in India and Burma—becomes an explicit argument in subsequent biographies of Judson and her counterparts. In the
1851 preface to new memoirs of Ann and Sarah Judson, Arabella W.
Stuart begins with the claim: "Among the many benefits which modern
missions have conferred on the world, not the least, perhaps, is the field
they have afforded for the development of the highest excellence of female character. . . . The missionary enterprise opens to women a sphere
of activity, usefulness and distinction, not, under the present constitution
of society, to be found elsewhere."[40] The cause of Western women's
rights and opportunities appears repeatedly in accounts of women missionaries, so insistently that by the twentieth century a biographer of Ann
Judson could begin by comparing Judson with Mary Wollstonecraft as
someone ranking "among the early protagonists of women's emancipa-
tion."[41] In the poetics of female missionary biography, the cause of converting the non-Christian or educating Indian women becomes complementary to the feminist cause of expanding Western women's work. In
St. John's words in India "He [God] opens to you a noble career" (360).

St. John's phrase "noble career" draws not only on the modern usage
of *career* as "a course of professional life or employment" but also on an
older meaning of the word as "the course of the sun or a star in the
heavens" or, figuratively, the height or "full swing of a person's activity."[42] As his adjective implies, he considers the female missionary's
career to be one that allows full scope to the subject's powers; by setting
her sights on heaven, she surpasses what would normally be possible on
earth. St. John's language reiterates the point that Arabella Stuart made
when she described missionary work as developing the "highest excellence of female character," "distinction" as well as "usefulness."

By emphasizing opportunities for women's careers, I do not mean
to suggest that St. John Rivers is a proto-feminist or that male missionaries
viewed the work of their female counterparts as part of a worldwide
emancipatory project. On the contrary, many male missionaries treated
female education and the careers of female missionaries as of secondary

interest. In reporting to the Scottish Assembly in 1835, for example, the Reverend Alexander Duff, who called himself "The Assembly's First Missionary to India" and who was also known as the "Pioneer of Missionary Education,"[43] failed to mention anything about female education in India. Apparently he was later questioned on this topic and responded in an 1837 report, *Vindication of the Church of Scotland's India Mission,* by describing the Day School and Orphan School run by Mrs. Wilson in Calcutta. Despite Mrs. Wilson's remarkable work, Duff was willing to dismiss its effects as short-lived, given the state of Indian society: "little, very little, in the way of permanent beneficial result can, in the present state of things, be expected to result from the operations of such a seminary." Duff believed that the Scottish mission must devote itself primarily to the education and conversion of men, who, "as time rolls on, [will] become the heads of families themselves, and then will they be prepared, in many instances at least, to give practical effect to their better judgment," including the education of their wives and daughters.[44]

Needless to say, British women did not see their missionary activity as secondary. They pointed out that the Christian religion had originally been "a GOSPEL to the poor" and that women were the first to spread the Christian message. "It seems peculiarly appropriate," wrote Isabella Stuart, "that woman, who doubtless owes to Christianity most of the domestic consideration and social advantages, which in enlightened countries she regards as her birthright, should be the bearer of these blessings to her less favored sisters in heathen lands."[45] However much we may balk at this rhetoric of Western superiority, it nonetheless reminds us that women educators in the East did not accept a rhetoric of gender or class inferiority. Missionary memoirs written by women insist that female education in India is crucial, that it may be "the most powerful form of agency available to women."

"The most powerful form of agency available to women" is not, of course, the language of nineteenth-century autobiography but Deirdre David's phrase in *Rule Britannia: Women, Empire, and Victorian Writing* (1995), used to describe Jane Eyre's project of "rehabilitating the colonizer" by marrying Rochester. David has written powerfully of the "two historical imperatives in the colonial politics of the 1830s and 1840s, rehabilitating the colonizer . . . and converting the colonized."[46] She argues that rehabilitating the colonizer came first, converting the colonized second, and that Jane Eyre's choice of the former represents the more powerful option of the two. My reading of missionary memoirs questions David's hierarchy. I suggest that it is precisely the issues of female agency and new careers for women that such auto/biographies of the 1830s and 1840s contest. Jane Eyre chooses woman's mission at home, marriage to and reform of Rochester. Female missionaries to India chose woman's mission abroad, commitment to all women's "elevation" and the opportunity for "honorable distinction." At mid-century it was unclear which choice was the better, the more powerful or productive for women.

What is clear, however, is that women missionaries and their memoirists developed a new form of Victorian life writing, one that represented women taking heroic action, women engaged in serious work outside the home. As a biographer, Arabella Stuart was quick to note the absence of such literature (indeed, of any women's biography) and thus the literary innovativeness of her work: "How few of the memoirs and biographical sketches which load the shelves of our libraries, record the lives of women!" Margaret Wilson noted, too, the possibilities for a new "species of biography" that recorded the "lives of distinguished females" who would otherwise have been "deprived" of "honorable distinction." [47] These auto/biographers depict themselves and other women in heroic modes—braving long ocean voyages, enduring the physical hardships of life on mission posts, living without the companionship of English-speaking women, facing customs and practices that would have shocked their European counterparts. Moreover, they show women taking heroic action in political crises, even intervening in military campaigns. Both Ann Judson and Sarah Boardman, for example, faced attack and imprisonment during the British invasion of Burma in the late 1820s, when all Europeans, whatever their nationalities or sympathies, were suspect by Burmese rulers. Both women aided European prisoners (including their husbands), intervened with Burmese officials, and served as translators between the British and Burmese. Their biographers emphasize the heroic *difference* of their characters and actions: "Females, who in this country of order and security, tremble at the idea of being left for one night alone in their strong and guarded dwellings, may perhaps conceive the feelings of Mrs. Boardman on being thus left." [48] There is no evidence that Sarah Boardman trembled.

Missionary memoirs taught their readers to regard their subjects in a heroic light, to venerate women missionaries as they would male heroes. As the genre developed during the nineteenth century, it increasingly came to incorporate exemplary scenes of veneration—as in the *Reminiscences* (1885) of Marilla Hutchins Hill, where Mrs. Bacheler, wife of a Baptist missionary, visits Serampore, "the birth-place of Indian missions," and pays pious tribute at the graves of her predecessors: "My heart thrilled with emotion, and it was with a kind of reverential awe that I ascended the steps of the Ghat and walked over the ground once hallowed by the footsteps of Harriet Newell, Ann Hazeltine Judson, Henry Martin, and others, whose names are written in heaven." Male readers, too, were expected to pay tribute, as does Dr. Bacheler in visiting the "grave of sister Phillips" at Sambhalpur, where he reflects that "she died with her armor on, bearing a noble testimony to the blessedness of the Gospel," and that "her influence had not died with her, but had been felt across the ocean in her native land." [49] The fact that Dr. Bacheler thinks first of Mrs. Phillips's influence at home rather than in India suggests that missionary memoirs constructed monuments to female heroism as much as to Christian evangelism and that, given the early deaths of their subjects, they had significant impact on the shape of Victorian women's lives.

Dr. Bacheler's meditations also suggest, if unwittingly, a historical reason for the early impact of missionary memoirs on nineteenth-century women's life writing. As he thinks of Mrs. Phillips's tragic death, he associates it with "the removal of Harriet Newell," the young woman who accompanied Ann Judson to India as the first female missionary but whose death virtually on arrival prevented her from contributing much to Indian missions. For Bacheler, nonetheless, "the influence of her death still continues to be felt, fanning, in many a heart, the missionary flame." [50] Bacheler points to the fact that the early deaths of women missionaries produced heroic memoirs ahead of their time—that is, historically prior to accounts by women professionals such as Tonna, Martineau, and Cobbe, who lived full life spans.

In more practical though no less heroic terms, female missionary memoirs showed women at work. Although professional concerns would later come to dominate the autobiographies of Harriet Martineau (1877), Frances Power Cobbe (1895), Margaret Oliphant (1899), and Jane Ellen Harrison (1925), work is virtually unrepresented in early nineteenth-century life writing by women. As Helena Michie has argued, citing Anna Jameson, "After all that has been written, sung, and said of women, one has the perception that neither in prose nor in verse has she ever appeared as a laborer."[51] Unlike other genres, and particularly in contrast to Indian travelogues like Emma Roberts's *Scenes and Characteristics of Hindostan* (1835) and Fanny Parks Parlby's *Wanderings of a Pilgrim in Search of the Picturesque* (1850), which represented middle-class British men and women at leisure, missionary memoirs depicted and discussed women's labor.[52] Women missionaries devoted large sections of their journals and histories to work—in education, in language acquisition and translation, in home visitation and medical aid.[53] Although such accounts of work sometimes sink under heavy religious rhetoric or virtually disappear in the unedited letters transcribed by their memoirists, these life histories nonetheless give prominence to women's achievements beyond maternity and domesticity.

The rhetoric of heroism and emphasis on women's work underwrite St. John's proposal to Jane Eyre. In many missionary memoirs, as in Brontë's novel, the decision to become a missionary is framed as a choice between heroism and domesticity—or, more precisely, between noble if sometimes tragic heroism and natural if also more easy domesticity. When Sarah Boardman's husband died and she faced the choice of staying at her mission post or returning home, she framed her dilemma this way: Would she (1) "devote herself to her domestic duties, manage her household, educate her darling boy, and in quiet seclusion pass the weary days of her widowhood," or (2) "looking abroad on the spiritual wants of the people around her, . . . continue to employ her time and faculties in instructing and elevating those in whose service her husband had worn out his life," or (3) "take her child, her 'only one,' and return to the land of her birth, where she still had dear parents, brothers and sisters, who would welcome her with open arms"? Boardman decided that to adopt either the first or third course would be to succumb to her "natural disposition" and "a strong tendency to self-indulgence."[54] In other words, she rejects the "natural" feminine desires for domesticity and maternity—in what is virtually a parody of nineteenth-century sentimental language—for the superior if demanding course of heroism. So, too, Ann Judson refused to abandon the missionary compound at Rangoon during the British-Burmese War, despite "dangers on every hand" and "bitter pains and persecutions." [55]

In *Jane Eyre* St. John's proposal—and Jane's refusal—similarly represent a choice between heroism and domesticity, though with more skepticism about the former and more advocacy of the latter. In chapters 33–34, the scenes in which Jane learns of her inheritance and hears St. John's proposal, the two characters quarrel over her future and, specifically, over the matter of her "employment" (343). Jane wants to spend her newly acquired time and money on domestic activities. When St. John asks, "What aim, what purpose, what ambition in life have you now?" (343), she responds that her "first aim will be to *clean down* Moor House from chamber to cellar," then prepare the rooms for the return of Diana and Mary, and then "solemnis[e]" certain "culinary rites" with Hannah (343–44). Her mock-religious rhetoric displeases St. John, who insists that she ought to look "higher" than "domestic endearments and household joys," that she ought to "look beyond Moor House and Morton, and sisterly society" (344). In Jane's usage, however, the rhetoric is not simply mock-religious, even if the tone is light. For her the domestic is the site of spiritual peace and personal development; "sisterly society" is the goal and haven she has sought.

Despite her sympathy for Jane's position, Brontë treats St. John and his heroic vision with considerable respect. When Jane suggests, for instance, that he marry Rosamund and "relinquish" his "scheme" to become a missionary, he legitimately objects:

(329)

> *"Relinquish! What! my vocation? My great work? My foundation laid on earth for a mansion in heaven? My hopes of being numbered in the band who have merged all ambition in the glorious one of bettering their race—of carrying knowledge into the realms of ignorance—of substituting peace for war—freedom for bondage—religion for superstition—the hope of heaven for fear of hell? . . . It is dearer than the blood in my veins. It is what I have to look forward to and to live for."*

Few modern readers share St. John's passion for missionary work, and his linguistic explosion may reveal a wariness of its extremes, just as Jane's mock-religious language may register an ambivalence about domesticity.

Yet St. John's vocation was deeply respected by the church and congre-
gations he served. As the almost hagiographic biographies of the first missionaries to India attest, these pioneers inspired young clergymen to embrace the missionary cause. After reading the *Memoir of the Rev. Henry
Martyn* (1814), the most celebrated of Evangelical missionaries to India,
one future Scottish missionary had a conversion-like experience: "I was
immediately smitten like Saul to the ground, and under the oppression
of what was mightier than any human hand, I was led for many weeks to
cry day and night, 'Lord, what wilt thou have me to do?'"[56] St. John,
too, describes a version of this experience; after feeling despair about his
clerical work in England, he tells Jane, "my powers heard a call from
heaven to rise, gather their full strength, spread their wings, and mount
beyond ken" (318). As Jane comes to recognize, his appropriate destiny
is India, just as hers is Thornfield: "He could not—he would not—re-
nounce his wild field of mission warfare for the parlours and the peace of
Vale Hall" (324).

To reformulate the debate between Jane and St. John, we might say
that what is at stake are different values in two new forms of Victorian
autobiography, the missionary and the domestic. Missionary autobiography associates itself with the heroic—as Jane puts it, St. John "was of
the material from which nature hews her heroes" (346), and he thus
incorporates the rhetoric of epic heroism as he recounts his spiritual
struggle to Jane Eyre. Missionary autobiography emphasizes vocation—
as St. John demonstrates when he relinquishes marriage to Rosamund
Oliver because he prizes more his "great work," his "foundation laid on
earth for a mansion in heaven" (329). Male missionary autobiography in
particular depends on a corresponding kind of female autobiography—
as St. John reveals when he tells Jane he needs a wife "fitted to my vocation" (357). He needs someone willing to enact a version of the memoirs
of Victorian clergymen's wives who accompanied their husbands to India—wives who opened schools for girls, who gained access to women
of the zenana, who initiated their own or supported their husbands' efforts in translation and publication, who were not only "helpers amongst
Indian women" (355) but husbands' helpers, too.[57]

Jane insists on a different direction for women's autobiography—
the domestic memoir, or what I have called the domesticated spiritual
autobiography. In her view, women's lives (and, by implication, life writ-

ing) naturally concern themselves with the domestic—as Jane insists when she places value on "domestic endearments and household joys" (344), on her need for a family, on "the calm of domestic life" (346). "The parlour is not his sphere" (346), Jane acknowledges, thinking of Rochester; but it is her own. Women's autobiography in Jane's estimate worries less about "vocation," more about "love." "I have no vocation," Jane tells St. John (354), even as she claims authority in matters of the heart and hearth, and "scorn[s] the counterfeit sentiment" he offers (359). Women's autobiography asserts, moreover, an independent status for itself, not simply a complementary or secondary relation with masculine autobiography. Jane desires "recesses in my mind which would be only mine" (359), even as she recognizes her connections with others.

Despite the intensity of St. John and Jane's debate, and despite the reader's sympathy with Jane's decision, Brontë balances the merits and demerits of their positions with remarkable justice. "He is right to choose a missionary's career" (346), Jane admits after observing his response to the newly refurbished Moor House. For St. John cares little if at all about "the humanities and amenities of life" or "its peaceful enjoyments" (345); he seems happy only when he aspires, only when he has "performed an act of duty" (347). In contrast, Jane finds happiness in "merry domestic dissipation" (347) with her newly discovered cousins. When she tells St. John, "I do not understand a missionary life" (354), she is not simply making excuses; rather, as she explains to Diana, she represents "the feelings and claims of little people" (366), people for whom St. John's "own large views" are incomprehensible and whom he "pitilessly" (366) forgets as he pursues his heroic schemes. In effect Jane articulates a rationale for domestic life writing, for the values and uses of auto/biography that hundreds of ordinary Victorian women expressed when they chose to devote their lives to—and write about—the home.

Most critics who discuss Jane's rejection of St. John's proposal treat it as a rejection of "patriarchy" and all that this term negatively contains—whether, in Adrienne Rich's terms, a "patriarchal religion" that encourages a "feminine urge toward self-abnegation" or, in Helene Moglen's, a "Victorian denial of the dignity of human passion" or, in Gilbert and Gubar's, "a pillar of patriarchy" who preaches "the Carlylean sermon of self-actualization through work."[58] Yet as Deirdre David's analysis of *Jane Eyre* as postcolonial text implies, Jane's decision to reform

Rochester, to become a "governess of Empire," does not escape the patriarchal frame, even if Jane carves out a "powerful form of female agency" within it.[59] Reforming the male colonizer by engaging in woman's mission at home can scarcely be said to avoid patriarchy any more than converting the colonial subject avoids patriarchy by extending woman's mission abroad. I would note, moreover, that Jane's rejection of St. John's proposal is as much literary as it is social or political; it reveals Brontë's desire to retain features of the domestic novel and its nonfictional counterpart, the domestic memoir, that female missionary autobiographies minimize or even omit.

One feature is the courtship and romance of the female subject; another is the valorization of the domestic setting. If one asks a modern reader why Jane rejects St. John's proposal, the answer will come back, "She does not love him." ("Nor does he love her" might be a second answer.) Although this response oversimplifies Jane's complex reasoning in her dialogues with St. John, in fact the novel makes "love" the pivot on which her decision turns. "I scorn your idea of love," Jane tells St. John when she finally refuses him, "I scorn the counterfeit sentiment you offer" (359). Jane claims an expertise in romantic desire that St. John, for all his heroic virtues, lacks: he cannot discern "real" from "counterfeit." While such expertise of the heart is fundamental to domestic literature, it is minimized in the memoirs of women missionaries, where other intellectual and moral qualities—"skill in the mastery of unknown and difficult dialects," "tact in dealing with the varieties of human character," "ardor and perseverance in the pursuit of a noble end," and an "exalted Christian heroism and fortitude, that braves appalling dangers, and even death in its most dreadful forms"—take precedence.[60] In missionary memoirs, the romantic experience of the subject may be acknowledged, but it is overbalanced by other considerations.

In the *Memoir of Mrs. Margaret Wilson,* for instance, the early chapters concentrate on those matters of character and training that prepared Margaret Bayne for missionary life, including her study of "the romance of Indian mythology and philosophy" and her "research in Hindostán."[61] When her marriage to John Wilson is introduced, her husband-editor links the couple's "mutual regard and affection" with their individual "aspirations and purposes" to serve God: "With the fullest confidence in her capacity to minister to my happiness, and, through God's assistance, to contribute in an eminent degree, by her rare endowments of nature and grace, to the advancement of the Redeemer's kingdom in India,— . . . I invited her to be the sharer of my joys and sorrows, of my toil and its reward." Much like St. John Rivers in both his egoism and his heroism, Wilson imagines his wife's decision to be motivated by duty: "She had humbly and faithfully prosecuted the work of self-examination, asking counsel in fervent and persevering prayer; the result of which was, that she considered it her duty to grant a cheerful acquiescence to my proposal." However, other sections of the *Memoir,* including Margaret's letters, suggest that the Wilsons enjoyed a happy, affectionate partnership and that, for Margaret at least, love motivated her decision to go to India. Yet as Wilson's overly careful language reveals, the form of the missionary memoir prescribed a commitment to "the future glory and perpetuity of the kingdom of God" over the earthly experience of domestic bliss.[62]

A few memoirs even hint that this "future glory" was all-important and that the female missionary may have fallen in love in order to get to India. Sarah Boardman, née Hall, was fascinated with missions long before she found a clergyman who shared her passion. "It is my ardent desire," she wrote to a friend, "that the glorious work of reformation may be extended. . . . How can I be so inactive, when I know that thousands are perishing in this land of grace; and millions in other lands are at this very moment kneeling before senseless idols!" "The enthusiastic Sarah" (the phrase is her biographer's) found her husband by publishing an elegy on the death of Colman, one of the first Baptist missionaries to India, in a religious magazine, where the poem "touched and interested" Colman's successor, George Dana Boardman.[63] Sarah Hall eventually married Boardman, served with him for years in India and Burma, and after his death married Adoniram Judson, another missionary. Although her biographer insists on the affection between Sarah and her two husbands, it takes little scrutiny to discover that for Sarah Hall missions took priority over marriage, duty over love.[64]

Brontë rejects this hierarchy—or, at least for Jane, makes human love more important than religious duty. This reversal of priorities may stem from psychological or ideological motives—psychological in that Brontë's own desperate need for love informed her fiction, ideological in that her response to missionary tales critiques the heroic model and evangelical aggressiveness they promulgated.[65] However satisfying these explanations may be to modern readers, the novel itself explains its different priorities in terms of "nature." As Jane analyzes St. John's disciplined refusal of Rosamund Oliver's love, "at once so heroic and so martyr-like," she concludes: "he could not bound all that he had in his *nature*—the rover, the aspirant, the poet, the priest—in the limits of a single passion" (324). Later, as she listens to his plea for joint missionary work, she see the limitations of this nature: "the analysis of his *nature* was proceeding before my eyes. I saw his fallibilities" (358). When she refuses him, it is because "our *natures* are at variance— . . . the very name of love is an apple of discord between us" (360, emphasis mine). This repetition points to the differences in human natures, some that can best be satisfied by love, others for which love is secondary or incidental.[66]

The focus on love and domestic happiness in *Jane Eyre,* as in other women's life writing, allows Brontë to represent, as Nancy Armstrong has argued, "the unseen desires of women." [67] It gives expression, in Brontë's terms, to "the feelings and claims of little people" (366), those ordinary subjects normally excluded from heroic autobiography and from public, *res gestae* memoir. It also allows Brontë to retain (or re-create) a second important feature of Victorian domestic fiction and memoir: the home as site of a new Eden.

In the final scenes of *Jane Eyre,* Brontë returns her heroine not to Thornfield, the site of temptation and trouble, but to a house named Ferndean, a natural, edenic setting. As Gilbert and Gubar argued long ago, Ferndean is Brontë's most significant revision of Bunyan and the narrative of spiritual pilgrimage: "Here, isolated from society but flourishing in a natural order of their own making, Jane and Rochester will become physically 'bone of [each other's] bone, flesh of [each other's] flesh.' . . . Not the Celestial City, but a natural paradise, the country of Beulah 'upon the borders of heaven,' where 'the contract between bride and bridegroom [is] renewed,' has all along been, we now realize, the goal of Jane's pilgrimage." [68] This revision of spiritual autobiography opens up enormous possibilities for women's life writing, as it domesticates a traditional religious genre by shifting the focus away from a heavenly paradise and toward an earthly, domestic setting, and thus legitimates, even valorizes women's narratives of domestic experience.

In order to reach Ferndean, however, Jane must revise not only Bunyan but the original biblical narrative of missionary enterprise: St.

Paul's account of his mission to the gentiles in the Acts of the Apostles. As Jane recognizes the contrary desires informing St. John's life and her own, she counters his proposal with an equally biblical, if also startling, model of her womanly destiny. Instead of India, she reinserts Thornfield (ultimately Ferndean) as the promised land of her pilgrim's progress and the site of woman's mission. Brontë nicely makes this substitution using two biblical allusions, the first to the Macedonian call in Acts 16:9, the second to the miraculous release of Paul and Silas from prison in Acts 16: 25–26. The double substitution—literarily, a duplicity—suggests an ambivalence about the generic revisions she is making.

In the first allusion, when St. John asks Jane to serve in India, Jane admits that "it was as if I had heard a summons from Heaven—as if a visionary messenger, like him of Macedonia, had announced, 'Come over and help us!'" (354). In the second, after Jane has heard the voice of Rochester crying "Jane! Jane! Jane!" she explains that "the wondrous shock of feeling had come like the earthquake which shook the foundations of Paul and Silas's prison: it had opened the doors of the soul's cell, and loosed its bands" (371). Both experiences are visionary; both come at moments of spiritual crisis; Jane analyzes both using biblical passages (from the same chapter of the Book of Acts, no less). Yet the second, the call from Rochester, stands as the authoritative climax to Jane's spiritual autobiography. Why?

It is tempting to suggest that the second episode represents better applied hermeneutics, a better example of autobiographical interpretation in that Jane's choice of biblical passage is more relevant to her situation or more aptly applied to her experience or more complex in its resonances. Indeed, since the release of Paul and Silas from prison in Acts 16:9 includes a rebellion against Roman authority and the salvation of a nearly lost soul, it seems closely attuned to Jane's action, which similarly rejects established authority and includes Rochester's redemption. Yet this explanation does not finally hold, for both biblical passages are valid in their historical and cultural contexts; Jane might legitimately have chosen woman's mission abroad or woman's mission at home. The difference seems to be that, in the second case, Jane voluntarily *chooses* her destiny, autobiographically and hermeneutically. As autobiographer, she consciously makes the story of Paul and Silas's release from prison a parallel to her own life story. For Victorian women, *Jane Eyre* thus makes the feminization and domestication of the missionary narrative available as a literary corollary of woman's mission at home.

Yet, while the novel constructs a domestic version of spiritual auto-biography, it also registers an ambivalence about the direction it has taken. Brontë creates Ferndean in place of Bunyan's Celestial City, re-writing the missionary memoir to legitimize Jane's mission at Ferndean, but she returns, in the final two paragraphs of the novel, to St. John Rivers as a missionary to India, revising Bunyan a final time and reading St. John as "the warrior Greatheart, who guards his pilgrim convoy from the onslaught of Apollyon." As Carolyn Williams has suggested, this rhetorical move "honors his vocation from a safe distance, accepting and even admiring for another what is rejected for herself."[69] Brontë's rhetoric may even suggest that Jane has knowingly made a lesser, more ordinary choice.

Jane's admiration for St. John includes a recognition that "his is the ambition of the high master-spirit" and that he "represents the first rank of those who are redeemed from the earth" (398)—a final acknowledg-ment of his place in a heroic tradition. Despite the potential irony of a man "ambitious" in the spiritual realm, Jane's language does not under-mine the vocational choice St. John has made; if anything, Jane repeats the rhetoric of missionary memoirs and sermons as if to commemorate his death in advance. In a funeral oration in remembrance of Harriet Newell, the "first martyr to the missionary cause from the American world," the Reverend Leonard Woods defined the Christian missionary in terms that anticipate the character of St. John Rivers:

> *The* Christian Missionary, *whose motives are as sublime as his office, forsakes all for Christ in a* remarkable *sense. The proof which he gives of devotion to Christ, is indeed of the same nature with that which other Christians give; but it is higher in* degree. *Others forsake the world in* affection, *but enjoy it still. He* renounces the *enjoyment, as well as the* attachment.[70]

Woods commends Harriet Newell and her husband as models that the most dedicated of his listeners might follow, even as he offers a more accessible alternative to those who might simply "imitate her humility, self-denial, and faith" in order one day to "dwell with her for ever" in heaven.[71] In the final paragraphs of the novel, Jane similarly designates

St. John as one whose devotion is different in degree, one "called, and chosen, and faithful" (398). Her inclusion of a domestic fact—that "St. John is unmarried: he will never marry now" (398)—suggests that he has fully renounced earthly attachment, a renunciation that other characters in the novel are not called upon to make.

Jane, like Diana and Mary Rivers, marries. These women find their blessing in marriage and domesticity: "I hold myself supremely blest," Jane says, "blest beyond what language can express" (396). The fact that St. John represents the extraordinary case, Jane, Mary, and Diana the ordinary, "the feeling and claims of little people," leaves the missionary memoir as a genre possible to an extraordinary few (including women), whereas the domestic memoir becomes the genre available to many. In the literary history of women's life writing, *Jane Eyre* obviously got it right. It made possible a way of thinking about women's lives that incorporated the religious and moral concerns of traditional spiritual autobiography even as it validated their ordinary, everyday experiences.

Jane's assertion of independence as an autobiographer validates the readings of feminist critics who see in *Jane Eyre* the creation of a new feminist myth or a spiritual pilgrimage toward wholeness. In the final volume of the novel, Jane takes control of her account, not only in choosing married life with Rochester but also in explaining her choice within a framework of biblical models (Jesus in Gethsemane, Mary at the Annunciation, David exorcising the evil spirit from Saul), all of which valorize woman's mission at home.[72] Yet those critics who have registered worry or wariness about the domestic myth Brontë inscribes or the generic residues she leaves unincorporated have a point, too. If *Jane Eyre* contributes to a new tradition of autobiography for Victorian women, it does so by domesticizing an older, spiritual form—by transferring its concerns from the realms of the religious and sublime to the more generally moral, by refocusing its concerns but also taming its ambition, and by substituting a woman's domestic and romantic life for the Celestial City as the site of aspiration.

IV

"For My Better Self":
Auto/biographies of the Poetess,
the *Prelude* of the Poet Laureate,
and Elizabeth Barrett Browning's
Aurora Leigh

Aurora Leigh is not, by any strict definition, the autobiography of
Elizabeth Barrett Browning. Unlike her eponymous heroine, Elizabeth
Barrett was not born in Italy of an English father and a Florentine mother;
she was not orphaned at age thirteen, raised by a spinster aunt, or (so far
as we know) proposed to by a wealthy English cousin. To pursue her
career as a writer, she did not move to London, take up residence in an
attic garret, "a chamber up three flights of stairs," or write "with one
hand for the booksellers" to keep body and soul together.[1] Nonetheless,
critics of all persuasions have read *Aurora Leigh*, at least in part, as an
autobiographical work—in Herbert F. Tucker's formulation, "a veiled
autobiography, a reluctant novel, and an aspiring epic."[2] They have done
so not from critical naiveté but from a consciousness of the poem's deliberate exploitation of autobiographical conventions, from its fundamental
use of first-person narrative and self-reflection to its shrewd alternation
of "the standard, postmortem mode of autobiographical finish and the
serial mode of the diarist shaping forth a life in running installments."[3]

   In this chapter I read *Aurora Leigh* as an autobiography of the English
woman poet—not so much analyzing the narrative conventions or techniques on which such readings usually depend, but rather considering
the work in its literary and historical contexts as a rewriting of the

auto/biographies, fictional and historical, of two major Romantic figures. The first, Laetitia Elizabeth Landon, or "L.E.L," was one of Barrett Browning's most important female predecessors, perhaps the most prolific maker of biographical portraits of the poetess. The second, William Wordsworth, was the major (male) poet of the century, the author of its most important autobiography tracing the "Growth of a Poet's Mind" and the nineteenth-century predecessor against whom Barrett Browning measured her achievement—"a great poet and true," as young Barrett declared to Mary Russell Mitford.[4] My contention is that, in the opening books of *Aurora Leigh,* Barrett Browning self-consciously revises and corrects the myth of the poetess constructed in L.E.L.'s *History of the Lyre* (1829), as well as in the spate of biographies of Landon published after the poetess's mysterious death in 1838. In the opening books of *Aurora Leigh,* moreover, as in the poem's resolution, Barrett Browning grafts onto this feminine tradition a masculine tradition of poetic autobiography represented by Wordsworth's *Prelude,* published just six years before *Aurora Leigh.* In both cases, the point is not simply literary allusion or allegiance. Barrett Browning treats the life writing of Romantic poets as preliminary to her own—that is, as "toil co-operant" unto her greater end, as preparing the way, historically and literarily, for the work of the modern poet. In both cases she corrects Romantic paradigms of poetic development, in the process redefining and expanding the woman poet's place and purpose in Victorian literature and culture.

For half a century after Mary Robinson published her *Memoirs* (1801), no major woman poet, and arguably no minor one, published an autobiography—perhaps because of the scandal of becoming a public spectacle that autobiography entailed, perhaps because so much lyrical poetry was considered autobiographical anyway, perhaps (and most important) because the feminine poetic tradition addressed itself to the myth of the poetess rather than the development of the individual woman writer.[5] Autobiographies of women artists and authors necessarily required discussion of professional achievement, of vocation and career—something that early nineteenth-century women poets preferred to avoid. As Marlon B. Ross has argued, "whereas the male romantics [were] anxious to promote the vocational status of poetry-making, the woman poets [were] anxious to suppress the emerging relation between poetic activity and vocation," preferring instead to envision their writing as a extension of their femininity or domesticity.[6] Writing archetypal narratives or creating cultural myths of the poetess, whose verse was conceived as natural inspiration rather than achieved vocation, better suited these women's goals— goals that Barrett Browning meant to abandon.

Much Romantic and early Victorian women's poetry relied, none-theless, on what we might call "autobiographical associations," on a con-flation or confusion of the poet's self with the figure of the poetess who so frequently appeared in her verse. Poetesses and their publishers often encouraged this conflation through prefatory memoirs that linked bio-graphical details of the poetess's life with segments of her lyric verse or through frontispieces that displayed the woman poet in the stereotypic garb of the poetess (as in figures 3 and 4, both frontispieces to Landon's work, the first depicting her as Sapphic poetess, the second as medieval woman troubadour). Laetitia Landon, far more than Felicia Hemans, made this conflation the subject of her poetry as well as a tantalizing enigma of her public career. Landon's major works—from *The Improvisatrice* (1824) with its Sapphic poetess and *The Golden Violet* (1826) with its female minstrel from Provence to "Erinna" (1826) and "The Lost Pleiad" (1829) with their innocent young poetesses brought to despair or death by thwarted love—all rework the dominant myths of the poetess, re-writing her life history and thus the tradition of women's poetry. In Landon's oeuvre the epitome of this rewriting is *A History of the Lyre* (1829), which, as its title suggests, presents an archetypal account of the poetess, her verse, and her career.

At the beginning of *A History of the Lyre,* an unidentified male speaker looks at the portrait of a poetess and meditates on the function of memory and autobiographical self-construction:

> 'Tis strange how much is mark'd on memory,
> In which we may have interest, but no part;
> How circumstance will bring together links
> In destinies the most dissimilar.
> This face, whose rudely-pencill'd sketch you hold,
> Recalls to me a host of pleasant thoughts,
> And some more serious.— This is EULALIE.[7]

Figure 3. L.E.L. (Laetitia Elizabeth Landon) as portrayed by Daniel Maclise. Published in *Fraser's Magazine*, 1832. Courtesy of Yale University Library.

Figure 4. L.E.L. (Laetitia Elizabeth Landon). Portrait by H. W. Pickersgill, engraved by
H. Robinson. Published by Arthur Hall, Virtue & Co. Courtesy of Yale University
Library.

At the beginning of *Aurora Leigh,* the speaker, now a woman poet, meditates on the function of memory and autobiographical self-construction
in a simile alluding to Landon's poem but altering its import:

> *Of writing many books there is no end;*
> *And I who have written much in prose and verse*
> *For others' uses, will write now for mine—*
> *As when you paint your portrait for a friend,*
> *Who keeps it in a drawer and looks at it*
> *Long after he has ceased to love you, just*
> *To hold together what he was and is.*

(1:1–8)

Like Landon, Barrett Browning remarks on the function of memory,
which "hold[s] together" the subject, "what he was and is." Like Landon,
too, Barrett Browning analogizes portrait painting and autobiographical
writing—with L.E.L.'s "rudely-pencill'd sketch" and its capacity for
linking past and present becoming the portrait Aurora Leigh will create
in verse to construct a coherent poetic self and a new vision of the
woman poet.

Yet these opening passages are significantly different, and in the difference lies the germ of Barrett Browning's reconstruction of the Romantic poetess. In *A History of the Lyre,* it is the male lover who holds the
poetess's sketch and contemplates it for "a host of pleasant thoughts" and
the construction of his *own* history and identity, whereas in *Aurora Leigh*
it is Aurora who writes of herself for her "better self." She, not her male
audience, takes charge of the woman poet's autobiography. Landon's
analogy between autobiography and portrait painting is subordinated to
a simile ("As when")—as if Barrett Browning means to subordinate the
traditional function of feminine memoirs to the more pressing need of
the woman poet. There is a shift, in short, from a male viewer to the
female poet, from art produced to satisfy masculine desire to art intended
for the development of the woman poet, from a literary tradition of
biographical memoirs *about* women poets to a new tradition of autobiography *by* women writers (hinted at in the next allusion of *Aurora Leigh*
(ll. 9–13—to Wordsworth's *Immortality Ode* and *Prelude*). Barrett Browning corrects Landon's opening statement of purpose—and, more broadly,
the plot of *A History of the Lyre*—by taking auto/biographical forms identified with the Romantic poetess and reconfiguring them to serve the

Victorian woman poet. In so doing she revises the developmental narrative of the poetess as it appeared in Landon's works and in biographies about Landon published in the two decades before *Aurora Leigh*.[8]

Like many of Landon's poems, these biographies reproduced—indeed, they gave credence to—the myth of the Sapphic poetess, the most common early nineteenth-century myth of feminine poetic inspiration and production. As Glennis Stephenson has argued, the Romantic-Sapphic artist invariably associates her work with her body and depicts it "as the intuitive and confessional outpouring of emotion": "Words like 'gushing' and 'over-flowing' abound. . . . These women are . . . fountains, not pumps. The flow is from nature, not art. Usually the creative woman in these poems is betrayed and abandoned, and finds that with the loss of love the flow dries up." A poetess like Landon thus came to exemplify a debased or inferior form of Romanticism—"Wordworth's 'spontaneous overflow of powerful feelings' which, rather than being recollected in tranquility, [were] immediately spewed out on the page."[9] Angela Leighton has further pointed out that "although L.E.L. insists on art as an overflow of the female body, she also frequently freezes the woman into a picture, a statue, an art object"—something that occurs in *A History of the Lyre,* where the poetess Eulalie appears first as a "rudely-pencill'd sketch," finally as a marble monument. "Such frozen postures," according to Leighton, have "a way of turning the woman into a form of sexual or artistic property for the man."[10]

Landon's myths of the poetess—as *improvisatrice,* as statue or art object produced for man's pleasure, as abandoned woman—go back at least as far as the first nineteenth-century autobiography of a woman poet, Mary Robinson's *Memoirs* (1801), discussed in chapter 1. In the *Memoirs* Robinson, an actress turned author, describes scene after scene in which she dresses up and performs for her audience, usually described as male. Her daughter and editor links her mother's artistic production with improvisation. Maria Robinson recounts, for example, several episodes in which her mother "poured forth those poetic effusions which have done so much honor to her genius, and decked her tomb with unfading laurels"[11]—poems such as "Lines to Him Who Will Understand Them," in which Robinson bids farewell to Britain for Italia's shore; "The Haunted Beach," inspired by Robinson's discovery of a drowned stranger; and "The Maniac," written, like Coleridge's *Kubla Khan,* in a delirium excited by opium. And, of course, Robinson was the archetypal abandoned woman, the first of several mistresses of the Prince of Wales, left in the lurch without financial support or social protection when another woman took his fancy.

Robinson's combination of improvisation and performance influenced the next generation of women writers, even if only as a cautionary tale. Generically a *chronique scandaleuse,* her *Memoirs* narrates the story of a popular actress who became the prince's mistress and turned professional writer when he abandoned her. Second-generation Romantic women poets, including Landon and Felicia Hemans, sought to avoid the scandal and self-aggrandizement of this form of life writing. They did not publish their own autobiographies, but in good early Victorian fashion let their lives be written for them—by family members, close friends, or other women writers who could testify to their feminine as well as literary virtues.[12]

We can nonetheless detect traces of Robinson's *Memoirs* in the biographies of Landon—and in just the features that Stephenson and Leighton point to: the poetess as *improvisatrice,* gushing forth her effusions like a natural spring; the poetess as statue, frozen into an artistic posture before the gaze of the male viewer; the poetess as abandoned woman, achieving fame but losing love. These were poetic myths that Barrett Browning inherited and resisted—not only because she, like Hannah More and Anna Barbauld before her, wished to assume the "sociomoral" role of the woman poet, writing as "the conscience of culture,"[13] but, more important, because Landon's poetess represents a case of arrested development.

Biographies of Landon as Sapphic poetess began appearing as early as 1839, the year after her death, with Emma Roberts's "Memoir of L.E.L.," included in the posthumously published *"The Zenana" and Minor Poems.* According to her friend and fellow writer, "While still a mere child, L.E.L. began to publish, and her poetry immediately attracted attention. . . . She rushed fearlessly into print, not dreaming for a moment, that verses which were poured forth like the waters from a fountain, gushing, as she has beautifully expressed it, of their own sweet will, could ever provoke harsh criticism." Laman Blanchard, who brought out *The Life and Literary Remains of L.E.L.* in 1841, similarly treats her poetry as natural productions, "just as the grass that sows itself." Like other biographers who would follow, Blanchard associates Landon with the title character of *The Improvisatrice,* noting that the heroine of that poem was "youthful, impassioned, and gifted with glorious powers of song; and, although introduced as a daughter of Florence . . . she might be even L.E.L. herself; for what were the multitude of songs she had been pouring out for three years past, but 'improvisings'?"[14] When William Howitt published his biographical *Homes and Haunts of the Most Eminent British Poets* in 1847, he, too, associated Landon with her *improvisatrice,* suggesting that "the very words of her first heroine might have literally been uttered as her own":[15]

> *Sad were my shades; methinks they had*
>   *Almost a tone of prophecy—*
> *I ever had, from earliest youth,*   (2)
>   *A feeling what my fate would be.*

Such associations had, of course, been encouraged by Landon herself, who, after translating the poetical odes of Madame de Staël's *Corinne* for its English publication, took to appearing in the Sappho-Corinne mode, dressed in Grecian costume with her hair done à la Sappho (figure 3), and then continued writing and rewriting the Sappho-Corinne myth, including the version in *A History of the Lyre.*

The myth of the poetess as *improvisatrice* gave certain advantages to the woman writer: it linked her to the cult of genius and her work to inspired rather than mechanical or pedantic production. But it had obvious disadvantages: in its emphasis on the poetess's naturalness and her youthful, sometimes even infantile poetic effusions, it tended to restrict her to an immature stage of development and to militate against more mature literary production. All of the major Romantic and Victorian women poets—Robinson, Hemans, Landon, Barrett Browning, and Rossetti— were infant prodigies, young geniuses who could recite hundreds of lines of verse as children (Hemans) or who composed poems and stories almost before they learned to hold a pen (Landon) or who published volumes of ambitious verses in early adolescence (Robinson, Hemans, Barrett Browning, Rossetti). This myth of youthful genius, as Norma Clarke has pointed out, worked against the development of the woman poet's career—and serious treatment of her poetry—once she move beyond youth into middle age.[16]

Despite the identification of Landon with the *improvisatrice* of 1824—and later with Erinna (1826) and Eulalie, the poetess of *A History of the Lyre*—Roberts and Blanchard both insisted that readers should not simply equate Landon with her imaginary counterparts, particularly not with the tragic Sapphic poetess who achieves fame but is unlucky in love. Roberts, who lived with her at 22 Hans Place, insisted that Landon was not a solitary, melancholy genius but a cheerful, domestic woman: "It may indeed be said, to L.E.L.'s honour, that she retained, to the last moment of existence all the friends thus domesticated with her, those who knew her most intimately being the most fondly attached." The tales of unrequited love were, in Roberts's view, "the production of a girl who had not yet left off her pinafores, and whose only notion of a lover was embodied in a knight wearing the brightest armour and the whitest of plumes."[17] Blanchard declared that

> no two persons could be less like each other in all that related to the contemplation of the actual world, than 'L.E.L.' and Letitia Elizabeth Landon. People would in this, as in so many other cases, forgetting one of the licenses of poetry, identify the poet's history in the poet's subject and sentiments, and they accordingly insisted that, because the strain was tender and mournful, the heart of the minstrel was breaking.[18]

On this point they were again taking their cue from Landon, who, in the preface to the volume that includes *A History of the Lyre,* wittily disclaimed the biographical link that so many of her readers assumed: "If I must have an unhappy passion, I can only console myself with my own perfect unconsciousness of so great a misfortune."[19]

Yet such proclamations of domesticity and disclaimers of Sapphic tragedy, most written after Landon's mysterious death by an overdose of prussic acid and intended to offset rumors of suicide, have the strange effect of reinforcing the third feature of the myth of the Romantic poetess—that of model or statue, of the poetess as a performer who strikes a pose for the pleasure of her audience but to her own detriment. The plot of *A History of the Lyre* reinforces this conclusion. Like many of Landon's works, it presents an inspired poestess, half-Italian, half-English, who spends her daytime hours in solitude, awaiting inspiration, and her nights in company, performing for her audience and winning great fame. She meets a man who listens and gazes raptly but who, in the end, abandons her for a more conventional, domestic Englishwoman. In *A History of the Lyre* the Englishman tells the tale of his encounters with Eulalie and of his eventual marriage to Emily. Landon adds the touch of having Eulalie create her own statue, "a sculptured form" that becomes a funeral monument:

> *"You see," she said, "my cemetery here:—*
> *Here, only here, shall be my quiet grave.*
> *Yon statue is my emblem: see, its grasp* (231)
> *Is raised to Heaven, forgetful that the while*
> *Its step has crush'd the fairest of earth's flowers*
> *With its neglect."*

Landon thus recognizes that the poetess sacrifices herself in performance for men: for their erotic pleasure, obviously, but also for their corporate benefit in that she does not interfere with (or intervene in) the patriarchal structures that allow Eulalie to die solitary and Emily, her passive domestic counterpart, to marry and reproduce English culture. In *A History of the Lyre,* far more than in earlier poems, the poetess becomes complicit in her own death.

Of the early biographers, only Howitt seems to have noticed the element of self-destruction in Landon's life and work. Although he presents it only as a possibility, he speculates that L.E.L. must have seen her fate "from earliest youth" and understood the danger of the poetic myths she was creating:

> *Whether this melancholy belief in the tendency of the great theme of her writings, both in prose and poetry; this irresistible annunciation, like another Cassandra, of woe and destruction; this evolution of scenes and characters in her last work, bearing such dark resemblance to those of her own after experience; this tendency, in all her plots, to a tragic catastrophe, and this final tragedy itself,—whether these be all mere coincidences or not, they are still but parts of an unsolved mystery.*[20]

Despite the tentative phrasing, Howitt was not a believer in "mere coincidences." His treatment of Landon's death makes it clear that he found foreshadowings in her poetical and fictional work of her tragic end. He recognized, as I believe Elizabeth Barrett did also, that Landon's self-construction as a Sapphic poetess, a reincarnation of Corinne, destined her for an early end—that Landon more or less wrote herself into a fatal plot.

Elizabeth Barrett was a careful reader (and admirer) of Landon's poetry, and she read carefully as well Blanchard's 1841 biography of the poetess. In a letter to Mary Russell Mitford, she compared Landon with Hemans, concluding that "if I had those two powers to choose from—Mrs. Hemans's and Miss Landon's—I mean the *raw* bare powers—I would choose Miss Landon's." Yet Barrett also believed that Landon had not fully realized her promise or power. To Mitford she added, "I fancy it would have worked out better—had it *been* worked out—with the right moral and intellectual influences in application." [21] How might Landon's life or career (the *it* is ambiguous) have been better "worked out"? Barrett Browning's more sustained commentary on Landon comes, I suggest, in the opening books of *Aurora Leigh,* where she acknowledges yet rejects the auto/biographies of the poetess who preceded her. [22] In these books she gives to Aurora the "right moral and intellectual influences" and then shows, in later books, how the life of the woman poet might look under their sway.

I have already noted that, in allusions to *A History of the Lyre* and *The Prelude,* Aurora determines to write an autobiography of her poetic development, as Wordsworth had done and Landon had failed fully to do. Her allusion to Wordsworth's poetry—

> *I, writing thus, am still what men call young;*
> *I have not so far left the coasts of life*
> (I:9–13)   *To travel inland, that I cannot hear*
> *That murmur of the outer Infinite*
> *Which unweaned babies smile at in their sleep . . .*

—claims partnership with an undebased Romantic tradition and a masculine form of autobiography. [23] Aurora Leigh is still young enough that she can recollect Wordsworthian joy and usefully trace "the growth of a poet's mind," providing evidence, to adapt Wordsworth's phrase, that "May spur me on, in [wo]manhood now mature, / To honorable toil"

(*Prelude*, 1:625–26). This turn to a Wordsworthian form of autobiography swerves from Landon's self-construction of the poetess as erotic object and performer for men's pleasure.

In *Aurora Leigh* Barrett Browning also abandons the model of the female poet as *improvisatrice*. In book I Aurora admits that she, like other young poets, often wrote spontaneously and effusively:

> . . . *Many tender souls*
> *Have strung their loses on a rhyming thread,*   (1:945–47)
> *As children, cowslips.*

Although she figures such rhyming as natural, she is not content to remain in this juvenile artistic state:

> . . . *Alas, near all the birds*
> *Will sing at dawn—and yet we do not take*   (1:951–53)
> *The chaffering swallow for the holy lark.*

In books II and III, taking the lark as her counterpart as other Romantic poets had taken the skylark, nightingale, or redbreast, Aurora traces her development beyond the stage of natural effusions toward mature poetic production.[24] Midway through she notes: "So life, in deepening with me, deepened all / The course I took, the work I did" (3:334–35).

In that "deepening" one crucial influence is Aurora's discovery of and immersion in her father's books, "the secret of a garret-room" (1:833), the masculine literary tradition. In this discovery Aurora "chance[s] upon the poets" (1:845), learns the meaning of "imperative labour" (1:880), and determines her vocation. These details more likely derive from Felicia Hemans's life or Barrett Browning's own than from Landon's. Although Landon's biographers insisted on "her devotedness to reading," which "was only equalled by the readiness with which she acquired whatever she chose to commit to memory, and the accuracy with which she retained whatever she had once learned,"[25] Hemans was the Romantic poetess who acquired the reputation for enormous classical learning. Hemans's Victorian biographer William Michael Rossetti, not one given to overpraising women poets, notes: "Her accomplishments were considerable, and not merely superficial. She knew French, Italian, Spanish, Portuguese, and in mature life German, and was not unacquainted with

Latin."[26] Barrett added Greek to these linguistic achievements, making herself the equal of the best male classical scholars. Both Hemans and Barrett began their careers with publications in a classical mode, Hemans with *The Restoration of the Works of Art to Italy* (1816) and *Modern Greece* (1817), Barrett with *The Battle of Marathon* (1820). And in the preface to *The Battle of Marathon* and other early volumes, as Vivienne Rundle has suggested, Barrett addressed her relationships "with her father, with her readers, and with the poetic tradition within which she was attempting to situate herself."[27]

Yet in tracing Aurora's career, Barrett Browning avoids reproducing the early phases of Hemans's or her own life, instead deriving the most important details from Landon's literary career. The effect is to treat the life of the Romantic poetess as a stage in the development of the Victorian woman poet—as a case of ontogeny recapitulating phylogeny. This tactic allows Barrett Browning to acknowledge the achievements of her predecessors but with the implication that she, representative of the next generation, will progress further.

In book III, for example, Aurora moves to an attic room in London, to "a certain house in Kensington" and "a chamber up three flights of stairs" (3:160, 158).[28] Barrett Browning never lived in a writer's garret, but Landon certainly did—at 22 Hans Place, Brompton, in an attic space invariably described in the biographies as a "homely-looking, almost uncomfortable room, fronting the street, and barely furnished."[29] So, too, Barrett Browning makes Aurora a hack writer of prose as well as an aspiring poet. It was Landon, not Barrett Browning, who churned out reviews for the *Literary Gazette* and whose biographers mention, usually as evidence of her wide knowledge, her enormous prose production.[30] Like Landon, Aurora works "with one hand for the booksellers / While working with the other for myself / And art" (3:303–5). Even Aurora's popularity with her readers suggests Landon's early career. The fan mail "with pretty maiden seals" from girls with names like Emily (3:212–13) or the "tokens from young bachelors, / Who wrote from college" (3: 215–16) recall both the sweet domestic bride of *A History of the Lyre* and the anecdote related by Edward Bulwer-Lytton and repeated in virtually all of L.E.L.'s biographies:

> *We were young, and at college, lavishing our golden years, not so much on the Greek verse and mystic character to which we ought, perhaps, to*

have been rigidly devoted, as "Our heart in passion, and our head in
rhyme." At that time poetry was not yet out of fashion, at least with us
of the cloister; and there was always in the reading-room of the Union a
rush every Saturday afternoon for the "Literary Gazette;" and an im-
patient anxiety to hasten at once to that corner of the sheet which con-
tained the three magical letters "L.E.L." And all of us praised the
verse, and all of us guessed at the author. We soon learned it was a
female, and our admiration was doubled, and our conjectures tripled.
Was she young? Was she pretty? And—for there were some embryo
fortune-hunters among us—was she rich?[31]

Such details in book III not only allude to Landon's life but signal more
generally, I think, the determination of Aurora, like other early Victorian
women writers, to pursue a professional career. In the 1820s, 1830s, and
1840s many women, like Landon and Roberts at 22 Hans Place, Harriet
Martineau in Fludyer Street, and George Eliot at 142 Strand, moved to
lodgings in London to signal their professional aspirations, and they were
not above writing reviews, translating foreign literature, or doing other
hackwork to provide the financial means needed to support their literary
careers. Aurora's life as a "city poet" represents this new, if not quite glorious, stage in the nineteenth-century woman writer's professionaliza-
tion.[32] It makes visible what the myth of the Romantic poetess hides: the
real, hard labor of the literary woman's life.

The differences from Landon's life are also significant, however—
most notably Aurora's unsullied reputation and her unwavering commitment, despite early fame, to produce high art. Landon's reputation had
come to ruin (or close to it) with rumors of illicit liaisons with William
Jerdan, editor of the *Literary Gazette;* William Maginn, the heavy-drink-
ing Irish journalist associated with *Blackwood's* and *Fraser's;* and Daniel
Maclise, the painter. Although they name no names, the early biographers acknowledge these "atrocious calumnies," in Howitt's phrase,
invariably to refute them. Nonetheless, the biographers admit that Landon's public persona, "the very unguardedness of her innocence," and
her lack of concern "about the interpretation that was likely to be put
upon her words" contributed to the problem.[33] So did her fictions of the
poetess. Eulalie in *A History of the Lyre* confesses that she is more like
the "Eastern tulip" with its "radiant" yet short-lived colors than the pure

"lily of the valley" with its "snowy blossoms." In contrast, Aurora declares unequivocally,

I am a woman of repute;
No fly-blow gossip ever specked my life;
(9:264–68)   *My name is clean and open as this hand,*
Whose glove there's not a man dares blab about
As if he had touched it freely.

As she begins her career, Aurora self-consciously resolves to live "holding up my name / To keep it from the mud" (3:311–12).

More important to artistic development, Barrett Browning revises Landon's attitude toward fame, work, and sustained poetic achievement. Eulalie, like Erinna before her, laments that she has lost the desire (or perhaps she lacks the ability) to sustain her work:

I am as one who sought at early dawn
To climb with fiery speed some lofty hill:
His feet are strong in eagerness and youth
His limbs are braced by the fresh morning air,
And all seems possible:—this cannot last.
The way grows steeper, obstacles arise,
And unkind thwartings from companions near.[34]

But whereas Eulalie laments that early fame has proved a fatal opium—

I am vain,—praise is opium, and the lip
(228)   *Cannot resist the fascinating draught,*
Though knowing its excitement is a fraud,—

that she can "no longer work miracles for thee [fame]," and that now "Disappointment tracks / The steps of Hope," Aurora determines that she will progress beyond simple "ballads," a form identified with the Romantic poetess, and work her way up through the generic ranks that have long challenged English male poets: from pastoral through georgic to epic. Indeed, one can read the opening monologue of book V as Aurora's response to Eulalie's tragic lament in *A History of the Lyre*. Aurora presents a counterargument that women poets can indeed "last" as "The way grows steeper, obstacles arise, / And unkind thwartings from companions near." Significantly, too, Barrett Browning turns Eulalie's admission of inadequacy into Romney's critique of the female poet's limitations (in 2:180–225 and 4:1115–24, 1159–68, 1202–11).[35] In *Aurora Leigh* it is the male critic who denigrates the woman poet's abilities and achievements, not the woman poet who self-destructs.

What Barrett Browning does not alter or avoid is Landon's psychological insight that the woman poet longs for, perhaps even needs, the approval of her male reader. In *A History of the Lyre* Eulalie performs for large audiences but in particular for the pleasure of the Englishman who follows her about for a year; when he leaves Italy without offering marriage, she more or less "hang[s] [her] lute on some lone tree, and die[s]."[36] Aurora confronts the issue of male approval in book V, where she not only lays out her plan for progress up through the generic ranks but also identifies the primary obstacle to her achievement:

> —*I must fail*
> *Who fail at the beginning to hold and move*   (5:30–32)
> *One man—and he my cousin, and he my friend.*

Aurora fears "this vile woman's way of trailing garments," yet determines that it "shall not trip me up" (5:59–60).

If Landon framed the issue in erotic or romantic terms, Barrett Browning reframes it to emphasize professional and aesthetic concerns. Aurora admits her loneliness as a woman writer and her envy of male artists who are rewarded with love, whether of a mother or of a wife. But the need for love, we should note, is not peculiar to the *woman* artist but includes male artists such as Graham, Belmore, and Gage, all of whom rely on domestic affection (5:502–39). Aurora expresses her desire for Romney's approval in rather different terms—that is, in terms of the poet's vocation and specifically the woman poet's terrain: Is her work, contrary to what Romney believes, equal to that of the social activist? Shall the woman poet be confined, as in Romney's view at the end of book IV, to "the mythic turf where danced the nymphs" (4:1161), or shall she treat, in her "imperative labour" (1:880), the whole range of human experience and passion that Aurora details at the beginning of book V? In Barrett Browning's poem it is Aurora's view, not Romney's opinion or Landon's precedent as poetess of lyric love, that finally determines the career of the woman poet—and the plot of the remainder of the poem.

After book V, very little of Landon's life and works informs *Aurora Leigh*—except, most significantly, that Barrett Browning revises the conclusion to *A History of the Lyre,* a conclusion some biographers thought Landon had enacted in her life. Eulalie, Sappho-like, dies an abandoned woman; Aurora lives to marry Romney. Eulalie's history is told only after her death by her male admirer; Aurora Leigh's is written at the height of her power by the poet herself. If the marriage ending of *Aurora Leigh* has been controversial among contemporary feminist critics, primarily for seeming to succumb to the conventions of the marriage plot,[37] it looks different in its historical and generic contexts. In the context of women's autobiography, it represents a determination to write one's own life and not let others construct one's self. In the context of biographies of the nineteenth-century woman poet, it represents a writing against tradition, a rejection of Landon's dying for (male) pleasure, and a progression from feminine poetess to woman poet.

Barrett Browning is famous for having written, "I look everywhere for grandmothers and see none."[38] Perhaps Landon, born in 1802, only four years before Barrett, was too close in age to be considered a literary "grandmother." Perhaps Dorothy Mermin is right that, in making such a comment, Barrett Browning was ignoring "the popular 'poetesses' who adorned the literary scene," as they did not represent "the noble lineage with which she wished to claim affiliation."[39] But perhaps between her statement to Robert Browning in 1845 and the writing of *Aurora Leigh* a decade later, she owned up to the existence of the women writers who had influenced her, if only (or primarily) as negative examples. Whatever the case, when Barrett Browning came to write her autobiography of the new woman poet, she framed its plot and many of its features in terms of the female literary figures of the preceding generation. If in revising *A History of the Lyre* she lets Eulalie's lyre stay hanging on a tree and gives Aurora instead a Gideon's trumpet, "a clarion" to press "on thy woman's lip" (9:929), she nonetheless acknowledges, in the scope and density of her allusions, the importance of Landon's work in the tradition of nineteenth-century women's writing.

As Barrett Browning's allusion to "that murmur of the outer Infinite" suggests (1:12), *Aurora Leigh* also considers the woman poet in relation to her male counterpart and incorporates (as it interrogates) the Romantic masculine model of poetic development best known through Wordsworth's "Self-biography" *The Prelude*.[40] Wordsworth was, for young Elizabeth Barrett, the preeminent English poet, the "poet-priest / By the high altar, singing prayer and prayer / To the higher Heavens."[41] Kathleen Blake has enumerated the many ways in which Barrett Browning identifies herself with Wordsworth, adopts his Romantic aesthetics, and aligns her poetic autobiography with his: in "her valuation of childhood, the loss of mother, then father, a turning toward nature, early poetic aspirations and self-doubts, a confrontation with social ills, the attraction of revolutionary or philanthropic hopes."[42] Yet for all the thematic parallels between Wordsworth's autobiography and Aurora's, the most essential features of the Wordsworthian paradigm, those ideological elements that define his particular Romanticism—the guiding role of Nature in the poet's development, the negative (or at best neutral) importance of the city, the sequential progress of love of nature leading to love of man and to a civic poetry—are questioned and modified in *Aurora Leigh*.

To begin with, Barrett Browning inscribes the Wordsworthian myth of Nature as "mother nature"—a moral teacher, protector of the child's psyche, and maternal substitute—not once but twice in *Aurora Leigh,* first in the account of Aurora's childhood in the Tuscan hills, "the mountains above Pelago" (1:111), and again in the account of Marian Erle's birth in the Malvern Hills, "in a hut built up at night / To evade the landlord's eye" (3:832–33). In both narratives, examples of nature's beneficent influence repeat scenes from *The Prelude* with genuine appreciation. But in the first Barrett Browning treats the myth of a maternal, nurturing nature with skepticism about its origins as a masculine literary construction, and in the second she considers its possibilities, negative as well as positive, in shaping the lives of the working-class poor. It is the need for repetition, I believe, that registers Barrett Browning's consciousness of the difficulties of the Wordsworthian model for the modern woman poet and her intention to revise the developmental sequence of *The Prelude*.

When Aurora's mother dies, her father removes his child from Florence and resettles in a Tuscan village. His rationale derives from literary mythology:

(1:112–17)

Because unmothered babes, he thought, had need
Of mother nature more than others use,
And Pan's white goats, with udders warm and full
Of mystic contemplations, come to feed
Poor milkless lips of orphans like his own—
Such scholar-scraps he talked, I've heard from friends[.]

Aurora's language reveals an ambivalence about poetic myths of "mother nature." On the one hand, "the white walls, the blue hills, my Italy" (1:232) nurture the young girl, and the "vocal pines and waters" become "confederate" with books, which Aurora's father also brings with him, as the "strong words of counselling souls" (1:187–89). On the other hand, Aurora distances herself from her father's beliefs with the phrase "he thought," as if to register the myth of mother nature as a masculine conception, not one fully or unequivocally shared by the mature woman poet who narrates her autobiography. With "scholar-scraps" Aurora suggests fragments of truth, patriarchal or academic learning that only half-comprehends the function of real mothers or the relation between mother nature and humankind.[43] Barrett Browning thus incorporates the two great teachers of Wordsworth's *Prelude,* nature and books, into her poem, giving Aurora the credentialing experiences of the Romantic poet, yet questioning the adequacy of the model.

With the domesticated nature that replaces the Italian hills as Aurora moves to England and into puberty, Barrett Browning admits to an even greater ambivalence about the adequacy of the Wordsworthian model for the *English* woman poet. The landscape of Aunt Leigh's country house is clipped, controlled, and utterly domesticated with its lime tree, broadly sweeping lawn, "shrubberies in a stream / Of tender turf" (1:583–84), and line of elms that "stopped the grounds and dammed the overflow / Of arbutus and laurel" (1:587–88). This domestic English garden is not paradise but purgatory. England's is "Not a grand nature," Aurora laments: "Italy / Is one thing, England one" (1:615, 626–27). The verbs Aurora associates with Italian nature—cleaving, leaping, crying out for joy or fear, palpitating, panting, and (finally) "waiting for / Communion and commission" (1:615–25)—all suggest that the aspiring young Englishwoman will not find the Wordsworthian sublime in her homeland, that her hope lies in deviating from English domesticity and reclaiming a larger European landscape and literary tradition.

In these early scenes Barrett Browning adopts the views of Germaine de Staël in *De l'Allemagne* (*Germany,* 1813), even as details of Aurora's birth and experience derive from Staël's "Italian" *Corinne* (1807)—that "immortal book," as young Barrett had called it.[44] In her work of comparative literature, Staël had characterized English literature and culture as thoroughly domestic: "Domestic affections holding great sway over the hearts of the English, their poetry is impressed with the delicacy and solidity of those affections." Staël had also judged, as a consequence, that English poetry had lost "the principle of terror, which is employed as one of the great means in German poetry."[45] *Aurora Leigh* reproduces these views to the extent that it locates the young poetess within an English country house and makes her early verse pastoral or weak georgic (poetry that Romney, incidentally, dismisses as "happy pastorals of the meads and trees," with little relevance to the "hungry orphans" and "beaten and bullied wives" of modern urban life, 2:1201–10). Yet for all that her depiction of English culture concurs with Staël's, Barrett Browning never fully endorses Staël's judgment. For one thing, *Aurora Leigh* does not dismiss the beneficial influence of a specifically domesticated nature. Once Aurora has moved to the city, she regrets her loss of the English countryside—"A hedgehog in the path, or a lame bird, / In those green country walks" (3:147–48)—and she acknowledges its restorative power: "I seem to have missed a blessing ever since" (3:150). For another, in thinking about the domesticity and femininity of English poetry, Barrett excluded Wordsworth from such categorizations as Staël proposed: to Mary Russell Mitford she cited Coleridge as saying "that every great man he ever knew, had something of the woman in him, with one exception: and the exception was Wordsworth."[46] By excluding Wordsworth from feminization, Barrett Browning can maintain—and claim the advantages of—a domestic tradition of English verse, while simultaneously incorporating the power of masculinity and the Wordsworthian sublime into her version of the poetic tradition.

Why should Barrett Browning, then, repeat certain natural scenes from Wordsworth's autobiography in her minibiography of Marian Erle? Repetition, as J. Hillis Miller notes, can involve contradiction or counterpart, the latter "a strange relation whereby the second is the subversive ghost of the first."[47] Unlike Aurora's narrative of childhood, Marian's tale, told "with simple, rustic turns" (4:151), seems more directly to echo Wordsworth's belief in nature as moral teacher and protector of the child's innocence and integrity. If Wordsworth grew up in Nature,

(1:297–300)

> *as if I had been born*
> *On Indian plains, and from my mother's hut*
> *Had run abroad in wantonness, to sport*
> *A naked savage, in the thunder shower,*

Marian, too, is "born upon a ledge of Malvern Hills," not in an imaginative Indian hut but in a less idealized "hut built up at night / To evade the landlord's eye, of mud and turf" (3:830–33). If Wordsworth spent his infancy beside the "ceaseless music" of the Derwent, which gave him

(1:279–81)

> *Amid the fretful dwellings of mankind*
> *A foretaste, a dim earnest, of the calm*
> *That Nature breathes among the hills and groves,*

so the less fortunate Marian, at three, would "run off from the fold,"

(3:884–91)

> *And, creeping through the golden wall of gorse,*
> *Would find some keyhole toward the secrecy*
> *Of Heaven's high blue, and, nestling, down, peer out—*
> *Oh, not to catch the angels at their games,*
> *She had never heard of angels—but to gaze*
> *She knew not why, to see she knew not what,*
> *A-hungering outward from the barren earth*
> *For something like a joy.*

If Wordsworth learned his moral lessons from Nature's "fearless visitings" or her "Severer interventions, ministry / More palpable, as best might suit her aim" (1:352, 355–56), so Marian "dazzled black her sight against the sky" and "learnt God that way" (3:892, 895):

(3:898–901)

> *This grand blind Love, she said,*
> *This skyey father and mother both in one,*
> *Instructed her and civilised her more*
> *Than even Sunday school did afterward.*

Marian's childhood is more explicitly Wordsworthian than Aurora's, its narrative more imitative of the early scenes of *The Prelude,* the tone more appreciative, less ironically distanced from its Romantic model.

In making Marian the more direct descendant of the child Wordsworth, Barrett Browning validates the Wordsworthian model but also demotes it to a simpler or lower phase of development. She may have intended to associate Marian's simple rustic life and response to nature with the "naive" poetry of Friedrich Schiller's "Über naive und sentimentalische Dichtung" (1795–96). In Schiller's classic formulation, nature in "naive" states of civilization, as in their literatures, "inspires us with a sort of love and respectful emotion, not because she is pleasing to our senses, or because she satisfies our mind or our taste, . . . but merely because *she is nature.* This feeling is often elicited when nature is considered in her plants, in the mineral kingdom, in rural districts; also in the case of human nature, in the case of children, and in the manners of country people and of primitive races." In the Schillerean dichotomy, Aurora would in turn be associated with "sentimental" or "modern" poetry in that "nature, in our time, is no longer in man, and . . . we no longer encounter it in its primitive truth." For Schiller this loss in modern experience is less a loss than an opportunity: "the end to which man tends by civilisation is infinitely superior to that which he reaches through nature."[48] Aurora's distance from Marian—and Wordsworth—represents in these terms an advance on *The Prelude,* an opportunity for progress and perfection.[49] Writing at a distance from Wordsworthian myth, Aurora can recognize its values and limitations, while also seeing the direction in which modern poetry should go.

Yet such an evolutionary interpretation of Barrett Browning's repetition—an interpretation that makes Wordsworth in the "masculine" literary tradition preliminary to the new woman poet in the same way that L.E.L. is preliminary in the "feminine"—obscures a more potent reason for reproducing versions of Wordsworth's childhood in both female characters' lives. In both cases, we might note, nature fails. In Marian's case, nature cannot protect her from a derelict mother or the evils of city life; in Aurora's, nature is simply inadequate to the task of the modern city poet. Both cases are intertwined and essential to Barrett Browning's critique and revision of Wordsworth.

Despite the moral lessons that Marian gleans from nature and despite the psychological integrity that her experiences with nature and books consolidate, as a young woman she is virtually powerless against evil parents or the social and economic complexities of urban life. This difference of gender Wordsworth only dimly acknowledges in *The Prelude,* primarily in the tales of Mary Robinson, Maid of Buttermere, and in scenes of London life in book VII. In contemplating Mary Robinson's sad case, Wordsworth muses on their almost identical childhoods in nature:

For we were nursed—as almost might be said—
On the same mountains, children at one time,
Must haply often on the self-same day
Have from our several dwellings gone abroad
To gather daffodils on Coker's stream.

(7:42–46)

This feminine countertale, a minibiography of an "artless daughter of the hills," shows the limits of nature's maternal nurture. Nature cannot save Mary from the "spoiler," "'a bold bad man'" who lies and seduces her, as it has saved Wordsworth from other evils.[50] But Wordsworth passes over this lack, recording only that Mary has returned to her native habitation and now "lives in peace / Upon the spot where she was born and reared; / Without contamination doth she live / In quietness, without anxiety" (7:320–23). As Lawrence Kramer suggests, Wordsworth transforms Mary into a "pastoral Proserpina," "a perpetually innocent child of earth, a figure of renewal and pastoral innocence."[51]

To a female reader, however, as to a Victorian sensitive to the question of the "fallen woman," Wordsworth's treatment of the Maid of Buttermere's tale reveals some strange inadequacies. In *The Prelude* Wordsworth imagines Mary egotistically as a version of his younger self or emblematically as a version of disrupted but restored childhood innocence;[52] yet he neither considers the difference of gender nor imagines a life story for Mary *after* seduction nor thinks about her illegitimate child in any terms other than death:

Beside the mountain chapel, sleeps in earth
Her new-born infant, fearless as a lamb
That, thither driven from some unsheltered place,
Rests underneath the little rock-like pile
When storms are raging. Happy are they both—
Mother and child!

(7:324–29)

Such happiness is death or death-in-life. In contrast, in Marian Erle's narrative, Barrett Browning writes beyond the "fall," making the social and economic causes of the "fallen woman" a matter of inquiry and imagining an afterlife for Marian's babe (if not quite for Marian herself).[53] It is the burden of *Aurora Leigh*, books VI–VII, to extrapolate from the half-told tale of *The Prelude*, book VII, a more adequate account of the fallen woman's experience; to recognize the gaps in Wordsworth's understanding and fill them; and thus to remake the Romantic poet into a modern poet cognizant of sexual politics and modern urban experience. Aurora must recognize the repetition—the sameness as well as difference—in Marian's life story and her own.

Such recognition includes a shift of the poet's interest from nature to city. In *The Prelude* the Maid of Buttermere's tale falls within Wordsworth's "Residence in London"—that is, he recalls it by seeing (or hearing of) a play at Sadler's Wells, *Edward and Susan, or The Beauty of Buttermere*, and he associates it with his first encounter with an urban prostitute:[54]

> *I heard, and for the first time in my life,*
> *The voice of woman utter blasphemy—*
> *Saw woman as she is to open shame*
> *Abandoned, and the pride of public vice.*
> $(7:384-87)$

Wordsworth's flight from the fallen woman is part of his larger flight from the city. As he admits in his "meditation" on "such spectacle" (7:393–94), he later feels "a milder sadness" rather than sheer distress, but he never gets beyond "grief / For the individual and the overthrow of her soul's beauty" (7:395–97). To put it starkly, Wordsworth never comes to terms with city life. When he summarizes his response to London and its place in his poetic development, the judgment is extreme:

> *Oh, blank confusion! true epitome*
> *Of what the mighty City is herself*
> *To thousands upon thousands of her sons,*
> *Living amid the same perpetual whirl*
> *Of trivial objects, melted and reduced*
> *To one identity, by differences*
> *That have no law, no meaning, and no end—*
> *Oppression, under which even highest minds*
> *Must labour, whence the strongest are not free.*
> $(7:722-30)$

The city defies the power of the poetic imagination to make sense of it. Even if, as critics sucn as Lucy Newlyn have eloquently argued, Wordsworth's response to London was actually more ambivalent, including a recognition of "the vitality of London that nourishes his 'riper mind,' " [55] the fact remains that *The Prelude* does not credit the city with any significant force in shaping the poet's mind or art.

Nor is the city associated in *The Prelude* with any creditable form of autobiography. As Mary Jacobus and Laura Marcus have argued, "Wordsworthian 'value', which must remain untainted by textual commodification," is "dependent upon the casting-out of the prostitute (Book VII of *The Prelude*) who stands not only, as in DeQuincey's autobiography, for disreputable confession and commodified selfhood, but in her 'painted bloom', for literary figuration, seduction or solicitation by Romantic personification itself." [56] By opening up *Aurora Leigh* to Marian Erle's story, even making it essential to the poet's own, Barrett Browning casts off not the fallen woman but fear of autobiography as a disreputable genre and the early nineteenth-century taboo against self-writing or any such self-display by proper women.

I have already suggested that Barrett Browning transplants Aurora from country to city to valorize the movement of professional women writers of her generation from provincial towns to London as artistic center. I would now add that Barrett Browning moves Aurora from country house to urban garret to insist upon the imaginative resources of the city and to underscore the necessity of the poet's engagement—not just encounter—with urban experience. It was no coincidence, I think, that when young Elizabeth Barrett cited an exemplary poem in defense of Wordsworth against criticism that he was a third-rate versifier, she chose the sonnet "Composed upon Westminster Bridge, September 3, 1802":

> *Earth has not anything to show more fair;*
> *Dull would he be of soul who could pass by*
> *A sight so touching in its majesty. . . .* [57]

Aurora Leigh is not dull of soul. Her visionary moments in the city are not occasional, as are Wordsworth's, but integral to her development. She in effect recognizes what Wordsworth only reluctantly acknowledged: that it is the interchange not of the human imagination and nature but of the imagination and any aspect of the visible world that counts.

When in book III Aurora takes up residence in a garret chamber, "up three flights of stairs" (3:158), she becomes quite explicitly a city poet. Aurora's prospect is of "slant roofs and chimney-pots," of "the great tawny weltering fog," of "Spires, bridges, streets, and squares" (3:177, 179, 181)—the prospect vision of nineteenth-century London. Aurora's inspiration is not blocked, she is not one "in city pent" (as Wordsworth imagined the young Coleridge to be), nor does she lack visionary experience. "Your city poets see such things / Not despicable" (3:186–87), Aurora reports. Her account of her early days in London ends with a visionary moment as dramatic as that in Wordsworth's ascent of Snowdon:

> . . . *sit in London at the day's decline,*
> *And view the city perish in the mist*
> *Like Pharoah's armaments in the deep Red Sea,*
> *The chariots, horsemen, footmen, all the host,*
> *Sucked down and choked to silence—then, surprised*   (3:195–203)
> *By a sudden sense of vision and of tune,*
> *You feel as conquerors though you did not fight,*
> *And you and Israel's other singing girls,*
> *Ay, Miriam with them, sing the song you choose.*

Harking back to the first Hebrew poetess and aligning herself with inspired epic and epideictic poetry, Aurora here answers Romney's earlier denigration of women's verse as merely "the cymbal tinkle in white hands" (2:170). She counters his assertion that Miriam ought to sing only "when Egypt's slain" (2:171)—that is, after Moses, the male leader, has done his work. Aurora insists that the poet's *vision* does the work, and celebrates it, too.

In the new model of poetic development and literary career that Barrett Browning constructs, this vision must occur in the city. As a young poet, Aurora must get past believing that her finest poetry will be "natural" or "landscape" poetry, that it will recollect her experiences in nature, whether in Italy or in England, whether autobiographical or fictive. The generic progression that Aurora outlines for herself in book V begins with "ballads" and "sonnets," then continues with a "descriptive poem called 'The Hills'" (5:90). Is this, we might ask, a Wordsworthian progression from the "lyrical" ballads of 1798 through the more sustained consideration of nature's work in *The Prelude* of 1805? Or is this a typically feminine progression from "ballads" (5:85) to the extended "pastorals" (5:130) that women poets such as Mary Howitt, Mary Mitford, and even Elizabeth Barrett herself wrote in the 1830s?[58] Book V of *Aurora Leigh* is ambiguous: Aurora's early work is not fully Wordsworthian in that it lacks "thoughts that lie too deep for tears," nor yet is it traditionally feminine in that Aurora aspires to the greater achievement of classical nature poetry, to what "well the Greeks knew" (5:96). Aurora dismisses her ballad writing as too easy: "the ballad's race / Is rapid for a poet who bears weights / Of thought and golden image" (5:84−86), and she criticizes her pastoral as verse only of "surface-pictures—pretty, cold, and false / With literal transcript" (5:131−32). The great poetry that she sets herself to write is instead epic—not the historical matter of Britain (in a swipe at Tennyson) or that of any ancient or medieval subject but an epic of modern life:

> ... *this live, throbbing age,*
> *That brawls, cheats, maddens, calculates, aspires,*
> (5:203−7)   *And spends more passion, more heroic heat,*
> *Betwixt the mirrors of its drawing-rooms,*
> *Than Roland with his knights at Roncevalles.*

Aurora's *ars poetica* in book V recalls Wordsworth's deliberation on epic themes in *The Prelude* (1:146−228). But Barrett Browning renounces historical subjects—the sorts of subjects Wordsworth enumerates and she herself chose in such early works as *The Battle of Marathon* (1820), *Prometheus Bound* (1833), and *A Drama of Exile* (1838)—and instead dedicates Aurora to the writing of a new epic, "the burning lava of a song" that celebrates "The full-veined, heaving, double-breasted Age" (5:215−16).[59]

Although Aurora commits herself to this new poetry in book V, she does not write it immediately. Like Wordsworth at the beginning of *The Prelude,* she suffers a blockage. Aurora's blockage is distinctly un-Wordsworthian, however—not only in the pivotal place it gives to human love but in its misprision of the role of nature in the inspiration and production of poetry. At the end of book V, distressed by her unrequited if unacknowledged love for Romney, Aurora sells her father's books (in what has long been read as a rejection of the masculine poetic tradition) and heads to Italy, her maternal homeland. Her invocation of Italy expresses an expectation of what the maternal landscape can do for the woman poet:

> *And now I come, my Italy,*
> *My own hills! Are you 'ware of me, my hills,*
> *How I burn toward you? do you feel tonight*
> *The urgency and yearning of my soul,*
> *As sleeping mothers feel the sucking babe*
> *And smile?*
>
> (5:1266–71)

Aurora expects the nurturance, psychological and poetical, that she has never had in England—an expectation derived from novels like *Corinne* or the "Italian" verse of the English poetesses. As it turns out, in Italy Aurora finds neither the nurturance nor the inspiration she seeks; Italy's hills "go / [Their] own determined, calm indifferent way" (5:1273–74). Expectations of the maternal homeland, of Italy as autobiographical and poetical origins, turn out to be unfounded.

What I am suggesting, to state it paradigmatically, is that the final books of *Aurora Leigh* reject both the Wordsworthian myth of nature as the primary source of poetic inspiration and the feminine myth of Italy, so dominant in the writings of Staël, Robinson, Hemans, and Landon, as the origin of women's poetry. At the beginning of *The Prelude*, Wordsworth escapes "From the vast city, where I long had pined / A discontented sojourner" (1:6–7), and, once returned to nature, feels poetic inspiration return:

> *For I, methought, while the sweet breath of heaven*
> *Was blowing on my body, felt within*
> *A correspondent breeze, that gently moved*
> *With quickening virtue, but is now become*
> *A tempest, a redundant energy,*
> *Vexing its own creation.*
>
> (1:33–38)

At a parallel narrative moment, Aurora escapes London and "the marriage bells of Romney" (7:397), and on a ship bound for Genoa feels "the wind soft from the land of souls" (7:467). But while this Italian breeze and the landscape of her childhood possess a restorative power—

> *I could hear my own soul speak,*
> *And had my friend—for Nature comes sometimes*
> *And says, 'I am ambassador for God'—*
>
> (7:464–66)

they produce no correspondent breeze of poetic inspiration. Once in Florence, the homeland of Landon's *improvisatrice,* "that land, / Where the poet's lip and the painter's hand / Are most divine," Aurora sits quiet as death, producing nothing.[60] While watching a Tuscan sunset or resting in her villa on "a perfect night, / Until the moon, diminished to a curve, / Lay out there like a sickle for His hand / Who cometh down at last to reap the earth"—at such times, she admits, "ended seemed my trade of verse" (7: 1298 – 1302). Although Aurora tries to rationalize this quietude as divine—"With God so near me, could I sing of God?"—her language betrays other sources of silence, of why she "did not write, nor read, nor even think" (7: 1305 – 6): a lost future, a spoiled life ("like some passive broken lump of salt / Dropped in by chance to a bowl of oenomel, / To spoil the drink" [7: 1308 – 10]), a waiting for death (the moon as grim reaper, as "sickle" of God).

The problem of poetic inspiration—or its lack—is one that all Romantic biographies of the poet or poetess address, from Mary Robinson's semi-autobiographical *Sappho and Phaon* (1796) to Landon's archetypal histories of the poetess to Wordsworth's greater odes and "self-biography" tracing the "Growth of a Poet's Mind." Indeed, in the final books of *The Prelude* Wordsworth explicitly raises the question of how the "Imagination," once "Impaired," can be "Restored."[61] This is the question that Barrett Browning poses in the final books of *Aurora Leigh*—not for herself (apparently she never suffered from writer's block) but for her archetypal woman poet. Wordsworth's answer involves the two primary "attributes" of nature—"emotion" and "calmness" or "peace and excitation"—that support the poetic imagination, at once stimulating it with "That energy by which he [the poet] seeks the truth," while also soothing or preparing it with "that happy stillness of the mind / Which fits him to receive it when unsought" (13 : 1–10). Barrett Browning's answer reworks the Wordsworthian formula by dividing those primary "attributes" between nature and man rather than assigning them to nature alone. In nature, Aurora finds "calmness" and "peace," but too much of it. She needs man—and, specifically, one man—to provide the "emotion" and "excitation" that will stimulate her to write great poetry.

Barrett Browning brings nature and man, peace and excitation, together in the final scene of *Aurora Leigh,* a scene that rewrites the climactic episode of *The Prelude,* Wordsworth's ascent of Mount Snowdon. In ascending Snowdon, the poet experiences a landscape that seems "the type / Of a majestic intellect" (14:66−67), one that reassures him of the power of the imagination. This Wordsworthian landscape—with Moon "hung naked in a firmament / Of azure" (14:41−42), "a silent sea of hoary mist" covering all but the tips of "headlands, tongues, and promontory shapes" (14:43, 46), and beneath "the roar of waters, torrents, streams / Innumerable, roaring with one voice / Heard over earth and sea" (14:59−61)—emblematizes the ideal relation of the human mind and nature. In it the imagination not so much usurps as "feeds upon infinity," "broods / Over the dark abyss" (14:71−72)—the latter image suggesting a repetition in poetic creation of original, divine creation and a reminiscence of *Paradise Lost* (1:20−22), where the Holy Spirit broods over Chaos and makes it fertile.

The closing landscape of *Aurora Leigh,* books VIII–IX, transforms Wordsworth's seascape into a cityscape. Instead of the Irish Sea disappearing in a "hoary mist," the city of Florence, seen from the hills above, disappears in shadows:

> *Gradually*
> *The purple and transparent shadows slow*
> *Had filled up the whole valley to the brim,*
> *And flooded all the city, which you saw*   (8:34−39)
> *As some drowned city in some enchanted sea,*
> *Cut off from nature . . .*

The sound heard from below is the roar not of waters but of the Duomo bell and "twenty churches [that] answer it" (8:46). There is a "golden moon" overhead (9:841)—but described fully only *after* Aurora and Romney embrace. Once again, Barrett Browning insists on the city as an equally valid and historically more likely source of the Victorian poet's inspiration. Yet if this cityscape provides Aurora with the "peace" and "calmness" that can restore her imagination, the "emotion" and "excitation" of Wordsworth's formula come from elsewhere. The seascape provokes a passionate, erotic desire to "leap and plunge":

> *And find a sea-king with a voice of waves,*
> *And treacherous soft eyes, and slippery locks*   (8:41−44)
> *You cannot kiss but you shall bring away*
> *Their salt upon your lips.*

This erotic figure of Aurora's imagination puts man back into the originary scene of inspiration and creation; he provides the excitement that
nature on its own lacks.

As Dorothy Mermin has suggested, Aurora's vision of a "sea-king,"
a male version of the mermaid, "establishes her as the speaking subject
whose desire elicits its object." [62] When Aurora imagines, Romney appears. This scene of a powerful *female* imagination revises, as I have already
argued, the finale of Landon's *History of the Lyre,* in which the poetess,
however inspired in personal solitude or public performance, cannot successfully move the man she loves. It also revises, if perhaps unconsciously,
those scenes in *The Prelude,* book VII, in which erotic desire is seen as
antithetical (or at best irrelevant) to the poetic imagination. But the
most significant revision of the Wordsworthian model of poetic development comes in Barrett Browning's insistence that the new woman poet
follow out the implications of what Wordsworth claimed to know (that
love of nature leads to love of man) and what her womanly experience
has taught (that "man" includes both a single man, Romney, and Man, all
humankind).

For all Wordsworth's attempts to show a progression from his early
love of nature to his mature concern for humankind, the dramatic scene
on Mount Snowdon omits man, and the subsequent exposition of the
poet's progress from "the ways of nature" to "the works of man and face
of human life" to his "Faith in life endless" (14 : 198, 202, 204) seems less
convincing as a result. In *Aurora Leigh* Barrett Browning never fully endorses the Wordsworthian progression, Aurora's earliest memories making human love more foundational than love of nature and her final vision
suggesting a simultaneity rather than a hierarchy or sequence. Nonetheless, Aurora moves, as does Wordsworth, from a moment of personal vision to a concern for humankind itself, and her vision fully recognizes
that "face of human life." Just as Wordsworth on Snowdon finds an emblem of the ideal relation of nature and the human mind, so Aurora finds
in marriage to Romney an emblem of ideal human relations and of man's
work for other men.

It is a traditional emblem drawn from the Song of Songs, one of
love and spousal union: [63]

> First, God's love.
> And next . . . the love of wedded souls,
> Which still presents that mystery's counterpart.
> Sweet shadow-rose, upon the water of life,
> Of such a mystic substance, Sharon gave
> A name to! human, vital, fructuous rose,   (9:881–90)
> Whose calyx holds the multitude of leaves,
> Loves filial, loves fraternal, neighbour-loves
> And civic—all fair petals, all good scents,
> All reddened, sweetened from one central Heart!

Aurora's emblem reverses Wordsworth's order, beginning with divine love, then moving to "the love of wedded souls," and finally expanding into all varieties of human love: familial, brotherly, neighborly, and civic.[64] It responds to the despair of *The Prelude*, book XI, where, in the aftermath of the French Revolution, Wordsworth images the era as "a budding rose" that "did not wake to happiness" (11:121–23); Aurora's emblematic rose promises a full bloom even in the nation or *civitas*. And it allows Barrett Browning to bring together the anticipated endings of her generic mix: the traditional marriage of domestic fiction, the apocalyptic union of English epic, and, in a moment of autobiographical revelation, the happiness of her own marriage to Robert Browning.

Finally, Aurora's vision and union with Romney allow Barrett Browning to incorporate, if only provisionally, a difficult, sometimes excluded aspect of English poetic autobiography: the politics of poetry. Daniel Riess has written persuasively of the depoliticizing of poetry in Landon's volumes of the 1820s: *The Improvisatrice, The Troubador, The Golden Violet,* and (I would add) *A History of the Lyre.* Whereas Staël's *Corinne* and other writings of the Coppet circle on which Landon drew used literature to engage in political debate (to attack, for example, the "dead" neoclassicism endorsed by the Napoleonic empire), Landon's adaptation of the story of Corinne represents, in Riess's view, "a testament to her shrewd skill at transforming potentially controversial Romantic works into a non-polemical Romanticism suitable for the mass market."[65] In *The Contours of Masculine Desire: Romanticism and the Rise of Women's Poetry* Marlon B. Ross views this retreat from politics, notable in More,

Barbauld, and other early nineteenth-century women writers, as part of a larger separation of women's poetry and the sphere of "feminine desire" from Romantic male poetry and "the masculine terrains of power."[66] In *Aurora Leigh* Barrett Browning puts the politics back into women's verse, returning to Staël's seminal model and repoliticizing Landon's derivative histories. In the debates between Aurora and Romney in book II over how best to ameliorate social ills; in the class satires of book IV, where "Saint Giles" meets "Saint James" at Romney and Marian's wedding; in the drawing-room gossip of book V, where Sir Blaise's Anglo-Catholicism meets Mister Smith's German Rationalism; in the political commentary of book IX, where Aurora and Romney discuss (and sometimes dismiss) feminism, socialism, communism, Comteanism, and other political isms—in these and other passages, *Aurora Leigh* resists the gendering of poetry that her female predecessors had so readily accepted, indeed encouraged, as they carved out a niche for women's verse.

Barrett Browning's relation to Wordsworthian politics is less straightforward. In general terms, *Aurora Leigh,* like *The Prelude,* responds to the nineteenth-century debate over poetry's worth: Is it important and influential work, or is it, as Utilitarians thought, a pleasant but trivial activity? Aurora calls it, in what may be a response to Ford Madox Brown's famous mid-Victorian painting *Work,* "imperative labour" (1:880), superior to the work of "common men" who "Lay telegraphs, gauge railroads, reign, reap, dine / And dust the flaunty carpets of the world / For kings to walk on" (1:870–72). The poem engages, to borrow Ross's terms, the "conflict between the romantic desire to view poetry as an influential kind of work that shapes material life through its immaterial power and the utilitarian desire to view poetry as a pleasing, but essentially superfluous activity that distracts men from the real work of technological advancement, economic growth, and sociopolitical progress."[67] In this cultural debate Barrett Browning asserts, with Wordsworth, the power of poetry to shape human lives. This is the lesson Romney learns through the destruction of Leigh Hall and his socialist schemes, then through his reading of Aurora's poetry. In asserting poetry's power, Barrett Browning assigns it to a source even more "immaterial" than Wordsworth's: "God's love" rather than nature. (It is as if nature itself were too dangerously material in an overly material age.)

More specifically in terms of contemporary politics and political movements, *Aurora Leigh* reproduces the pattern of *The Prelude* in its movement from an enthusiastic but wrongheaded politics to a more mature understanding of how social and moral progress might occur. At the end of his "Residence in France," books X–XII, Wordsworth describes a civic despair induced by the Terror of the French Revolution:

> *I lost*
> *All feeling of conviction, and, in fine,*   (11:302–5)
> *Sick, wearied out with contraries,*
> *Yielded up moral questions in despair.*

Although he recovers his moral equilibrium, and even at the end of *The Prelude* reasserts his "hopes of good to come" (13:63), he still rails against political rulers and social theorists, including Adam Smith, who "Plan without thought, or buil[d] on theories / Vague and unsound" (13:70–71). In *Aurora Leigh* Romney replaces Wordsworth, and socialist schemes become the narrative equivalent of the French Revolution. Romney suffers from Wordsworth's naive political enthusiasm and then from his political despair. At the end of the poem it is Romney, like Wordsworth but unlike Aurora, who rails against political and social theorists:

> *"Fewer programmes, we who have no prescience.*
> *Fewer systems, we who are held and do not hold.*
> *Less mapping out of masses to be saved,*   (9:864–69)
> *By nations or by sexes. Fourier's void,*
> *And Comte absurd—and Cabot puerile."*

Apparently Aurora the *poet* has already absorbed the lesson of *The Prelude,* thus avoiding the false steps that Romney, a nonreader of poetry, inevitably takes. Or perhaps, as a *woman* unobligated to enter the political arena, she never fully faces the temptation of politics to which such men as Wordsworth (or such characters as Romney) succumb.

How one chooses between these two possibilities depends, I think, on which genre of *Aurora Leigh* one chooses to emphasize and how Barrett Browning's politics appear from that generic perspective. Critics who read the poem primarily as domestic fiction tend to see in the differences between Aurora and Romney, as in their marriage, a reinscription of traditional gender roles, a capitulation to patriarchy, a conservative ending to Aurora's life story. Ellen Moers's disappointment in *Aurora Leigh* as "a good second-rate novel" stems, for all her celebration of Barrett Browning and her reintroduction of the work to the feminist canon, from this generic emphasis; in the novelistic tradition, the poem's closure seems conventional, even conservative, scarcely political.[68] Herbert Tucker's more generous reading depends on its attention to epic dimensions. In the "consecrated elements" of Aurora's final epic vision—"the 'jasper-stone as clear as glass' and the jeweled heavens of the last lines"—Tucker finds a "crystalline *Bildung* . . . precipitated out of the poetic solution in which Aurora's selfhood has been dissolved, diffused, and suspended for a kind of re-creation to which the traditional bildungsroman gave little play." Emphasizing the *Bildungsroman* form rather than Victorian domestic fiction, Tucker sees epic as renovating the novel by "expanding the horizons of domestic fiction beyond merely human engagements, through the edification of the bridal New Jerusalem, to espouse a sacred civic trust."[69] Thus Aurora, we might say in response to my initial formulation, has not only absorbed the political lessons of *The Prelude* but also reconceived the tactics of epic as a public, civic-minded genre.

Reading *Aurora Leigh* as autobiography may produce yet the most encouraging view of Aurora and her creator as poetically and politically engaged. By choosing to include politics in the narrative of Aurora's development, Barrett Browning breaches the boundary between the realms of masculine and feminine writing and, unlike the poetesses before her, moves into the masculine terrain of politics and publicity. That Barrett Browning should introduce politics not only into women's poetry but also into a woman writer's *autobiography* is especially significant, given the deep resistance to self-display that More and Barbauld, Joanna Baillie and Hemans reveal. (Hemans, for example, was so excessively concerned with violating codes of proper femininity that when her sister, Harriet Owen, composed a memoir to preface Hemans's posthumous poems, "Owen initiate[d] her memoir by protesting the indecorousness of writing a memoir of a woman who wished her life to remain private." By comparison, Landon was comfortable with self-display—and hence an easier poetess for Barrett Browning to adapt.)[70]

When Aurora determines to write of herself "for my better self" (1:4), she knows that she violates a feminine code of early nineteenth-century women writers against *auto*biography, yet she characterizes her act not as self-violation but as self-improvement. That her improvement extends beyond the self and encompasses the civic body we can determine from the final vision of the poem—a vision of the New Jerusalem that represents not a domestic Eden, the traditional feminine realm, but rather a new world "whence shall grow spontaneously / New churches, new economies, new laws / Admitting freedom, new societies / Excluding falsehood" (9:946–49). Except perhaps for the final section of Harriet Martineau's *Autobiography,* with its prophetic "Last View of the World," there is no autobiographical conclusion quite so engaged with the public good or quite so insistent about the need for the woman writer to move out of the private and into the civic realm.

V

Family Business: Margaret
Oliphant's *Autobiography* as
Professional Artist's Life

Margaret Oliphant's *Autobiography* seems split between two traditions of Victorian life writing: between a professional author's account of
her aspirations and public achievements and a domestic memoir of Oliphant's life as a daughter, sister, mother, and pillar of the family. At least
literary critics have tended to read the *Autobiography* this way. From Annie Coghill's 1897 obituary essay in the *Fortnightly Review,* which posits a
sharp separation between Oliphant's work, "given to the public," and
"her life," given "for her children first, and after them for the small circle
of loving and intimate friends," to more recent analyses that see in the
text "an irresolvable conflict between femaleness and writing" or treat
the subject positions of "mother" and "woman writer" as mutually incompatible, the *Autobiography* has seemed to demonstrate the tensions
within the life of the nineteenth-century woman writer. In Gabriele
Helms's words, writing an autobiography led Oliphant "to the formulation and inscription of numerous tensions and contradictions." [1]

The origins of these tensions have been explained either biographically (as resulting from individual experience) or culturally (as part of
larger historical circumstances). Read biographically, the *Autobiography*
shows the marks of its unusual composition. Oliphant began writing the
narrative for her children, particularly for her younger and favorite son,
Francis, known as Cecco; but before it was completed, both of her sons
died: Cyril in November 1890, after what became part I was completed,
Cecco in October 1894, just as she brought part II to a close. Thus when
the work was half-finished, the audience changed, and with it the autobiographical genre. As Oliphant ruefully noted, what she had intended

for a loving domestic circle, for a child "to read with tenderness, to hide some things, to cast perhaps an interpretation of love upon others, and to turn over all my papers with the consciousness of a full right to do so," had to be reconceived as a professional memoir for the general public. "How strange it is to me to write all this," she reflected when she returned to the manuscript after Cecco's death, "with the effort of making light reading of it, and putting in anecdotes that will do to put in the papers and make the book sell! . . . I feel all this to be so vulgar, so common, so unnecessary, as if I were making pennyworths of myself." [2]

Read as a cultural document, the *Autobiography* displays another, more common set of tensions. Throughout the work, Oliphant narrates incidents of family crisis that led to artistic compromise; in Dorothy Mermin's formulation, while Oliphant's maternal strength "may have empowered her as a woman she felt that it enfeebled her as a writer." [3] As Oliphant reached the turning point of her career, for example—with her Carlingford series successfully launched, her histories of the religious leader Edward Irving and the French politician Montalembert securing her reputation as a biographer, and a steady flow of articles in *Blackwood's Edinburgh Magazine* providing financial security and status as a reviewer—her brother Frank filed for bankruptcy, and the support of his family, including the expensive education of his son, fell upon Oliphant's shoulders. As she tells the story, the crisis demanded that an irreversible decision be made: support her family or uphold her artistic standards. "I never did nor could," Oliphant explains, "hesitate for a moment as to what had to be done. It had to be done, and that was enough, and there is no doubt that it was much more congenial to me to drive on and keep everything going, with a certain scorn of increased work, and metaphorical toss of my head, as if it mattered! than it ever would have been to labour with an artist's fervour and concentration to produce a masterpiece" (125). This incident, with its structure of family responsibility in conflict with artistic aspiration, becomes evidence in most critical readings of the *Autobiography* of the cultural predicament of the woman writer. "For middle-class women of the nineteenth century," according to Mary Jean Corbett, "living 'a literary life,' in the sense that term might hold for Mill or Dickens or Trollope, was almost impossible—and so, of course, was writing one." [4]

Without attempting to deny such tensions, I want to reconsider the

Autobiography in literary-historical rather than biographical or cultural terms—that is, as a kind of autobiography written by women artists in the nineteenth century—and to argue that Oliphant did indeed write a "literary life." I believe that when she came to compose her personal narrative in 1885, she had conceived of a union of two autobiographical traditions frequently considered incompatible. She imagined a version of the Victorian domestic memoir that would incorporate the professional artist's life story by making it part of a chronicle of the family's professional achievement. Her memoir, intended for "my boys," could be seen, then, less as a private or individual document than as a collaborative family history, including her own literary achievement as well as her sons' entry into the profession of letters.[5] This reconception of the woman writer's memoirs was meant not to display the tension between motherhood and authorship but rather to resolve it.

In order to make this argument, I need to distinguish between the kinds of professional artist's autobiography that Oliphant did not intend to write—indeed, that she disdained—and a kind of family memoir that had a long, distinguished literary tradition and that Oliphant used as the basis of her own work. What Oliphant did not intend was a reminiscence of professional literary life of the sort her contemporaries S. C. Hall and William Howitt had published in *A Book of Memories* (subtitled *Of Great Men and Women of the Age, from Personal Acquaintance*) and *Homes and Haunts of the Most Eminent British Poets*.[6] These volumes drew on a lesser writer's acquaintance with the more famous and, in their implicit acknowledgment of inferior status, represented the sort of hackwork that Oliphant resisted as "making pennyworths of myself." Neither did Oliphant intend a professional life story in the mode of Harriet Martineau, with its "heroic" account (the adjective is Oliphant's) of a lone woman writer's struggle to publish her work and achieve fame.

As we know from Oliphant's 1877 review, virtually everything about Martineau's book offended her: its disrespectful treatment of parents and "desecration of th[e] home"; its "posthumous assault" on friends and acquaintances in its pages of petty criticism; its misguided choice of a "foolish" American editor; and, above all, its self-important mode of self-presentation.[7] Oliphant's criticisms of Martineau's *Autobiography* are not merely matters of taste; they are matters of ideology. Martineau conceived her life in typically individualistic terms of personal progress and professional success; Oliphant espoused a more collaborative and familial approach to literary work typical of women writers of her generation. If we consider those few passages of Martineau's *Autobiography* that Oliphant praises, we can recognize an incipient version of the ideology that would later underwrite her own account. In one, a description of Martineau's childish attempts to write books, Oliphant praises the "pretty account of her first publication." In another, an account of Martineau's entry into professional authorship, Martineau's *Autobiography* firmly separates the feminine, domestic work of making shirts from the masculine, professional work of writing books. In the *Blackwood's* review, however, Oliphant refuses to acknowledge this distinction, instead concentrating on the domestic setting and reading into the incident "the pleasant atmosphere of family life."[8] That "atmosphere of family life," with its assumption of the compatibility of the domestic and professional, was what Oliphant valued in autobiography and in the form known today as the domestic or family memoir.

In her work for *Blackwood's Edinburgh Magazine,* Oliphant reviewed over a dozen domestic memoirs, both in their seventeenth- and nineteenth-century manifestations. She wrote a series on literary autobiography in seven parts in 1881–83, over half of which focused on domestic memoirs, and during the 1870s and 1880s in her columns "New Books" and "The Old Saloon" she reviewed virtually all of the important memoirs of Victorian women artists who were her friends or contemporaries. From these critical analyses we learn what Oliphant valued most about autobiography—and what she disliked. She valued, for example, the childhood reminiscences of writers—"infinitely more interesting and charming to the imagination" than their accounts of books produced and honors won (Mary Somerville); she disliked memoirs that included "so many chapters of dry detail" as to make a great man's life seem utterly dull (George Grote) or that quoted correspondence of a "consistent and unvarying intellectual strain" instead of showing the "more genial and natural" domestic life (Sara Coleridge); and she especially disliked memoirs that revealed "all the scandals and pseudo-revelations which literary scavengers delight to shovel out," approving instead those editors whose "family pride and affection" made them "lock up their skeleton in a closet" (Coleridge).[9] These preferences were to influence her own account, with its emphasis on childhood and domestic experience and its relative omission of professional development. From her reviews, too, we learn that Oliphant understood that styles of authorial self-presentation change, going in and out of fashion with the times.[10]

In the *Blackwood's* autobiography series, Oliphant came to terms with the literary traditions of the genre, delineating them (as perhaps the first critic to do so) and distinguishing among their different purposes and effects.[11] In the opening article on Benvenuto Cellini, she distinguishes between *res gestae*, the autobiographies of important public figures who "leave behind a record of many things worth knowing, clear up, perhaps, some historical mysteries of [their] period, and keep the incidents of [their] own [lives] alive among men," and the "domestic records" of persons over whose head "these events have passed" but whose account "widens our experience of human nature" and is thus as "interesting and instructive as any other part of the perennial drama." In her sixth article, on the seventeenth-century memoirs of Lucy Hutchinson and Alice Thornton, Oliphant virtually defines the genre of domestic memoir:

> *Mrs Hutchinson's memoirs were not intended for the public. The compilation of family histories was a fancy of the time. In the leisure of widowhood and age, when her children were out in the world and her noonday over, a woman who had been full of fancy and vivacity all her life—without leisure, in the vicissitudes of an active career, for more than a copy of verses now and then, or a religious meditation jotted down among the simples in her recipes-book—would amuse herself in the ease of her later days by writing down all that happened, if not to herself, "to your father," in all the principal chapters of his existence.*[12]

Here are the key elements: an autobiography written by an older woman, a mother, for the purpose of conveying family memories, attitudes, and achievements, her own as well as the family's.[13] Oliphant's comments on Lucy Hutchinson's memoir suggest just how much she admired this domestic genre, with its emphasis on family values and a network of familial relationships. She notes admiringly that Lucy describes her parents "with all the affectionate panegyric which was general in those days," though she adds (perhaps recalling Harriet Martineau) that "now, were such a chronicle made," the writer, "clear-sighted and impartial, should set before the reader the defects of his progenitors."[14]

Despite the contrast between an idealized "then" and a debased "now," and despite the relegation of domestic memoirs to a historically remote "fancy of the time," domestic memoirs continued to be written—indeed, they flourished—in the Victorian era. Wives of diplomats, politicians, civil servants, clergymen, and others carried on the tradition of family history, incorporating their personal lives into the predominantly public accounts of their husbands' achievements. More particularly, in a Victorian version of the form, ordinary wives and daughters wrote reminiscences of domestic life in middle-class homes for their children and grandchildren, implicitly asserting the value of the domestic as equal to that of the public. Domestic memoirs flourished among the families of professional artists and authors, as Oliphant well knew. She reviewed versions for *Blackwood's* in 1873 and 1874 with the *Memoir and Letters of Sara Coleridge* and the *Personal Recollections of Mary Somerville by her Daughter Martha Somerville;* in 1879, in the column "Two Ladies," with the *Memoirs of the Life of Anna Jameson, by her Niece, Geraldine Macpherson,* and Fanny Kemble's *Records of a Girlhood;* again in 1889 with *Mary Howitt: An Autobiography, edited by her Daughter Margaret Howitt;* and in 1890 with the *Life of Harriet Beecher Stowe.* Even more than her 1881–83 series on autobiography, these memoirs were personally and professionally influential on Oliphant. In a letter to John Blackwood included in her *Autobiography and Letters,* she notes that Somerville "recalls to me my mother and even my own recluse childhood" (244), and in the early pages of her autobiography Oliphant quotes Somerville's memoirs (to the effect that "one does not, to one's consciousness, change as one's outward appearance and capabilities do," 13).[15] Mary Howitt, too, appears in Oliphant's autobiography as "a mild, kind, delightful woman" who nonetheless frightened the younger writer with stories "of many babies she had lost through . . . too much mental work" (36). Geddie Macpherson, editor of Anna Jameson's memoirs, was a close friend in Rome at the time Oliphant's husband died and a frequent companion on Oliphant's European travels. What these women's lives—and Oliphant's reviews—suggest is a version of what Janice Carlisle has called specular autobiography.

Specular autobiography, according to Carlisle, is a form of life writing that sees, comprehends, even creates the self by mirroring (often with distortions) the life of another.[16] In such autobiography, the writing subject reviews her life not simply in its own terms but primarily in comparison with others. Usually, when Oliphant's life has been considered in comparison with those of other women writers, the choices have been

Charlotte Brontë and George Eliot—a critical practice that has left Oliphant looking "small, very obscure, . . . rather a failure all round."[17] More recently, however, Joanne Shattock has suggested that such comparisons, the instigating occasions for writing the *Autobiography,* might lead us to more complex, even revisionary conclusions: "It was Oliphant's strength as an autobiographer that she was able to lift herself out of her self-pity and to write an autobiography which was not, as were Eliot's and Martineau's, structured as success stories, the emergence of public women."[18] Assuming Shattock's approach but not necessarily concluding that Oliphant's account represents a story of failure, we might look instead to the memoirs of the women writers about whom Oliphant wrote as a source of her autobiographical form and her beliefs about a woman writer's work.

These domestic memoirs are a typical Victorian hybrid of auto/biography. The *Personal Recollections* of Mary Somerville (not a literary figure but a pioneering woman of science, remembered now as the person for whom Somerville College, Oxford, was named) contain, in her daughter's words, "recollections of past times, noted down by my mother during the last years of her life," with selected letters "to eminent men and women" and a daughter's dutiful testimony to "her [mother's] simple and loving disposition."[19] This is the form Oliphant seems to have had in mind when she wrote that her autobiography was intended for her children "to read with tenderness, to hide some things, to cast perhaps an interpretation of love upon others, and to turn over all my papers with the consciousness of a full right to do so" (81). It would have been her sons' prerogative (and duty) to edit the manuscript for publication, adding as they saw fit selected letters and biographical details.[20]

Like Somerville's *Personal Recollections,* Anna Jameson's *Memoirs* and Mary Howitt's *Autobiography* combine personal reminiscences with letters and biographical transitions added by the editor, in the first case a niece, in the second a daughter. Jameson's *Memoirs* (1879) was assembled almost twenty years after her death from journals, letters, and the memories of her niece Geraldine Macpherson—in large part to counter the negative portrait included in Martineau's *Autobiography* (1877). Howitt's *Autobiography,* begun for her children, was completed just before her death for serial publication in *Good Words* and later amplified for book publication.[21] Even more than Somerville's, these memoirs display the communal origins of the domestic genre. In old age Howitt wrote her "Reminiscences" (the title she chose for *Good Words*) with her daughter Margaret at her side, sifting through, selecting, and editing the family letters.[22] The final text includes not only Mary Howitt's life story but an interpolated account by her husband, William, about his childhood and family origins, a preface about both parents written by Margaret, and, along the way, an account of the family's professional achievements. Since William and Mary Howitt were well-published poets and journalists, their daughter Anna Mary was a prominent painter in the 1840s and 1850s, and their daughter Margaret a professional translator, this autobiography represents a family memoir *cum* professional artist's life.

What the autobiographies of Somerville, Jameson, and Howitt offered were incipient versions of the professional woman's life written as domestic memoir—not only a formal model but (despite Oliphant's dismissal of "theory") an ideological model for the woman artist's work. In her 1879 review of Jameson's *Memoirs,* which she paired with the actress Fanny Kemble's *Records of a Girlhood,* Oliphant articulates this ideology before discussing the books themselves. At stake are two questions about women's professional work: the historical moment at which it becomes professional and the philosophical relationship between the professional and the domestic. Oliphant notes that "from the beginning of history, . . . whenever it has been necessary, women *have* toiled, have earned money, have got their living and the living of those dependent upon them, in total indifference to all theory"; she makes this assertion to counter "the present generation," who "considers itself to have invented the idea that women have a right to the toils and rewards of labour" and who act under "the delightful conviction of being themselves inventors, apostles, and missionaries of an altogether novel undertaking."[23] Here Oliphant registers her annoyance (as in the ironical phrase "delightful conviction") at professional women, younger than she, Jameson, and Howitt, who claim distinction as the first working women (and who do so vociferously) but whose claims are historically ill founded.

More crucial, because fundamentally contrary to Oliphant's conception of work, is the ideological position these younger women take: they lay claim to the "professional" by excluding or separating it from the "domestic." When Oliphant argues that "the greatest and most fundamental wrong done to women in this world is the small appreciation ever shown . . . of the natural and inevitable share of the world's work which they cannot avoid, and which no one can say they do not fulfil unmurmuringly," she is not falling into essentialism or anticipating an argument of modern feminism, that women ought to be paid for domestic labor. Rather, she means to argue against a conception of the woman writer (and, more broadly, woman worker) that achieves professionalism by breaking with domesticity. "So long as the occupations of mother and housekeeper are taken for granted as of no particular importance," Oliphant proclaims, "so long will all hot-headed and high-spirited women resent the situation." Her position entails not only the argument that maternal and domestic work ought to be valued, but also the stronger claim that women artists best conceptualize and realize their professional work when it proceeds from a domestic context.[24]

Oliphant found this model of professionalism in the lives of Jameson and Kemble, and it underlies her own *Autobiography*. In discussing Jameson, she seizes on a childhood incident in which Anna, well aware that her father, "an Irish miniature-painter of very considerable ability" but in pecuniary straits "unfortunately common enough in artists' households," gathers together her siblings and convinces them that they should "set out for Brussels, learn the art of lace-making, work at it at once successfully, and achieve in the shortest possible time a fortune with which to set their parents at ease in the future." This childhood anecdote anticipates the more serious moment when, at sixteen, Jameson goes out as a governess to support herself and family and, while accompanying her charges on a grand tour, writes the book that launches her career as an author, *Diary of the Ennuyée*. Domestic duty leads, almost naturally, to authorship. In recounting Kemble's entry into theatrical life, Oliphant re-creates an even more dramatic domestic scene. As a girl of nineteen, Fanny witnesses her mother's distress over the impending bankruptcy of the family and the close of Covent Garden theater, and she asks her father's permission to "seek employment as a governess, so as to relieve him, at once, at least of the burden of my maintenance." Instead of agreeing to governessing, the parents allow Fanny to try acting, and her performance in the role of Juliet saves the family from "domestic catastrophe."[25] Oliphant links these incidents, the stuff of artistic mythmaking, to the professional "artist-classes," which on "frequent occasions" allow "the loyal and dutiful daughter" to become "the mainstay and saviour of the falling house." The artist-classes are exempt from the usual Victorian dichotomies of masculine and feminine, professional and domestic. According to Oliphant, "it is art alone which (more or less) equalises the value of labour without respect of sex or circumstance."[26]

This view of the "artist-classes" informs Oliphant's own life writing—and, indeed, I suggest that her *Autobiography,* with its similar scenes of professional origins, represents the epitome of this Victorian tradition. Although she did not come, as did Jameson and Kemble, from an already established professional dynasty, her account suggests that she hoped to establish one, and her scenes of artistic origins underscore the relation between familial and professional work.

Oliphant's first autobiographical impulse—the much-discussed journal fragment in which she records "the turning-point" of her life when she faced, on the one hand, John Blackwood's rejection of her manuscripts and, on the other, "the children's dear little faces when I got home," only to go on that night to write the first story of her brilliant Carlingford series[27]—anticipates the pattern of domestic crisis spurring on (and legitimating) professional success. Even more thoroughly, if less dramatically, the chronological narrative of the *Autobiography* underscores the relation between domesticity and literary work. As Oliphant reconstructs her life, professional work seems naturally and necessarily to proceed from the domestic context.

Oliphant records three critical scenes of artistic origins—mythical, marital, material. In the first, she recalls that she began novel writing while her mother "had a bad illness" and she was in a state of "depression and sadness" over the breakup of an engagement. Writing fiction was an alternative to needlework, something "to secure some amusement and occupation for myself while I sat by my mother's bedside" (16). In this scene, the artistic mythmaking inserts itself into Oliphant's fiction: "I wrote a little book in which the chief character was an angelic sister, unmarried, who had the charge of a family of motherless brothers and sisters, and who had a shrine of sorrow in her life in the shape of the portrait and memory of her lover who had died young" (16–17). This myth, produced first in 1845 as the novel *Christian Melville,* again in 1890 as *Kirsteen,* also appears in the early pages of the *Autobiography,* albeit with less dramatic flourish. As Oliphant tells it, the "little book" pleases her ailing mother and older brother Frank; her fiction writing provides work for the alcoholic Willie, who becomes her amanuensis and later publishes the novel under his own name; and her writerly career gives an alternative direction to a family history of crisis and failure. "This wonderful event," the publication of her first novel, she reports, "must have come most fortunately to comfort the family under new trouble" (19).

Ideologically, Oliphant treats the acts of writing and publishing not as the beginning of an independent professional career but as a collaborative, familial effort. Her mother and brother Frank, as readers and critics, become as crucial as the writer herself: "They were part of me, and I of them, and we were all in it" (23). From this insight emerges an extended analysis of the place of writing in the lives of women artists of her generation: that it "ran through everything" yet "was also subordinate to everything"; that "writing a book" proceeded in the same way as "making a shirt"; that, by occurring around the family worktable, writing became naturalized rather than "artificial"; that it was not, as in Austen's generation, a matter of family embarrassment but rather a cause for pride: "mine were pleased to magnify me, and to be proud of my work" (24). Despite the commonplace terms it employs, what is striking about this analysis is its historical sensitivity. Oliphant recognizes that the "meaning" of women's writing from Austen's generation to hers has changed and, by implication, that it changes for subsequent generations. Yet she also insists on a continuity in her own self-conception, one rooted in domesticity.[28] "Up to this date, 1888," she insists—that is, up to the moment at which she writes the first section of her autobiography—she has located her writerly work within the family circle: "My study, all the study I have ever attained to, is the little second drawing-room where all the (feminine) life of the house goes on" (24). As the parenthetical insistence on "feminine" life makes clear, Oliphant rejects a "masculine" conception of the professional writer's career (à la Martineau) or a life story that would reconceive her experiences in modern terms that separate the domestic from the professional. Despite the tensions registered, at root Oliphant imagines authorship and domesticity as connected.

This authorial self-conception continues in the account of Oliphant's marriage, which includes a second scene of writerly origins. Oliphant's reticence about her courtship and marriage to Frank Oliphant has caused much speculation about the happiness of their union, but a pivotal detail, generally overlooked, comes in the form that Frank's proposal takes: that he and Margaret should "build up the old Drumthwacket to-gether" (28). The Wilson-Oliphant union was conceived, as were many marriages among the professional artist-classes in the early nineteenth century, as a family-based and dynasty-building arrangement. The art historian Deborah Cherry has discussed the importance of family net-works in the training and support of nineteenth-century painters, male and female alike: "From the later eighteenth century the practice of art was . . . shaped by kinship links, intermarriage, familial training and an increasing professionalisation. Artist dynasties assisted in the formation of an occupational group with strong familial and professional ties." [29] While family groups were particularly common among painters (and, of course, Frank Oliphant was a painter as well as a stained-glass designer), such groups were also significant among novelists, journalists, and editors, where training, support, and the exchange of professional information were equally crucial. William and Mary Howitt, Oliphant's friends, were one well-known unit at mid-century, as were others in Oliphant's Lon-don circle: the S. C. Halls, both writers; the history-writing Strickland sisters and fiction-writing Marryat sisters, the latter daughters of the ad-venture novelist; the Gillies sisters, one a writer, the other an engraver; and the Chorleys, a family of translators, writers, and editors of a success-ful literary annual. When in her "Reminiscences," for example, Howitt recalls her acquaintance with the Chorley family, she describes them as a literary unit: "the gifted Quakeress, Jane Chorley, her highly-endowed children, William, John, Henry, and Mary Ann, forming the literary staff of the 'Winter Wreath.' " [30] At her marriage Oliphant may have been un-certain about the *kind* of professional family tradition she and Frank might build, but that she had "the old Drumthwacket" in mind becomes evident from her subsequent comments about the family achievements of the Wilsons (one of whom became president of University College, Toronto, the other Regius Professor of Technology in Edinburgh) and her family connections with Dr. David Moir, the famous "Delta" of *Blackwood's Magazine* (28−29).

In this context Oliphant's narrative of her wedding day—the day also on which the proofs of *Katie Stewart* arrived [31]—reiterates her concep-tion of writerly work as familial in origin and intention. The imaginative source of the novel, her first published by Blackwood, was familial, being "a little romance of my mother's family, gleaned from her recollections and descriptions" (30). The dedication to her mother insists on the importance of her maternal inheritance:

> *My Dear Mother,*
> *This story, which you have told to me so often, I offer to you again*
> *unchanged except in form. To the clear memory and vivid apprehension*
> *which have made "Katie Stewart" a living personage and authority to*
> *me all my life, I owe many another good thing but few pleasanter than*
> *the stories and recollections of that time long ago which connected the*
> *extreme age of "Auntie Morison" with my dear mother's early youth.*[32]

At the time of her wedding, Oliphant had even hoped that her new husband would draw the illustrations for the Christmas edition of the novel, thus making the book truly a family project.[33] Perhaps most important, the novel effectively established her career as a woman of letters in that it forged a personal and professional link with the Scottish publishing house that was to be her primary source of income and outlet for literary work for over forty-five years. As Oliphant puts it, "I received proofs of this story on my wedding day, and thus my connection with the firm of Blackwoods began" (31)—as if she had "married" the Blackwoods, too.

Finally, this family-based conception of work underlies the early scenes of the Oliphant marriage, which represent what might be called the material or physical origins of their artistry. Although Oliphant dismisses the London artistic society to which Frank introduced her as a "strange disappointment and disillusion," not all "beautiful conversation, all about books and the finest subjects," as she had expected (33), she nonetheless reminisces about the authors and artists within their professional circle, painters such as George Lance and Alexander Johnstone, writers such as the Halls and the Howitts, women artists such as the painter Rosa Bonheur, the actress Charlotte Cushman, and the novelist Dinah Mulock. These reminiscences remind us, as they would have reminded her sons, of the professional artist-class of which the Oliphants were a part, even if the intellectual judgment on that class is severe.

In contrast, Oliphant gives a scene (really a composite) of "true society" in which the young couple, after the day's work, visit "the house of another painter uninvited, unexpected, always welcome" (40). On first reading, her description might seem to separate professional work from domesticity—in that she recalls "the men above" as they "smoked and talked their subjects, investigating the picture of the moment," while "we women talked below of our subjects, as young wives and young mothers do" (40)—except that Oliphant records an architectural feature of painters' houses that inevitably merged the professional and domestic, noting as well that she went on these visits "with my work" (40). All painters used "the drawing-room proper of the house, the first-floor room, for their studios" (40); in her own house in Ulster Place, she used "the little back drawing-room" for her work, the "dining-room of the house being Frank's painting studio" (44).

This work arrangement recalls a specific moment in the history of the professional artist-classes, among painters especially but also among journalists and novelists, in which work went on within the home, not at a different location. As the art historian Will Vaughan has explained, from the beginning until the middle of the nineteenth century, painters transformed their houses to incorporate their studios and salesrooms; the ground floor became the workplace, the sales place, the place of contact between the artist and his audience.[34] This practice, adopted after the days of patronage and before the days of the art dealer, made most artists' studios de facto into family businesses, where they would work, often with their sons, wives, and daughters sharing space with them. It is a practice, moreover, that makes the commonplace notion of separate spheres irrelevant.

If the Oliphants' combination of painting and writing was atypical (though Oliphant notes in *The Victorian Age of English Literature* a similar combination in the Opie and Hofland families), it nonetheless reminds us that the narrative of a woman writer's separation from her family to pursue a literary career in London—so prominent in Martineau's *Autobiography* and John Cross's *Life* of George Eliot—was not necessarily the norm, nor was the ideology of a "professional career" widely accepted among women writers in the mid–nineteenth century. Martineau's account makes a point of separating her literary work from the common needlework of other women; Oliphant's refuses a clear distinction between the two. Martineau's account narrates the successful emergence of an individual author; Oliphant's aims, at least initially, at the history of a professionally ambitious family group. Martineau's account may be more readily recognizable as a professional author's autobiography, but Oliphant's account, like her reviews, means to challenge both the ideology of that familiar genre and its historical dominance.

When Oliphant thus sums up, in this segment of her *Autobiography*, the "happy moments which I can recollect," describing the happiest as a "curiously common and homely" moment in her young married life when she looked out her bedroom window, "the glimmer of the outside lights, the room dark, the faint reflection in the glasses, and my heart full of joy and peace" (44–45)—she is not privileging domesticity or maternity over literary or professional life. Within a house that combined workroom and study with bedroom and nursery, she is registering a moment without tension, "a sensation of that sweet calm and ease and peace" (45). That moment came, personally and historically, during what she termed, in her review of Mary Howitt's autobiography, "a halcyon time" when writers like the Howitts (and herself) provided "simple, wholesome, and good" reading for the public and earned a "respectable income," "every condition of Grub Street being totally absent." [35]

By arguing that the form of Oliphant's autobiography suggests family ambitions and even a desire to incorporate her sons' literary development into her life story, I know that I run counter to the conventional view of family matters. Oliphant scholars have never treated Frank Oliphant's artistic career seriously, nor have they considered her sons, Cyril and Cecco, to be exemplars of vocational achievement, largely because of their failure to attain their professional aspirations: Cyril as a barrister or as personal secretary to the governor of Ceylon, Cecco as a librarian in the British Museum. Officially, the Oliphant men failed because of health, Frank giving up his stained-glass business when his consumption was diagnosed, Cyril being sent back from Ceylon "on doctor's orders," Cecco passing his civil service examination but failing the physical requirement. Yet aside from poor health, assumptions about their "character"—especially a sneaking suspicion that the sons were morally and mentally ne'er-do-wells who preferred living off their mother's income rather than taking on hard work to earn their own—have contributed to the sense of family failure. As one of Oliphant's contemporaries recalled, writing of Cyril, "no more melancholy decadence than that of the vivid sparkling Eton boy into the elderly and deprecating loafer, dawdling about Eton and Windsor, could be imagined." [36]

Yet this is the biographer's judgment, not the autobiographer's perspective. The *Autobiography* constructs a different version of the family's artistic achievements. Despite the frustration Oliphant registers at her husband's lack of business sense (43) or the despair she admits when writing about his fatal illness, when she "had to go on working" while he, "unable for any exertion, s[at] silent," not giving "a word, a cheerful look, to disperse a little the heavy atmosphere of trouble" (52–53), her *Autobiography* faithfully records his major artistic work: his paintings of King Richard and the Prodigal Son (42), his unfinished Machiavelli (52), his Italian scene of "a group of lads from the country," and his two final sketches (61). Whatever the "black holes" in the *Autobiography,* to borrow Merryn Williams's phrase, Frank Oliphant's artistic career is not one of them.[37]

With the sons the case is more complex. During their brief lives Cyril and Cecco achieved a modicum of literary success, the latter especially by becoming a regular contributor to the *Spectator* and *Blackwood's* and by producing a steady stream of literary work for the ten years he lived after his degree taking from Balliol. As Oliphant puts it in the final pages of her account, "My Cecco . . . righted himself and overcame— not in time enough to save his career at Oxford, but so as to be all that I had hoped" (148–49). What had she hoped? The *Autobiography and Letters* suggest a literary career. When Oliphant began composing her life history, she had reason to believe that Cecco might inherit her literary mantle; indeed, it is possible to argue that his first professional publication (in the *Spectator* in 1884) motivated her retrospective account of her own career (begun in February 1885).

During her sons' adolescence Oliphant seems to have hoped (perhaps even expected) that one or both would enter the profession of letters. When in 1862 she wrote a letter of congratulations to William Blackwood, founder of "Maga," on the birth of his grandson, she noted that she hoped to send congratulations again "on the still more auspicious occasion when the 'little Editor,' who, I have a conviction, was specially born for the Magazine, takes up the old ensign"; she added, "I hope by that time I shall have a cadet too, able to do better work than his mother" (188). A decade later, when she took on the extra burden of her brother Frank's family and resigned herself to producing second-rate work, she wrote to William Blackwood that she made this sacrifice "with my eyes open, not deceiving myself on the subject"; again she added, "One of my boys, perhaps, may take up my imperfection and make it into something worthy to live" (238). And, in a Christmas letter to the Blackwoods in

1875, just after Cyril entered Oxford and a year before Jack Blackwood would do the same, she noted with pleasure that Cyril had "formed a friendship with a young brother (he thinks) of Major Lockhart" (252), son-in-law and biographer of Walter Scott—just the sort of friendship that would please a mother who had conceived of herself as a female Scott and who hoped for a family tradition in literature.

Perhaps inevitably, Oliphant's sons set their sights on different professions, Cyril in the law, Cecco in the British Museum. When these opportunities fell through, they turned to literature—Cyril with a little success, Cecco with greater aptitude and discipline, and hence greater success. Testimony to the sons' literary achievements is well represented in the authorized 1899 edition of the *Autobiography and Letters*—so well that we might say that one "ending" of Oliphant's life story fulfills the familial imperative of its beginning.

From the letters selected, we know that Oliphant set Cyril to work as her collaborator when she realized that he had neither the aptitude nor the discipline to pursue the law. Two years after he took a second at Balliol and after he gave up his legal studies, she wrote to William Blackwood that he was working on "my Leopardi" but "like all inexperienced writers, has got a mass of material accumulated through which at present he is floundering, not seeing how to get it into bounds; but he is hoping to send the first portion, which of course he left to the last, ready soon" (310). Nothing more about Cyril as author or collaborator appears in the letters until 1890, the year of his death, when Blackwood published his slim volume on De Musset in its Foreign Classics for English Readers series. Only then, when death made proof impossible, does a letter from Cecco suggest that his brother had a "rare talent" for "verse translation" and that the two of them had "formed a plan of another work which would bring out this rare talent in the same way" (377). Oliphant herself seems to have been more ambivalent about Cyril's literary abilities: her judgment in the *Autobiography* concludes that, in the De Musset volume, "much was so well done, and yet some so badly done" (148).

With Cecco, Oliphant was right to have more hope. Although he had a passion for heraldry and wished to find a librarianship that would allow him to indulge it, from the beginning of his adult life Cecco assumed the role of author. By July 1884, when he was twenty-five, Oliphant was writing to Annie Coghill that Cecco had "entered the band of critics, and had a paper in the 'Spectator' the other week," and, she added, "I hope will get on in that way" (319). She certainly encouraged Cecco's writerly pursuits. Early the next year she wrote confidentially to John Blackwood about printing one of her son's stories: "Cecco, I believe, has begged to have his story put into type. Will you kindly let me be at the extra expense, for I want to give him a lesson in literature in this way,—this of course strictly between ourselves—but please humour me" (324). That lesson in literature seems to have taken, for by the end of 1885 Cecco's story "Grateful Ghosts" was in proofs for *Blackwood's Magazine,* and Oliphant was writing happily to the publisher: "I trust too that your last new contributor, Cecco, will give you and the public satisfaction, and that this may be the beginning of a long connection" (329). In a family letter to Annie Coghill she more soberly notes the publication of his story, as well as his review "Two Novels" in the *Spectator,* while adding that still "his soul sighs for the Heralds' College" (330).

Whether by Oliphant's direction or Annie Coghill's editorial decision, the final letters selected for the *Autobiography* repeatedly show Cecco in the role of author, writing to John Blackwood with proposals for articles, asking about deadlines, or collaborating with his mother on profit-making travel books. In terms of Margaret Oliphant's literary career, many of these letters are unnecessary: they reveal little about her essays or books, and, in their concentration on Cecco's career, they tend to deflect attention from the mother's professional achievement. In terms of a family memoir, however, the letters have the effect of constructing if not a family dynasty, at least a familial collaboration. Oliphant becomes the mentor—instructing her son in the ways of the literary world, ensuring that another generation of Oliphants will become a name in literature, building up the "old Drumthwacket" as Frank Senior had intended.

Was this vision of familial collaboration and achievement merely another of Oliphant's fictions? Perhaps given Cecco's health, but not given his abilities. His story "Grateful Ghosts" shows a penchant for suspenseful narration and humor; his critical essays on the medieval Scots poets Robert Henryson and William Dunbar in *Blackwood's* are scholarly and thorough, if sometimes less than engaging; his reviews of contemporary novels in the *Spectator* are competent, even insightful; his articles on travels in the Holy Land, eventually gathered into a small book, represent the kind of hackwork for which his mother was well known. The literary work Cecco pursued was uncannily in the familial mode: super-natural fiction, travel books, semischolarly essays, an endless stream of reviews. Contemporaries recognized the family connection. In a *Black-wood's* column published soon after Cecco's death, ostensibly reviewing his mother's recent novels but also serving as an obituary for her son, the writer concluded: "Mr Francis Oliphant was a writer finely endowed with talent and manifold accomplishments; and he wanted nothing but the blessing of health to make for himself a prominent place in contem-porary literature." [38]

We shall never know whether this evaluation of Cecco's talent was realistic or overly generous, or whether the *Autobiography*'s representation of the family's literary achievements was Oliphant's own or her editor's. Certainly, Annie Coghill, the editor, chose, after narrating Cecco's death, to include a description of the son's "quaint study," a description which reminds us that he was fundamentally a writer: "his chair still stood by the writing-table, and, left as when he had risen from his last day's work, the half-written page, and the pen laid down for ever, seemed only wait-ing for his accustomed presence" (408). Annie tells us, too, that the col-umn in *Blackwood's* written after Cecco's death included a favorable no-tice of the mother's work and "what she valued much more—a short but very just appreciation of such writings of Cecco's as had appeared in those familiar pages" (416). Annie Coghill's editorial work has been denigrated as "pious but misguided," [39] but in the matter of family history we have little reason to suspect Annie of doing anything other than fulfilling Oli-phant's wishes. In a letter to John Blackwood two months after Cecco's death, Oliphant mentioned the manuscript of her autobiography, noting that she had intended it for her sons but that it was still "a thing to be calculated upon." Coghill follows this letter with an insistent statement that she carried out Oliphant's intentions: "What Mrs. Oliphant says in these letters she repeated without word of change on her deathbed" (418). [40]

If it is a question of autobiographical self-construction or editorial reconstruction, Coghill insists that the *Autobiography and Letters* respects the former. Perhaps it is more accurate to conclude that the letters she selected provide one ending of a bifurcated autobiography. An alternative ending, more critical and self-reflexive, more willing to reexamine the professional ideology that motivated her writerly career, comes in parts III and IV, which Oliphant composed after her second son's death.

On 2 October 1894 Francis (Cecco) Oliphant died at Eton, and on 5 October 1894, with her son's body lying in a coffin in the next room, Oliphant narrated the story of the death of her husband, the other Francis Oliphant, at Rome. The *Autobiography* associates the two deaths, not just narratively but thematically: with the first, the hoped-for domestic partnership ended; with the second, the hoped-for family tradition in literature ended. Oliphant emphasizes the solitariness of her position in the aftermaths of both. After her husband's death, she was left with "my own faculties, such as they were, to make our living and pay off our burdens by" (64); more severely, after her son's, she is "all alone. I cannot write any more" (150). The second instance especially insists on the link between family and writing.

Oliphant did, however, continue producing an autobiographical manuscript after her son's death, shifting from domestic memoir to a more conventional, public account of her literary life. When she resumed on Christmas night, 1894, she registered the need for this change: "I feel that I must try to change the tone of this record. It was written for my boys, for Cecco in particular. Now they will never see it . . . and I am now going to try to remember more trivial things, the incidents that sometimes amuse me when I look back upon them, not merely the thread of my life" (64–65). Despite this explanation for her shift from private to public, from family circle to literary audience, I would argue that the generic shift within the *Autobiography* was motivated by a larger historical shift, one Oliphant discussed eloquently in her reviews and fiction, if only indirectly in terms of her personal history.

If Oliphant meant her autobiography to register an ideology of work common to professional women writers of her generation and class, she could not have written her account, even before the deaths of her sons, unaware of the fragility of this ideology, especially in its dynasty-building intentions. Most of the artists' memoirs she reviewed for *Blackwood's* included some account of the artists' children and, almost invariably, of their failure to continue the family tradition. Her review of Sara Coleridge's *Memoirs* speculates about whether a great poet can transmit his genius to the next generation and, noting the relative weakness of Coleridge's sons, posits rather fancifully that the talent went to the poet's daughter: "It seems more fit that the great efflorescence of a race should continue on the female side than that nature should go on forcing un-natural splendour out of an exhausted stock in the person of an heir-male."[41] In her review of *Anna Jameson's Memoirs* Oliphant noted with pleasure the transmission of professional training not to a son but to a niece, Geraldine Macpherson, whom Jameson encouraged to illustrate the *Legends of the Madonna and the Saints:* "In some corners of the etchings may be seen a tiny G. here and there, which stands for the younger helper, the child, the shadow, the biographer, whose name is now joined to hers in this last and doubly close union for ever."[42] As the diminutives suggest, Oliphant recognized that the transmission from Jameson to Mac-pherson was weak, even if she still took pleasure in recording the female line of inheritance. In Howitt's case the failure of parental ambition was more public and disturbing. Mary Howitt had trained her two daughters to become independent professional women, yet her autobiography re-cords the disaster of the elder Anna Mary's ambitions as a painter (she suffered a nervous breakdown after reading John Ruskin's criticism of her publicly exhibited *Boadicea*) and silently acknowledges the younger Mar-garet's failure to do much more than hackwork. Oliphant discreetly avoids the daughters' failures in her review, commenting instead on the aesthetic error of incorporating the "less interesting" memoir of the hus-band, William.[43]

At her best Oliphant was astute, even painfully self-critical about the professional ideology and dynasty-building intentions of artistic families. In what she labels a "digression" in her review of Jameson and Kemble, but what becomes a telling analysis of the artist-classes of which she, Jameson, and Kemble were a part, Oliphant discusses the "change in national manners" that led artists to aspire to be something more than "the attendant start of some noble or wealthy house" (209). This aspira-tion, apparent in the Kembles, she locates first in the career of Sir Walter Scott, who "wanted to establish a family, . . . to be a country magnate, and leave to his sons and grandsons after him (alas!) the inheritance of this magnificent position" (208). Oliphant reluctantly joins in the common verdict against the "foolishness" of this aspiration,[44] but she also defends Scott's determination "to be socially independent—to be the host and not the guest, to give and not receive" (209). In her conflicted assessment of Scott she reveals her own desire for social independence (as mistress of her own house and social circle, not just a literary lion put on display by a wealthy patron) and her own fond, if foolish, Scott-like desire to establish her sons and heirs. Both desires are confirmed in Oliphant's anecdotes of the many parties she hosted at Windsor, as well as in an expurgated passage of the autobiography, written just after her elder son's death, in which she compares her life, work, and achievements with Scott's. His story creates a "national brotherhood," she suggests, expressing her own thoughts and feelings as "a bigger me." [45]

The *Blackwood's* reviews further express her growing awareness that the domestic ideology which had motivated the professional women of her generation had declined from dominant to démodé. In her 1889 review of Mary Howitt's *Autobiography,* Oliphant looked back to their early days in literature as "a halcyon time," days when the public was "content with reading so simple, wholesome, and good as that provided for them by a writer like William Howitt"; as she recalls "the red and blue binding" of Mary Howitt's books "upon library shelves and booksellers' tables," she laments that they are now "dead—as herrings that are red, are all those pleasant volumes." [46] Surely she was also thinking of her own books; in a self-deprecatory phrase in the *Autobiography* she admits "at least half of them [should be] forgotten" (5).

In her 1890 review of *The Life of Harriet Beecher Stowe,* Oliphant wrote not only of dead books but of dead ideologies. Quoting an anecdote in which Stowe explains her reasons for becoming an author as unashamedly domestic—"With the first money I earned in this way [by writing], I bought a featherbed!"—Oliphant notes: "This admirable confession of poverty and virtuous striving and the prosaic uses of the literary gift, was considered engaging and delightful to the highest degree in those days." [47] She explicates Stowe's story with an astute discussion of the historical shifts in the self-conceptions of women writers—from the Romantic period, with "all the artistic enhancement which Corinne's flowing robes and lyre gave in a previous generation," to the mid-century domestic ideology that underlay Stowe's work and her own, to the fin-de-siècle rejection of domesticity and revival of models of genius: "Corinne and her lyre are coming back to displace the excellent wife and mother. . . . The whirligig of time turns round again." [48]

Given Oliphant's acuteness about the changes in literary and cultural fashions, we might consider the second half of her *Autobiography* (parts III and IV) as something more than a personal reaction to her son's death. It involves also an acknowledgment of—with a resistance to—this literary historical shift, a complex negotiation of her authorial self-presentation to an audience less enamored than it had once been with "the excellent wife and mother." We might see parts III and IV, I suggest, as a failure to write in the newly prescribed authorial mode; as a self-conscious refusal to do so; and as an analysis of the effects of her resistance, one that becomes a critique of the domestic ideology she so thoroughly had embraced.

The second half of the *Autobiography* fails in that Oliphant never really writes the conventional literary memoir that she tells herself she must. Although, as Elisabeth Jay notes, Oliphant "deliberately returns us to the formula of the more public memoir designed to secure an inheritance for her unmarried niece [Denny],"[49] this "return" is only partial, and Jay's statement is true only in the sense that Oliphant here recounts her meetings with the Carlyles and the Tennysons, her work on the biographies of Irving and Montalembert, her dining with Mrs. Duncan Stewart and the literary elite, and other such socioprofessional anecdotes. Yet the second half of the *Autobiography* also suffers from a pattern of narrative reversion in which Oliphant repeatedly forgets the literary matters she has been discussing and tells "baby stories" (86) instead.

As Oliphant recounts, for instance, the excitement over *Salem Chapel* and her early research for the biography of Edward Irving, she strays into a tale of Cecco's childhood illness. The associative train is easy enough to reconstruct: Jane Carlyle, whom Irving had tutored, was due to visit to discuss her childhood mentor; Cecco had just recovered from a convulsion before Carlyle's visit; and thus Oliphant associates her baby and the biography. Yet it annoys her that she cannot write of her literary work in the expected mode: "Here is a pretty thing. I should like if I could to write what people like about my books, being just then, as I have said, at my high tide, and instead of that all I have to say is a couple of baby stories. I am afraid I can't take the books *au grand sérieux*" (86). Similarly, she recounts her last visit to the Tennysons in maternal terms: "It was after Lionel's death, and after my Cyril's death" (138). She remembers Mrs. Tennyson as a mother who, like herself, had lost a son, and recalls

Lord Tennyson's delightful conversation and poetry reading, "glad and thankful that Cecco should see him so" (138). In these instances, as in others, the *Autobiography* filters its memories through a maternal lens.

It is possible, however, to read these reversions not as failure but as resistance to the more conventional form of artist's memoir that Oliphant disliked aesthetically and ideologically. In her reviews of the 1870s and 1880s she had repeatedly declared that memoirs of high-achieving men and women would be better pieces of literature if they said less about public achievement and more about domestic incident. She asked, in ironic wonder, how Mrs. George Grote, "a wife full of literary abilities," could have made "a dull book out of such a man's [her husband's] life": "a more arid and barren record of facts could not have been given to the world than this strange mixture of biography and autobiography, which ought to have been one of the most delightful volumes ever penned, and is one of the dreariest." Of Sara Coleridge's *Memoir* she concluded: "The filial and modest editor would have done more justice to this gentle memory, had she collected a handful of pleasant nursery letters, the mother's babbling to her children, or the girl's wayward visionary fancies, than can come out of all these philosophisings."[50] Given these views, Oliphant's reversion to "baby stories" reflects the triumph of personal taste and aesthetic judgment over cultural convention and market sense. Near the end of the *Autobiography,* after telling about her family's financial troubles and wondering if "such details would be of interest to the public," she comes to articulate this aesthetic view again: "as a matter of fact, it is exactly those family details that are interesting,—the human story in all its chapters" (122).

Beyond what I have called aesthetics, Oliphant's "reversions" also reflect a refusal to alter her sense of self. If Oliphant viewed her literary work as situated in and emerging from her domestic life, then to associate literary and domestic incidents in her *Autobiography* was to reproduce narratively what she intended professionally. Repeatedly Oliphant insists that she cannot write about her literary career as other well-known authors have done. On the one hand, she distinguishes herself from such writers as Charlotte Brontë, whose feminine preoccupation with romance differs from her own "fuller conception of life," her "man's view of mortal affairs," with its sense that "the love between men and women, the marrying and giving in marriage, occupy in fact so small a portion of either existence or thought" (67); on the other hand, she refuses the wholly professionalized approach of Anthony Trollope, whose *Autobiography* begins with his intention to speak not of "my private life" but "of what I, and perhaps others round me, have done in literature."[51] Oliphant conceptualizes herself and her work differently: "Trollope's talk about the characters in his books astonished me beyond measure," she noted after reading his *Autobiography,* "and I am totally incapable of talking about anything I have ever done in that way" (4).

Whether failure or resistance, the second half of Oliphant's account includes a remarkable self-critique, a critical analysis of the domestic ideology to which she had so faithfully adhered. Most obviously, this critique exposes the limitations that her commitment to home and family imposed on her literary career. Oliphant became, in her own terms, a Victorian Andrea de Sarto, with "perhaps more than one Lucrezia to take care of" (5−6). As several critics have pointed out, her *Autobiography* comes increasingly to show the effects of a "del Sarto pattern" on her literary production: early achievement and promise hindered by family crisis with artistic compromise and inferior books resulting.[52] Oliphant's self-critique is most powerful in her analysis of the family crisis of 1868, when, at the height of her Carlingford series, her brother Frank filed for bankruptcy and she assumed responsibility for his family. Although she asserts that "at my most ambitious of times I would rather my children had remembered me as their mother" (130), she also recognizes the conflicting desire to produce lasting work—and her failure to do so: "An infinitude of pains and labour, and all to disappear like the stubble and the hay" (130).[53]

I want to suggest, however, that the self-critique in the closing pages of the *Autobiography* works not only to expose the limitations of domestic ideology on Oliphant's literary work but, more startlingly, to explore its effects on the home itself. Writing in the 1890s, an autobiographer could easily record the tension between domestic and literary work knowing that it was acceptable, even fashionable to do so. For more than a decade Oliphant's female contemporaries had registered the obstacles they faced in their professional memoirs (e.g., Howitt's *Autobiography*), their autobiographical fictions (e.g., Mary Cholmondeley's *Red Pottage*), and the New Woman novel. What Oliphant did, a far more difficult task, was to consider the effects of her ideology of work on her sons and their failed careers.

In contemplating Cyril's wasted life, she debates whether her "dearest, bright, delightful boy" missed his footing because of "inherited tendencies" or environmental (that is, domestic) influences. It is the latter that preoccupy her. Was it her own "foolish way" of taking her "work very lightly," not "let[ting] them know how hard pressed I was sometimes" (148), that caused her sons to misunderstand the nature of work? Or was it her habit "of laughing at superior people, the people who took themselves too seriously" (148), that taught them to treat life parodically, mocking real intellectual labor instead of earnestly engaging in it? These questions strike at the heart of Oliphant's ideology: if literary work is naturalized, treated as an extension or a version of maternal and domestic labor, then how can sons understand or enter the literary tradition their mother wishes them to continue? Oliphant implies that they cannot, that the domestic ideology sufficient for her career was inadequate for theirs. She acknowledges (almost) that male writers need an alternative model to motivate their work.

In this matter Oliphant was, once again, a shrewd reader of literary history and Victorian autobiography. In Mary Howitt's *Autobiography* the mother records her commitment to training her daughters for artistic careers and her encouragement of Anna Mary's work as an illustrator of her parents' poetry and prose; indeed, as Oliphant surely knew, Anna Mary wholly embraced her mother's ideology of work, writing the classic mid-Victorian account of female collaboration in her novella *Sisters in Art* (1853).[54] Yet, as Oliphant also knew, Mary Howitt narrates a different approach to the professional training of her sons. Howitt tells how, early in the 1850s, her husband, William, took the boys out to the colonies to "learn what opening there might be on the Australian continent for our sons" and how they eventually distinguished themselves in commercial and political careers.[55] As Howitt's autobiography reveals, the model for male (literary) work shifted significantly from what Oliphant and Mary Howitt had assumed at mid-century; whereas the Howitts entered their literary careers as collaborators, their sons and daughters assumed different, gendered patterns of work. "So departs," concludes Oliphant, "the practice and acquaintance of the world."[56]

Anthony Trollope's *Autobiography,* which Oliphant reviewed for *Good Words,* reproduces a similar historical shift away from a feminine domestic ideology toward a masculine model of the profession of letters—a sort of literary phylogeny of the professional artist-classes. In his second chapter, "My Mother," Trollope records the literary life of a woman who worked, much as Oliphant did, late into the night to salvage her family's fortunes and whose novels were composed while she nursed her dying husband and her sons. Trollope pays tribute to Frances Trollope's ability to write in the midst of family crisis, to his mother's "power of dividing herself into two parts, and keeping her intellect by itself clear" (24). But in the very formulation of his praise—her "power of dividing herself," continuing her domestic duties while "keeping her intellect" distinct—he anticipates the gendered distinction between domesticity and literary labor that would dominate the next generation of writers, male and female both, and that explains his own decision to treat literature as a public profession, distinct from "my private life" (1).

Oliphant refuses to consider her life in Trollopean terms (though she was often called a "female Trollope" and though her comments in *Good Words* about this "prolific writer" anticipate her defense of industry in her own *Autobiography*).[57] She also refuses to register, within her family memoir, the historical shift that Trollope reproduces and that she elsewhere recognized had taken place. Even though Oliphant praises Trollope's life as leaving behind "the example of useful exertion," an example that did much "to restore character and credit to the literary profession,[58] she does not write of her son Cecco or his brief literary career in Trollope's masculine mode. Instead, with her closing paragraphs on Cecco's life, on how "he righted himself and overcame . . . so as to be all that I had hoped" (148–49), she amalgamates her son and her self: "I can hear myself saying 'Cecco and I.' It was the constant phrase" (150). The son becomes part of the maternal writing, part of the family business, the "old Drumthwacket," and when he dies, both die with him: "And now here I am all alone. I cannot write any more" (150).

VI

Mary Cholmondeley's Bifurcated Autobiography: Eliotian and Brontëan Traditions in *Red Pottage* and *Under One Roof*

MARY CHOLMONDELEY (1859–1925) wrote two autobiographies: the first, *Red Pottage* (1899), an autobiographical fiction tracing the vicissitudes of an aspiring young writer blessed with genius but trapped in a life of domestic drudgery; the second, *Under One Roof* (1918), a more cheerful domestic memoir of life in the Shropshire rectory where Cholmondeley grew up with seven brothers and sisters. Neither represents, by any traditional definition, a pure autobiography, the first because it fictionalizes the author's experience, the second because it fails to construct a coherent self and produces something closer to biography than autobiography with its chapters on her father, mother, nanny, and younger sister Hester.[1] Indeed, in both books Mary Cholmondeley claimed to be memorializing Hester, who had died before she could pursue a writerly career.

Yet Cholmondeley considered both books to be versions of her own life story, and her reading public recognized them as such. Shortly after the success of *Red Pottage,* a brief biographical preface began to appear in new editions of Cholmondeley's novels, pointing out the parallels between her life and her fictional *Künstlerroman*. Magazine articles also recognized the parallels. In a column, "Autobiography and Fiction—Mary Cholmondeley's Stories and Her Life," the reviewer noted, for example, that like her protagonist, the author had grown up in a provincial clergyman's house; that she had spent some of her early years in London with a distinguished and witty grandmother who introduced her to society life; that she suffered from poor health, and thus "her work," like Hester's, "has been done in the semi-retirement consequent upon semi-illness." [2]

Cholmondeley acknowledged an even more fundamental autobiographical basis for her work. Of *Red Pottage* she wrote in her private journal: "I was the book before it was written. Why did they not see me then as they think they see me now? I am the same woman." [3] In her letters, she referred to episodes in *Red Pottage* as well-remembered incidents from childhood, to her brother as the "real Dick Vernon," and to herself as (at least in part) the protagonist, Hester. "I suppose there is a good deal of me in Hester," she wrote to her friend and mentor Rhoda Broughton. [4] Two decades later, in *Under One Roof,* she wrote of that same self in relational terms, as the daughter and sister of the family members she so strikingly portrays, and, as I shall argue, of the sororal commitment she so guiltily felt she had betrayed.

In this chapter, however, I approach Cholmondeley's two autobiographies not in terms of their authenticity or fictionality but as they represent two distinct strains of late nineteenth-century women's life writing, one descended from J. W. Cross's *George Eliot's Life as Related in Her Letters and Journals* (1885), the other from Elizabeth Gaskell's *Life of Charlotte Brontë* (1855). The Eliotean strain, dominant in *Red Pottage,* concentrates on the intellectual and artistic development of the woman writer, struggling with domestic repression, separating herself from provincial life and mores, and ultimately winning fame for the work of her genius. The Brontëan strain, dominant in *Under One Roof,* focuses instead on the household as the nursery of genius, on the collaborative and familial origins of authorship, if also on the difficult responsibility that sisters bear for memorializing the lives and genius of siblings who have died young. In Cholmondeley these two strains are contradictory—or, more precisely, they produce different versions of the woman writer's development in relation to domesticity. Both accounts differ from the mid-century model of authorship that attempted an ideological reconciliation of the writerly and domestic lives and that I traced in chapter V in Margaret Oliphant's *Autobiography.* Both ultimately expose the tensions that Oliphant was at such pains to resolve.

Within a month of its publication in October 1899, *Red Pottage* had become a success and a scandal. In Britain 8,000 copies of its first edition sold out by early November and 10,000 copies of its second edition soon thereafter; in the United States, by May 1900 the book was selling at the rate of 1,500 copies a day. Critics and clergymen debated its merits in the periodical press and the pulpit. The *Spectator* columnist called it a "brilliant and exhilarating novel"; another reviewer, a "masterpiece" that "challenges comparison with Charlotte Brontë." At the same time, a religious periodical claimed it was "a libel on the High Church clergy," a London clergyman denounced Cholmondeley from the pulpit, and a church newspaper suggested that the nasty portrait of the Reverend Mr. Gresley was written as "a piece of spite" because she had been "jilted by a clergyman."[5] Young London intellectuals in Henry James's circle asked each other, "Have you Read Pottage?" Percy Lubbock recalls, "Off we went in lively argument. Wasn't she clever? wasn't she cruel?—but wasn't she wise and just?—she was very amusing at all events, and very powerful."[6]

The immediate success of *Red Pottage* came, in part, because of its sensational tale of adultery and its shocking plot of a clergyman who destroys his sister's art. *Red Pottage* narrates two generically distinct if thematically related plots: the melodramatic tale of Rachel West, an heiress who loves a man trapped in an illicit affair and doomed to die by his own hand, and the *Künstlerroman* of Hester Gresley, a gifted New Woman writer. But the critical success of the novel came also, I believe, because readers like Henry James and Percy Lubbock recognized in it a tale of genius unfulfilled, of an Eliot-like artist defeated by the repressive forces of bourgeois culture. Hester Gresley is a George Eliot stuck in provincial "Middleshire," forced to endure the stupidities of a clergyman's household, unable financially or emotionally to break with her family and take up an independent professional career. We might say that the novel retells the life of George Eliot—the life revealed by Eliot's husband, J. W. Cross, in *George Eliot's Life* (1885)—without the break with Robert Evans or the move to literary work in London. It depicts what happens to a young woman writer like Cholmondeley who models her literary self on Eliot but who cannot enact the plot of Eliot's life in her own.

The Eliotian dimensions of *Red Pottage* have been recognized before, though only partially explored. Percy Lubbock, Cholmondeley's friend and literary executor, noted that Emerson was her mentor in life, Eliot in literature. As the novelist who had "uplifted [English fiction] to a moral and an intellectual eminence," George Eliot became the model for writers of Cholmondeley's generation, the woman artist who confirmed Mary "in her wrestle with the shapes of her own imagination." According to Lubbock, Eliot was a model in more practical literary matters as well: the setting of Cholmondeley's novels in "Middleshire," the attempt at "full-coloured drama in homely places," and the mixture of "serious story" with "comedy of characters and manners."[7] Following Lubbock, modern critics, most notably Vineta Colby and Elaine Showalter, have discussed Eliotian techniques and themes in *Red Pottage*, including the use of epigraphs, several from Eliot, all in imitation of *Middlemarch;* the Eliotian concerns with egoism and sympathy; and a moral aesthetic committed to the growth of sympathy in the reader.[8]

It is the (re)construction of Eliotian authorship, however, that most strikingly emerges in *Red Pottage* and that concerns me in this chapter. For Cholmondeley takes Eliot's life story as presented in Cross's *Life* and, in combination with elements from *The Mill on the Floss,* Eliot's most famously autobiographical novel, redirects the tradition of the Victorian woman writers' autobiography and *Künstlerroman.*

To a Victorian reader, as to a modern one, *George Eliot's Life* gives the impression of a bookish young woman, of a powerful mind intent on intellectual and moral growth. This impression begins with Cross's "Introductory Sketch of Childhood," which includes a précis of Mary Ann Evans's familial origins but concentrates on anecdotes of book learning—indeed, the passion for books—characteristic of the future author. Cross seems to have garnered every bookish incident he could recall. From "the first present I ever remember having received from my father," a little book titled *The Linnet's Life* (1822), which young Mary Anne read "over and over again"; to her "passionate delight and total absorption in Aesop's Fables"; to her humorous turn for "a Joe Miller's jest-book, with the stories from which she used greatly to astonish the family circle"; to her discovery of Scott's *Waverley* and the Elia essays, between which she "divided her childhood allegiance," Cross turns the "Introductory Sketch" into a bibliographic essay on Eliot's youthful reading.[9] His emphasis on Eliot's passion for books is modified only by his discussion of "the religious side of her nature," which "developed to a remarkable degree" (1:23) under the tutelage of Miss Lewis at Miss Wallington's school. But even as he mentions Eliot's attraction to Evangelical doctrine and her "works of active charity," Cross stresses the fact that "she was always prosecuting an active intellectual life of her own" (1:33).

A concern for the life of the mind and a passion for books can, in a sense, be seen as a conventional feature of literary auto/biography: one thinks, for example, of six-year-old Felicia Hemans reading Shakespeare "while seated in the branches of an apple-tree" or reciting "whole pages of poetry after a single reading," or of Harriet Martineau, at age seven, discovering the "plain, clumsy, calf-bound volume of 'Paradise Lost'" that fixed her "mental destiny" for the "next seven years."[10] Yet *George Eliot's Life* altered the relative importance of these anecdotes in the tradition of women's life writing. Prior to Cross's *Life,* such anecdotes revealing a bookish inclination and foreshadowing a literary career had been complemented by details of the woman writer's domestic development: one thinks again of Felicia Browne falling in love with the romantic Captain Hemans of the Royal Welsh Fusiliers, whom she married at age sixteen, or of Harriet Martineau's describing her training in housewifery, typically required of middle-class girls: "I platted bonnets at one time, knitted stockings as I read aloud, covered silk shoes for dances, and made all my garments."[11] In *George Eliot's Life* such domestic elements are largely eliminated, whether consciously or not, by virtue of Cross's decision to relate Eliot's life "in extracts from her own letters" (1:38). We might say, in fact, that Cross's editorial decision—and the letters themselves—changed the way women writers understood their lives and their professional development.[12]

Because the letters begin in 1838, just before Eliot turned nineteen, they pass over childhood and immerse the reader in the rapidly developing mind and opinions of the future author. Because, moreover, the earliest letters come from a correspondence with Maria Lewis, Eliot's teacher, they dwell almost exclusively on books and the ideas found in them. As Gordon Haight has suggested, Maria Lewis was the first "to perceive the remarkable quality of her [pupil's] mind," and she became "more like an elder sister than a governess."[13] In the first letters to Miss Lewis, for example, Eliot reports on a visit to London, reflects on her reading of Pascal, Samuel Johnson, Philip Doddridge, Hannah More, and Edward Young, and meditates on the possibility of "becoming as eminently holy as St. Paul" (1:39–42). Even when she touches on less bookish matters, Eliot tends to moralize and intellectualize, as if all human experience were primarily a matter of thought. "For my part," she tells Miss Lewis, "when I hear of the marrying and giving in marriage that is constantly being transacted, I can only sigh for those who are multiplying earthly ties which, though powerful enough to detach their hearts and thoughts from heaven, are so brittle as to be snapped asunder at every breeze" (1:40). No doubt this was the sort of comment that provoked Margaret Oliphant to remark that Eliot had lived "in a mental green-house,"[14] but it (and the bent of mind it represents) allowed young writers like Mary Cholmondeley to assert the importance of their intellectual and spiritual growth, to the minimization of romantic and domestic interests.

If *George Eliot's Life* tells a bookish story, it also registers the importance of female friendships in the development of the woman writer—another important influence on Cholmondeley's work. Almost exclusively, the early chapters of the *Life* derive from Eliot's correspondence with Maria Lewis, Sara Hennell, Mrs. Bray (née Caroline Hennell), and Mrs. Pears (née Elizabeth Bray). The names of these women appear regularly and prominently in the text of the *Life,* another result of Cross's editorial policy, in this case the listing of dates and correspondents in the margins. Eliot's epistolary exchanges with female friends provided a genuine education; in effect, they were an alternative to a university curriculum or the provincial (and far inferior) schooling of her brother Isaac. The letters give detailed analyses of the books Eliot read, accounts of her "mental characteristics" (1:145), and early evidence of her aspirations as a writer. From the "doggerel lines, the crude fruit of a lonely walk," that she sent to Maria Lewis in 1839 to the anxieties and pleasures expressed in letters to Sara Hennell and Caroline Bray in 1844–45 as she translated Strauss's *Das Leben Jesu,* the letters show Eliot becoming an author. These early letters testify to the essential role of same-sex friendship in women's mental and moral development.[15] Without the companionship of such women as Lewis and Hennell as fellow intellectuals, Mary Ann Evans would never have become George Eliot—or so Cross's *Life* implies.

Whether or not Cross intended this point, the life history he constructed gives a remarkably original picture of the intellectual lives of nineteenth-century women. As we have seen, earlier autobiographies focus on the role of male mentors or companions in female development. Martineau's *Autobiography* describes its subject's intellectual growth in conjunction with that of her brother James, then as compensation for the loss of James during his college training. Barrett Browning's *Aurora Leigh* imagines a young woman's discovery of her paternal intellectual inheritance as a secret intellectual life unshared with other women. Oliphant's *Autobiography* concentrates on the family circle, mother and brothers alike, in tracing its subject's entry into the literary profession. Only Mary Robinson's *Memoirs,* written nearly a century earlier, holds out the possibility of a female intellectual community in its account of Meribah Lorrington's Sapphic academy—but then leaves that possibility unfulfilled as Robinson discovers the treacheries of professional literary women.

If Cross's *Life* depicts intimate friendships with women, it also underscores the necessity of a break with domestic life, as most of those earlier Victorian autobiographies did not. For Mary Ann Evans this break came naturally with the death of her father in 1849. Chapters I and II of the *Life* (covering the years 1838–46) chart young Mary Ann Evans's intellectual development as she reads books, records her responses, and exchanges views with her female friends. Chapter III, "Life in Coventry till Mr. Evans's death," then suggests, albeit subtly, that Mary Ann Evans needed to escape the restrictions of family life, that she needed to transcend her provincial origins, however helpful the Hennell-Bray-Pears relationship may have been in nurturing her literary, theological, and moral growth. Because Cross naturalizes this transition, making it the result of death rather than a conscious decision to leave behind her friends and family, *George Eliot's Life* glosses over the conflict between domestic duty and literary aspiration. In effect, the *Life* eliminates (or sequentializes) the conflict. Eliot appears first as dutiful daughter nursing her father through his final illness, then as independent thinker, editor, and writer taking up her career in London. Whether naturalized or not, however, the *Life* insists on a pattern of independent movement away from home followed by individualistic achievement in the professional realm.

When Mary Cholmondeley adapted the Eliotian pattern of authorship in *Red Pottage,* she could assume the importance of female friendship and intellectual companionship in the making of the woman artist, but she could not, as we shall see, naturalize the transition from domestic to professional life. Cholmondeley may have derived some of her high-minded sentiments about friendship from Emerson's essay "Friendship," perhaps even some of her cadences from Emerson's prose.[16] Indeed, Cholmondeley's sister Hester once caustically remarked in her journal, "N——was tried at luncheon by Mary's Emersonian views of friendship."[17]

Despite the Emersonian influence, the model of female friendship and the language of its expression in *Red Pottage* are decidedly Eliotian.

As in *George Eliot's Life,* the early chapters of *Red Pottage* focus on friendship between women as the source of artistic vocation and literary production. We meet Hester Gresley, the New Woman writer, first through Rachel West's passionate defense of her friend's novel *Idyll of East London,* then through the narrator's meditation on women's friendship:

> *Many sarcastic but true words have been said by man, and in no jealous spirit, concerning woman's friendship for woman. The passing judgment of the majority of men on such devotion might be summed up in the words, "Occupy till I come." It does occupy till they do come. . . . But nevertheless here and there among its numberless counterfeits a friendship rises up between two women which sustains the life of both, which is still young when life is waning, which man's love and motherhood cannot displace nor death annihilate; a friendship which is not the solitary affection of an empty heart nor the deepest affection of a full one, but which nevertheless lightens the burdens of this world and lays its pure hand upon the next.*[18]

Cholmondeley's commentary reproduces, in abstract and generalized form, Eliot's expressions of love and sorority in her letters to Sara Hennell and Cara Bray. Writing from Geneva, where Eliot went to recuperate after her father's death, she assured Sara: "Never make apologies about your letters, or your words, or anything else. It is your soul to which I am wedded; and do I not know too well how the soul is doubly belied—first by the impossibility of being in word and act as great, as loving, as good as it wills to be, and again by the miserable weaknesses of the friends who see the words and acts through all sorts of mists raised by their own passions and preoccupations?" (1:240). More confidently, writing from London after her return to England and her assumption of editorial responsibilities at the *Westminster Review,* Eliot told Sara: "It is impossible that I should ever love two women better than I love you and Cara. Indeed it seems to me that I can never love any so well; and it is certain that I can never have any friend—not even a husband—who would supply the loss of those associations with the past which belong to you" (1:277). This language of love between female friends that surpasses the marital bond and survives the maternal experience comes not from Emerson's essays or Eliot's novels but from Eliot's letters.[19]

In the friendship of Hester Gresley and Rachel West in *Red Pottage* Cholmondeley translates such sentiments into fictional form; indeed, her *Künstlerroman* envisions the effects of a powerful female friendship as Eliot's own novels never did.[20] For not only do Hester and Rachel offer mutual support during various emotional and financial crises, as women might be expected to do; their friendship more fundamentally initiates Hester's career as a writer. During childhood Hester introduces fiction into Rachel's otherwise "stolid, solid, silent" life as she tells stories of captive princesses and rescuing princes, of talking sparrows and magical trees, and as she commemorates through poetry their experiences, comic and tragic alike (29). During late adolescence Hester discovers her vocation through her love for Rachel—what Cholmondeley calls "the yearning of her soul" (37). As Ann Ardis has argued, in the closing scene of chapter VI, which includes a retrospective history of their friendship, "Cholmondeley presents Hester's love for Rachel as the primary motivation for her art."[21] Hester's "yearning" toward her friend "lit up something which had long lain colossal but inapprehended in the depths of her mind. . . . She saw, as in a dream, terrible, beautiful, inaccessible, but distinct, where her power lay" (37). This visionary moment is followed by the announcement: "A year later Hester's first book, 'An Idyll of East London,' was reaping its harvest of astonished indignation and adulation" (38). The narrative thus links sororal love with authorial production.

By arguing that the Hester-Rachel friendship in *Red Pottage* reproduces the Mary-Sara-Cara friendship of Cross's *Life*, I do not mean to exclude other autobiographical and literary influences. Mary Cholmondeley's sisters—Diana, Victoria, and Hester especially—encouraged and influenced her literary career. The dedication of her first novels, *The Danvers Jewels* and *Sir Charles Danvers,* to Diana—"To my sister 'Di' I affectionately dedicate the story which she helped me to write"—alludes less to collaborative writing than to emotional support during a period of "darkness and depression."[22] The dedication of *Red Pottage* to Victoria—"Good things have not kept aloof, / I have not lack'd thy mild reproof, / Nor golden largess of thy praise"—commemorates the friendship that bonded two sister-artists, one a writer, the other a painter.[23] Even the names of her protagonists—Diana of *Diana Tempest,* Hester of *Red*

Pottage—attest to the sisterly bonds that underlie Cholmondeley's fiction. And, more practically, we might credit Rhoda Broughton, as family friend, fellow novelist, and literary mentor, with initiating Cholmondeley's writerly career by taking the manuscript of *The Danvers Jewels* to her publisher, George Bentley, and encouraging its publication.[24]

More generally, Cholmondeley's thematics of sisterhood fulfills a feminist idea expressed as early as 1852 in Anna Mary Howitt's novella *Sisters in Art,* and one that flourished in the New Woman novels of the 1880s and 1890s. Howitt's novella argues the case for a women's art college as it depicts a group of women friends living and working together, "sisters in love and unity—as SISTERS IN ART." Howitt's three women protagonists win an artistic competition because together they combine "three truths rarely found so united in design—the natural, the scientific, and the artistic."[25] The novella thus rationalizes collaboration not only on the grounds of emotional or financial support but, more significantly, with the argument that collaboration produces superior artistic work. New Woman novelists may not have written so concretely about art colleges or so confidently about women's achievements, but they too embraced the ideology of women's collaboration. As Ann Ardis points out, the concerns of New Woman novelists differ from those of their male contemporaries and the high modernists who follow them: "[Cholmondeley's] characterization of Hester Gresley's deep love for Rachel West, her friend and her artistic subject, is to be contrasted with, for example, Joyce's oft-quoted characterization of the artist's godlike remove from his work in *Portrait of the Artist as a Young Man.*"[26]

If Cholmondeley rewrites *George Eliot's Life* by borrowing its scenes and sources of artistic origin, she does not complete its plot of artistic achievement: the move to London, the "marriage" to George Henry Lewes, the successful attempt at fiction, the growing fame as a novelist. As I have suggested, *Red Pottage* imagines a woman author whose life stagnates in the provinces, whose plot does not naturally release her from domestic duties. Like her creator, Hester lives for a while in London under the protection of an aunt, Lady Susan Gresley, just as Cholmondeley had lived with her grandmother, the "beautiful and witty" Mrs. Legard.[27] Yet despite an auspicious beginning, Hester never becomes an eminent writer. We might say that Cholmondeley asks, "Why didn't I become a George Eliot?"—a version of the question Margaret Oliphant posed while reading Cross's *Life,* as she wondered what she might have become had she not "been handicapped in life." [28] Cholmondeley does not handicap her woman artist by giving her a large family like Oliphant's to support, but she nonetheless imagines the obstacles to Hester's success as domestic.

In *Red Pottage* the conflict Hester faces emerges from a sibling rivalry, from the intellectual, religious, and aesthetic disagreements that separate Hester from her obtuse clergyman brother, James. Whatever its psychological basis, the conflict expresses itself domestically. Like many of Eliot's heroines, most notably Maggie Tulliver, Hester feels tied to her brother by bonds of affection and obligation; these bonds, which lead her to live with James and his family after the death of her aunt, hinder—and ultimately destroy—her art. Cholmondeley frames the conflict between domesticity and artistry in Eliotian terms, using an epigraph from *Middlemarch* to introduce the chapter that depicts Hester's predicament:

> *Only those who know the supremacy of the intellectual life—the life which has a seed of ennobling thought and purpose within it—can understand the grief of one who falls from the serene activity into the absorbing soul-wasting struggle with worldly annoyance.* [29]

In *Middlemarch* this sentence explains Lydgate's agony as he realizes that his romantic and domestic choices have undermined his professional goals. In *Red Pottage* its repetition suggests that women, too, have intellectual and professional ambitions that their domestic situations spoil. The epigraph neatly—and perhaps too simply—frames the tensions as a dichotomy: between artistry and domesticity, intellectual activity and worldly annoyance, patriarchy and women's creativity.

In the plot of *Red Pottage,* Cholmondeley leaves no doubt as to who or what destroys Hester's art. The villain is the Reverend James Gresley, the agent of patriarchy. In chapter 39 we read, in excruciating detail, the process by which James discovers, edits, mutilates, and then burns the proof sheets of his sister's new novel. All the emotional and intellectual differences that have separated sister and brother emerge in the process— from James's jealousy that Hester should dedicate the book to her friend Rachel and care "nothing of blood relations" (257), to the conventionality that causes him to misread passages of original thought for error, to his exaggerated amour propre that makes him bristle at Hester's critique of the clergy, to the theological dogmatism that leads him to mistake allegory for apostasy. As the reviewer for *The Spectator* said in one of the first notices of the novel, Hester Gresley "suffers a perfect martyrdom at the hands of her brother, a fanatically narrow-minded clergyman, and his devoted but equally exasperating wife." [30]

The fact that readers can so easily identify the villain—and view Hester as a victim—might lead us to note that *Red Pottage* departs from its Eliotian origins and wonder why Cholmondeley has simplified where Eliot would have complicated. In Eliot, villainy and victimization are never so clear, nor is agency so completely removed from the protagonist's hands. In *The Mill on the Floss,* Maggie Tulliver's love for her brother leads to both her heroism *and* her self-destruction. In *Middlemarch* Lydgate's emotional complexity leads to his fatal attraction to Rosamund but also displays itself in a "native warm-heartedness," a dread of "a future without affection," and a susceptibility—that of "a loving-hearted man"—to his wife's "words and tears." [31] In contrast, in the life story of the artist in *Red Pottage* Cholmondeley abandons Eliotian complexity and turns to the moral simplicity of melodrama.

We might interpret Cholmondeley's departure from Eliot in two somewhat contradictory ways: either as a desire to correct a flaw in *George Eliot's Life* or as a refusal to acknowledge a flaw in her own. Cross's *Life,* unlike the subsequent biographies of Eliot with which modern readers are familiar, avoids or obscures domestic disruptions. It eliminates the conflict between Mary Ann Evans and her brother Isaac; it glosses over the sharp religious dispute with her father that nearly sent Eliot into lodgings and that today we refer to as her "Holy War." [32] In Cross's version of his wife's personal history, domestic disruptions have little impact on Eliot's professional aspirations or development. Unlike the lives of her fictional heroines, Eliot's life emerges organically, without dramatic ruptures, with only the ordinary separations from home and family that result from marriage and death.

Cholmondeley must have read between the lines of Eliot's letters— and read Eliot's novels as the more accurate emotional autobiography. *Red Pottage* relies on Eliot's novel *The Mill on the Floss* rather than on Cross's *Life* when it plots the course of female development. It turns to the emotional economy of *The Mill* for its understanding of sibling love, rivalry, and repression, and it insists, at least in part, on the pathological basis of artistic creativity.

In *Red Pottage* Cholmondeley represents a relationship between personal pain and artistic achievement that she found in Eliot's life and that she also recognized in her own. Cholmondeley once said that her fiction emerged from pain and repression, not from happiness:

> *If I had been a pretty graceful girl who had danced herself into a fairly happy, entirely commonplace marriage, . . . I could never have arrived where I am today. It is not my talent which has placed me where I am, but the repression of my youth, my unhappy love-affair, the having to confront a hard dull life, devoid of anything I cared for intellectually, and being hampered at every turn I feebly made by constant illness.*[33]

Hester Gresley may not be quite so unhappy, but like Cholmondeley and like the young, awkward Mary Ann Evans, she faces "a hard dull life" devoid of romance and burdened by domestic drudgery. Hester's novels emerge as she confronts her pain and transforms it into art (as we know from passages of her new novel, which concern the soul's struggle "to clothe itself anew" and which are quoted by her brother as he mutilates the pages).[34] Hester can no longer achieve this transformation when her brother brutally intervenes; he reverses the process by inflicting too much pain and destroying his sister's work.

By making Hester's brother the obstacle to the woman writer's achievement, Cholmondeley targets patriarchal institutions—the bourgeois family, the Anglican church, the small English village—as the "problem." In so doing, she writes a powerful critique of what we today call Victorian domestic ideology. She also avoids, however, another possible explanation for Hester's predicament and her own failure to become George Eliot. She avoids the question of talent or genius.

Cross's *Life* had insisted that Eliot was no infant prodigy, that her intellect and moral sense developed slowly, if also surely: "Hers was a large, slow-growing nature; and I think it is at any rate certain that there was nothing of the infant phenomenon about her" (1:15). Like many subsequent biographers, Cross also insisted that Eliot possessed no innate aptitude for fiction, that she remained uncertain of her talents until late in life. He even reproduced her long essay "How I Came to Write Fiction" to show her ambivalence: "I always thought I was deficient in dramatic power, both of construction and dialogue . . . as the years passed on I lost any hope that I should ever be able to write a novel, just as I desponded about everything else in my future life" (1:414).

Cholmondeley does not allow such uncertainty to touch Hester Gresley, her woman writer. Like the child prodigies of Romantic poetry, Hester is gifted from birth with the arts of storytelling and versemaking. As an adult, when Hester struggles to complete her novel, she faces the petty domestic disturbances of the Gresley household, and she must strive mightily to make her art realize her high aspirations, but there is little sense that she will fail for lack of genius or will. Cholmondeley even frees her ideal artist from the heaviest of women's burdens—maternity—by separating biologically reproductive women such as Rachel from literarily productive women writers such as Hester. (In this detail, too, she follows *George Eliot's Life,* in which Eliot's books become her children—"the Mill," for example, "my youngest child.")[35]

In *Red Pottage* Hester's art becomes a sacred trust, a spiritual mission. The novel allegorizes Art as a modern Christ calling the woman artist to walk "upon the troubled waves of art" (154), and Hester's struggle is figured as the disciple's desire and fear: "She had trusted and doubted, had fallen and been sustained, had met the wind and the rain, after she had sunk in despair, and risen again, she knew not how, now at length a great wave—the last—had cast her half-drowned upon the shore. A miracle had happened" (154). Although the language of this allegory includes despair and faith, sinking and rising, there can be little doubt as to Hester's worthiness or her novel's worth.

It is usually suggested that Cholmondeley idealizes her woman writer in an attempt to memorialize her sister Hester, who died young. I suggest that Cholmondeley idealizes her woman writer as an apotropaic gesture, as a means of self-protection and psychological defense. In this interpretation of her writerly history, Cholmondeley is able to avoid, as autobiographers such as Oliphant could not, the troubling question of inferior achievement. She never need ask herself why her life was only partially Eliotian. The answer to the question "Why did I fail to become a George Eliot?" is made both simple and incomplete—simple in that the answer is "Victorian patriarchy"; incomplete in that the answer eliminates specific flaws or gaps in the writer's self, those matters of ability, temperament, and will that must necessarily be part of an individual's life story.

In *A Literature of Their Own* Elaine Showalter has argued that "most nineteenth-century women novelists seem to have found [George Eliot] a troubling and demoralizing competitor, one who created an image of the woman artist they could never equal."[36] In Showalter's account, which includes extensive documentation of attacks on Eliot by contemporaries, Mary Cholmondeley emerges as a rare admirer, not a detractor. Certainly, Cholmondeley admired Eliot—as we know from the plots of her early novels, her imitation of Eliotian techniques, and her comments to fellow writers. Yet we may wonder whether Cholmondeley's admiration and extensive imitation became possible only by reproducing selective features of Eliot's career and repressing or altering the differences from her own.

Red Pottage gives us an Eliotian version of Cholmondeley's life: a life of intellectual and aesthetic development, of enabling friendships with women and the occasional enlightened man, of devotion to art and the gifts of genius, if not finally of literary fame. When Cholmondeley returned to her life story two decades later, she produced a different account of her artistic development, this time in Brontëan rather than Eliotian terms.

When, at the climax of *Red Pottage,* James Gresley destroys the manuscript of his sister's novel, he tells his wife: "I have been reading the worst book I have come across yet, and it was written by my own sister under my own roof." The narrator ironically comments, "He might have added 'close under the roof,' if he had remembered the little attic chamber where the cold of winter and the heat of summer had each struck in turn and in vain at the indomitable perseverance of the writer of those many pages" (261). Mary Cholmondeley used a version of this key phrase, "under my own roof," as the title of a domestic memoir she wrote nineteen years after *Red Pottage. Under One Roof: A Family Record* (1918) tells a tale of life in a provincial rectory quite different from that in her autobiographical fiction. As she recalls the actual father, mother, and nanny who had raised her and her seven siblings, Cholmondeley rewrites the story of a woman artist's development in relational rather than individual terms and reconsiders her literary career—and her sister's—as Brontëan myth. *Under One Roof* is thus a corrective memoir, recreating the environment in which Cholmondeley grew up, redrawing the portraits of the provincial clergyman and his family, and revealing Cholmondeley's guilt about her abandonment of a sororal model of writing.

The corrective intention of *Under One Roof* is readily apparent in the portrait of Cholmondeley's father with which the memoir opens and in the sketch of her sister Hester, the aspiring young writer idealized in *Red Pottage*. The first section, titled simply "Father," portrays a clergyman who is virtually the antithesis of the fictional James Gresley. Whereas the Reverend Gresley is doctrinally narrow, literarily and socially conventional, the Reverend Richard Cholmondeley becomes—in his daughter's portrayal—a "last representative of a by-gone class of clergyman" (3), an incarnation of George Eliot's Mr. Irwine, with "all the distinction and kindliness of a Mr. Irwine and with it, what Mr. Irwine lacked, an abounding energy which naturally spent itself on his parish" (10).

Many of the details Cholmondeley includes in the portrait of her father seem intended to correct possible misapprehensions readers may have taken from her novel. In her memoir, for example, she pointedly notes that her father "lived on terms of lifelong sympathy and friendship with local nonconformists" (10) (as Gresley, who publicly called Dissenters "worms," did not), and she explains that her father instituted a second communion service on Sunday not to require double attendance (as Gresley did) but to accommodate parishioners who could not attend a morning service. Cholmondeley makes her father, in contrast to the verbally clumsy Gresley, the source of the family's literary talent and aesthetic sensibility, as she remembers him composing songs, accompanying himself on the piano, and building his children a toy theater. She even revises the anecdote about the parishioner who, answering a question about whether he believes in the devil, says: "Believe in him! I would not trust him for a moment!" In her autobiographical retelling, her father emerges as a clergyman of mild temper but firm faith: "Now, I won't have that old friend of my childhood taken from me" (16)—a reproof the fictional James Gresley could not have articulated.

Given this nostalgic, even hagiographic treatment of her father, we may wonder why Cholmondeley worried so much about the reception of her memoir. To Rhoda Broughton she confessed: "My little volume

'Under One Roof' will be out early in January to avoid the Christmas traffic in gift books. I rather tremble in my shoes as to what extent those two excellent men my brothers will think of it. They will I fear expect the 4 people dealt with to be portrayed as perfect characters: and I greatly fear that what seems to *me* character drawing will seem to *them* disloyalty."[37] One explanation for her fear is that, in characterizing her father as an old-fashioned clergyman, untrained in parish duties and untouched by crises of faith, Cholmondeley makes him appear ineffectual to modern eyes. A more likely reason is that the second section, "Mother," depicts a depressed woman temperamentally disinclined to rectory life, better suited to a career as a college don without children or domestic responsibilities, but unfortunately paralyzed after the birth of her eighth child, Hester—and thus scarcely the traditional maternal heroine of a Victorian family memoir. Certainly, Cholmondeley could not have feared her brothers' reaction to the third section of the memoir, "Ninny," a tribute to their "beloved nurse" (55), whose "boundless love" (66) embodied the words of St. Paul to the Corinthians: "Ninny's love indeed suffered long and was kind, did not seek its own, thought no evil, bore all things, believed all things, hoped all things, endured all things—*never failed*" (67, paraphrasing I Cor. 13:4–7).

Although the portrayals of her father and mother may have seemed disloyal, what Cholmondeley feared most, I suggest, is that her memoir revealed a more fundamental kind of disloyalty—a disloyalty to her sister Hester, to the literary life of the family, and to the domestic ethos that had instigated her own literary career. Cholmondeley explains in her introduction that she wrote *Under One Roof* to honor her sister Hester, who had aspired to become an author but whose illness and early death put an end to such plans. Writing the memoir is thus a commemorative as well as retrospective act. "For several years, as I had leisure," Cholmondeley tells us in the preface, "I worked, sometimes for months together, at arranging and sorting the great piles of her manuscripts, reading the diary and making copious extracts from it in hope of one day writing a memoir of her, and incorporating with it what seemed to be the best of her serried masses of poems, essays, stories" (xiii–xiv). Cholmondeley gave up on the project, however; she reached the conclusion that "the material for such a volume, even after diligent sifting, remained too immature, had not sufficient originality to justify publication" (xiv). What she does not reveal until late in the memoir is that she had promised Hester, on her deathbed, that she would "make a book of her best stories and essays for private circulation" (121)—a promise she did not keep. What she only partially reveals is that this promise emerged from a Brontëan model of authorship that had informed the Cholmondeley sisters' early lives and literary work—a model Cholmondeley had abandoned.

Those who knew the Cholmondeley family often pointed out the parallels between the Brontës' lives at Haworth and the Cholmondeleys' at Hodnet. Percy Lubbock noted, for instance, that Mary Cholmondeley fell into the English tradition of the novel-writing parson's daughter: "We know that there is no such hand at firing scandal with her novel-writing as the shy maiden-daughter of an English country parsonage. Before Mary there was Charlotte, the other clergyman's daughter from the north; and since Mary there is doubtless many another—there's Kate and Caroline, to be sure." [38] Hester's diary noted another parallel in meditating on a visitor's reaction to their lives in such remote, limited circumstances: "We are heavy and serious. . . . C—— [the visitor] says we are narrow, or rather we have been cramped, and never allowed fair play" (103). In *Under One Roof* Cholmondeley associates her siblings with the Brontës even more explicitly. As she recalls "we four sisters" racing "up and down the old schoolroom to get warm," "walking swiftly, our hands in our muffs," having "long discussions on books and people and Life," she imagines the Cholmondeley girls as a reincarnation of the Brontës: "Later on when I read Mrs. Gaskell's *Life of the Brontës,*" she adds, "I realized with surprise that other eager young women had walked up and down their old schoolroom just as we had done, before we were born" (102–3). [39]

Cholmondeley's slip—it is Gaskell's *Life of Charlotte Brontë,* not *of the Brontës*—reveals her difficulty as autobiographer: her memory insists on familial aspirations rather than singular achievement. [40] As Cholmondeley recalls growing up in Hodnet Rectory, her memory encompasses a *group* of sisters with intellectual and literary aspirations, at least one of whom besides herself produced an enormous quantity of literary work. In retrospect, Cholmondeley comes up against the fact that she was not alone in wishing to pursue an artistic career. This realization forces a paradigm shift: What would her past reveal if she considered her life within a Brontëan rather than Eliotian framework? Unlike *George Eliot's Life,* which traces the career of an extraordinary individual and which informs the narrative of *Red Pottage,* Gaskell's *Life of Charlotte Brontë* follows the development of a woman writer who was the center—and survivor—of an artistically gifted group of siblings.

In *Under One Roof* Cholmondeley reconsiders herself as a latter-day Brontë. Many of the details she includes in the memoir have precedents in *The Life of Charlotte Brontë,* to the extent that *Under One Roof* seems both influenced by Gaskell's work and celebratory of the model of authorship she depicts. Cholmondeley's memoir, like Gaskell's, includes a clergyman-father with literary talent and pride in his children's artistic accomplishments, as well as a faithful nurse (Tabby for the Brontës, Ninny for the Cholmondeleys) who replaces a dead or invalid mother. It depicts an isolated childhood in northern England (Yorkshire for the Brontës, Shropshire for the Cholmondeleys), which makes the children dependent on themselves for amusement and encourages them in exercises of the literary imagination. Most sadly, *Under One Roof* recounts a family history of illness that begins with the mother and infects the children, plaguing several of the sisters (including Mary) with asthma and ending in a consumptive death for Hester, as it did for all the Brontë children.

Beyond significant details, however, is the role that *The Life of Charlotte Brontë* creates for its central figure, a role that haunts Cholmondeley's reminiscences of her siblings.[41] Gaskell imagines Charlotte, the eldest surviving sister, as the instigator of the Brontës' literary production, the faithful nurse of her dying sisters, and finally the commemorator of their lives and work. *Under One Roof* reveals that Cholmondeley struggled with these roles, her Eliotian conception of authorship at odds with her Brontëan sense of domestic responsibility. As we can guess from *Red Pottage,* for many years Cholmondeley wanted to escape the life of the rectory—as Charlotte Brontë presumably did not, at least not according to Gaskell's *Life.*

The role of literary instigator and leader was one that Charlotte Brontë had consciously assumed. According to her preface to the 1850 edition of *Wuthering Heights* and *Agnes Grey,* published just after her sisters' deaths, Charlotte had discovered her sisters' literary talents and proposed joint publication. Gaskell repeats the story, in Charlotte's words, in the first volume of the *Life:*

One day in the autumn of 1845, I accidentally lighted on a MS. vol-
ume of verse, in my sister Emily's hand-writing. Of course, I was not
surprised, knowing that she could and did write verse: I looked it over,
and something more than surprise seized me—a deep conviction that
these were not common effusions, nor at all like the poetry women gen-
erally write.[42]

In this now-famous narrative of literary discovery, Charlotte persuades a
reluctant Emily to publish and encourages Anne, in whose poetry she
finds "a sweet sincere pathos," to join the venture. Gaskell emphasizes
Charlotte's tenacity in her pursuit of literary fame for the three sisters.
She describes Charlotte writing to publishers for advice, buying a book
about preparing a manuscript for the press, and negotiating details of
printing and advertising with their publisher, Aylott & Jones. When the
volume of poetry fails, Charlotte then suggests that the sisters try fiction,
informing Aylott & Jones that "C. E. and A. Bell . . . are preparing for
the press a work of fiction, consisting of three distinct and unconnected
tales, which may be either published together, as a work of three
volumes, . . . or separately, as single volumes" (292). In *The Life of Char-*
lotte Brontë Gaskell may celebrate the achievements of an extraordinary
literary family, but the title of her memoir quite rightly focuses on the
figure who made that achievement possible.

   In comparison with Brontë, Cholmondeley registers her failures—
sometimes clearly, sometimes less perspicaciously than she might. As the
eldest sister, she tells, in a Brontëan mode, of the romantic fiction-
making in which the sisters engaged, a practice that required Mary to
invent wild adventure tales whenever she returned home from social visits. When Cholmondeley describes this practice, however, she assumes
the active role of narrator to Victoria and Hester as listeners, and while
she suggests that these stories "possibly fired Hester to literary composition" (76), this insight comes far too late. Cholmondeley guiltily admits
that during Hester's lifetime she never discovered her sister's talent for
fiction-making: "I do not think that any of us realized in those days that
we had 'a chiel'—an affectionate but lynx-eyed chiel—'amang us taking
notes.' . . . After her death we discovered that she had left an enormous
mass of manuscript, including a diary in many volumes" (xiii). The for-

mulation here ("any of us") displaces responsibility for recognition of Hester's talent onto the entire family, whereas it might be seen as primarily Mary's. Charlotte Brontë had assumed that her sisters possessed literary talent similar to her own, and she "discovered" their work, we might say, because she thought of her own writing not as singular but as familial or sororal. Despite the fact that Hester began making books by the age of twelve—literally, creating volumes with such titles as "Hester Cholmondeley: My Travels on the Continent of Europe" and "Cholmondeley's Poetry Composed by Her"—and despite the fact that Hester won a prize in *Little Folks* magazine at age thirteen (79) and began contributing regularly to *The Sunflower,* a children's magazine, at age sixteen (89), Mary Cholmondeley seems to have been blind to her sister's literary aspirations.

What produced such blindness? For one thing, Cholmondeley's conception of authorship in the 1870s, when Hester was composing these many volumes, prevented her from seeing writing as a sororal enterprise; in her imitation of Eliot, Cholmondeley became so deeply immersed in her own development, in the model of singular achievement, that she failed others. Had she looked from a Brontëan viewpoint, she might have recognized her sister's talent. For another, we can speculate that Cholmondeley's reevaluation of her career from its end rather than in medias res, as well as her deep concern for her family's survival during the First World War, shifted her perspective as autobiographer from self to family unit.[43] (*Under One Roof,* after all, includes no section titled "Mary"; its approach is thoroughly relational.) Whether for these or other reasons, the 1918 memoir seeks to remind its readers of Cholmondeley's role as "ever-watchful nurse" of her dying sister and to restore her place as commemorator of the lives and literary work of her sisters, despite her confession that she initially failed.

The phrase "ever-watchful nurse" comes from *The Life of Charlotte Brontë,* as Gaskell describes Charlotte's care of Anne, "this youngest, last sister," in her final illness (363). Emily Brontë resisted the ministrations of her family; according to Gaskell, she "adhered tenaciously to her habits of independence. She would suffer no one to assist her. Any effort to do so roused the old stern spirit" (356). In contrast, Charlotte and Anne shared their final hours together as "nursing and dying sister." In Gaskell's words: "Charlotte had the comfort of being able to talk to her about her state; a comfort rendered inexpressibly great by the contrast which it presented to the recollection of Emily's rejection of all sympathy" (364).

Cholmondeley's narrative of Hester's death follows Gaskell's example closely; in fact, the insight that the Cholmondeley sisters resembled the Brontës irrupts within the narrative of Hester's illness. Just as Gaskell discusses Anne's constitutional delicacy, "a fact which perhaps made them less aware than they would otherwise have been of the true nature of those fatal first symptoms" (363), so Cholmondeley laments that Hester's asthma, a disease from which several of the family suffered, made them "lamentably slow to take alarm" (101). Just as Charlotte talks to Anne "about her state" (364), so Mary and Hester have "conversations" about "the betrayal of our Lord" (111), which produce Hester's lines: "Still, as of old, / Man by himself is priced. / For thirty pieces Judas sold / Himself, not Christ." And just as Gaskell inserts the last verses Anne composed,

> *I hoped that with the brave and strong*
> *My portioned task might lie;*
> *To toil amid the busy throng,*
> *With purpose pure and high. . . .*

so Cholmondeley inserts "a little poem" that Hester wrote "which shows how much more peaceful she had become":

> *The sudden sun has trampled on the sea*
> *A throbbing molten path, a wedge of gold*
(110) *That leads out, seeming limitless to me,*
> *Into the fogs that mingle sea and sky,*
> *Into the regions where thought cannot die.*

There is even a parallel between the two writers' novels, Brontë's *Shirley* begun "when there were three sisters living and loving" and then "taken up when one alone remained" (380) and Cholmondeley's *Diana Tempest* begun before Hester's illness and revised—following Hester's responses to the manuscript—after her death (121).[44]

Given this careful repetition of Gaskell's *Life,* we may wonder why Cholmondeley had so much difficulty fulfilling her final promise to Hester. Charlotte Brontë had commemorated her sisters' lives by editing their literary remains and writing a biographical preface that is partially a posthumous tribute. Gaskell is careful to insist on the "painfulness" of this task, quoting Charlotte's letter to Ellen Nussey:

> *Mr Smith [Brontë's editor] wishes to reprint some of Emily's and Anne's works, with a few little additions from the papers they have left; and I have been closely engaged in revising, transcribing, preparing a preface, notice, &c. As the time for doing this is limited, I am obliged to be industrious. I found the task at first exquisitely painful and depressing: but regarding it in the light of a* sacred duty, *I went on, and now can bear it better.*   (426)

In the introduction to *Under One Roof* Cholmondeley writes of a similar editorial attempt, but the difficulties she identifies are aesthetic rather than emotional. She speaks of "the great pile of manuscripts" as difficult to sort (xiii), of work that is "too immature" or "not sufficiently original to justify publication" (xiv), and of her fear that, in portraying Hester, she should be "tempted to suppress and emphasize, to entwine the myriad parti-coloured threads into a picturesque tapestry with an interesting figure in it" (xv). No word of grief or remorse is uttered. The literary task consumes her attention.

No one who has read the final section of *Under One Roof,* the section "Hester's Works," would disagree with the judgment that Hester Cholmondeley's literary remains are "immature." The poetry, stories, and critical excerpts show talent but not achievement. Yet the casuistry of the "Introduction" hides the more significant reasons why Mary Cholmondeley found it difficult to fulfill the commemorative task she set herself.[45] As Cholmondeley was later to observe in her novel *Prisoners Fast Bound in Misery and Iron* (1905), autobiographers rarely understand the truth of their own lives: "Do our whispered or published autobiographies ever deceive anyone except ourselves? We alone seem unable to read between the lines of our self-revelations. We alone seem unable to perceive the sinister ghost-like figures of ourselves which we have unconsciously conjured up from our pages for all to see."[46] Cholmondeley deceived (and continued to deceive) herself about Hester's talent and its relation to her own. As Deirdre d'Albertis has observed of the Brontës, Charlotte's posthumous account of her sisters concludes "with the surviving sibling performing the 'sacred duty' of wiping 'the dust off their gravestones' and leaving 'their dear names free from soil.' " [47] Because Cholmondeley had not discovered her sister Hester's talent or helped her to publication in her lifetime, it was yet more difficult twenty-five years later to perform the editorial task that Brontë had undertaken as a "sacred duty."

We may analyze this difficulty either biographically or historically. In biographical terms, Cholmondeley's decision to compare the sisters' lives with those of the Brontës places Mary firmly in the role of Charlotte, eldest sister and survivor, and Hester in the role of Anne, the youngest, weakest sister and least talented writer. However accurate this analogy may have seemed to Mary, it nonetheless avoids a possibility that Hester's extensive juvenilia make obvious to other readers: that Hester in fact possessed more literary genius than her eldest sister, that Hester was the "real" Charlotte Brontë. Modern readers who encounter the list of Hester's juvenile books and the samples of her writing recall the contents of Gaskell's famous fifth chapter in the *Life:* "Charlotte Brontë's catalogue of her juvenile productions, with specimen page—Extract from the introduction to 'Tales of the Islanders'—'History of the year 1829'—Charlotte's taste for Art—Extracts from other early writings in MS." [48] Hester's juvenile attempts at making books imitate Charlotte Brontë's literary remains. It is as if she, too, had read *The Life of Charlotte Brontë* and discerned the parallels, even before her eldest sister.

This possibility helps to explain why Mary Cholmondeley gave her ideal writer in *Red Pottage* the name Hester, yet also why she delayed so long in fulfilling the deathbed promise she had made. On the one hand, the character of Hester Gresley pays tribute to the literary talent that Mary recognized in her sister. On the other, by inventing a Hester Gresley for an autobiographical fiction, Cholmondeley confuses the distinction between self and sister and thus obscures the question of literary talent—obscures it so well that Rhoda Broughton, an old family friend, interpreted "Hester" as a fictional version of Mary's self. [49] The confusion of roles raises the question: Who truly inherited the Brontëan mantle? Which Cholmondeley sister corresponds to which Brontë sibling? It may have been psychologically necessary for Mary Cholmondeley in 1892, the year of Hester's death, to avoid articulating this question. Because she had not yet established her literary reputation, she may have been chary of initiating the career of another, even a favorite sister. An Eliotian release from domestic claims may have seemed requisite for imaginative freedom.

A harsher analysis might further point out that *Under One Roof* eliminates the villainy of *Red Pottage,* that it places the blame for the woman writer's failure on sisters, not brothers. Cholmondeley's memoir does not invoke patriarchy as the obstacle to women's achievement in literature or art. Rather, the problem (if we are to identify one) is an abandonment of sororal goals. Thinking biographically, we can understand why Cholmondeley found it easier in fiction to target patriarchal institutions, why she found it harder in memoir to avoid recognizing the obstacles that Hester had placed on her life. Hester's birth had invalided Cholmondeley's mother, shifting the burden of household management to Mary; Hester's death then added the responsibility of literary memorialization. In *Under One Roof* a quiet, anxious sifting and sorting of manuscripts replaces the dramatic burning of a manuscript in *Red Pottage.* The wretched James Gresley has no counterpart in the memoir, except perhaps in Mary Cholmondeley's fear of disloyalty or her unwillingness to repeat Brontë's "unremitting sense of duty to others, no matter the financial, emotional, physical, or professional costs to herself." [50]

When Cholmondeley finally came to do her "sacred duty" and compose an auto/biography portraying her dead sister, she had reached a point in her career when she could acknowledge her achievement as past and anticipate the literary work of the next generation. By 1918 the fame of *Red Pottage* had not exactly faded, nor had Cholmondeley ceased to care about the success of her fiction; but, as she put it, "my imagination has dropped dead into the great crevasse of the war." [51] From her surviving letters, we know that she helped several young London writers get started: she befriended the novelist Hugh Walpole before the war, and Percy Lubbock became a special favorite, as her correspondence with Henry Newbolt, editor of the *Monthly Review,* reveals in her gentle efforts to find an outlet for Lubbock's essays. Within the family, she took pride in the talents of her niece Stella Benson, daughter of her sister Essex, who became the author of some two dozen novels. To Macmillan, which had assumed copyright of Cholmondeley's early novels when Bentley sold his publishing firm, Mary wrote in 1917: "I have been greatly interested in the debut of my niece Stella Benson. She appears to me really gifted and original. I am glad to hear you are bringing out her second (as well as her first) book." [52]

It may be that Stella's success—Stella who had been named for the dead Hester [53]—made the question of the older generation's literary talent moot. It may be, too, that the continuing literary achievement of the Cholmondeley family enabled Mary to return to the origins of her own artistic development and reenvision her career not as singular or Eliotian but as part of a larger national and historical pattern of distinguished families of writers.

Afterword

It is tempting to read Chomondeley's trajectory—from an Eliotian version of the self as a unique, artistically gifted individual to a Brontëan reassessment of the writer as part of a familial or sororal group—as a historical trajectory as well. Might not Cholmondeley's reassessment in *Under One Roof* represent a fin-de-siècle return, at least among women writers, to a collaborative model of authorship? The joint literary ventures of such late nineteenth-century teams as Edith Somerville and (Violet) Martin Ross in fiction (two cousins) and Michael Field (Katharine Bradley and Edith Cooper) in poetry (aunt and niece) suggest that some women writers at least embraced an ideology of literary work as "shared enterprise, defying individualisation."[1] The collaborative autobiographies of the Women's Co-operative Guild, *Life as We Have Known It* (1931), further point to an awareness of the literary, social, and political uses of collective rather than individual life writing.[2]

Yet the historical record is not so simple, nor can Cholmondeley's autobiographical revision be treated as representative. Despite the active discussion at the end of the century about the values of collaborative literary work, the dominant attitude seems to have been that collaboration might suffice in genres dominated by plot (drama) or fact (journalism), but that it could never produce works of great depth or genius. As Walter Besant argued, in an essay that reduced feminine collaboration to mere supplement or inspiration for the male writer, "Neither in the study of the wanderings and development of the individual soul, nor in the development of character, nor in the work of pure and lofty imagination, is collaboration possible."[3] Besant's model privileged the lone writer of genius—among women, the example of Eliot.

Moreover, the tradition of the female *Künstlerroman* that Susan Gubar has traced from Victorianism into early modernism suggests that the Eliotian model of authorship held sway for most women writers until well into the twentieth century, especially in its distinction between domesticity and professionalism and in the division of biological reproduction from literary production that figures so prominently in *Red Pottage*. Gubar suggests that in autobiographies of the female artist, "artistic production and biological reproduction are either contradictory models furnishing alternative scripts or analogous, parallel paradigms."[4] Even in the Brontëan model as delineated by Gaskell, which allows for parallel development if not precisely "parallel paradigms," the relation between domesticity and professional achievement remains uneasy. Although Gaskell insists that Brontë fulfilled her responsibilities as a woman *and* as a gifted writer, she represents her subject's life as "divided into two parallel currents—her life as Currer Bell, the author; her life as Charlotte Brontë, the woman." The adjective "parallel" allows for compatible or complementary development, but "divided" acknowledges the tensions. Gaskell admits that controlling or reconciling the "two parallel currents" was a challenge for Brontë, as it was for all Victorian women writers: "There were separate duties belonging to each character—not opposing each other; not impossible, but difficult to be reconciled."[5]

If Cross's *Life of George Eliot* reconciled the currents by making them sequential—that is, if Cross minimized the tensions by making provincial familial life seem naturally to precede Eliot's professional London career—his auto/biography of Eliot also opened the way for the division between biological reproduction (the woman's role) and literary production (the writer's role). Cholmondeley's division of female characters into Rachel (the reproductive woman) and Hester (the productive literary genius) represents one version of this division. Mary Howitt's *Autobiography,* published in 1889, four years after Cross's *Life,* presents another version in its division of Howitt's career as emerging from wifely and maternal impulses versus the obstacles children create for the literary woman. The most frequently quoted passage in Howitt's *Autobiography* emphasizes the division—indeed, turbulence—of the "two parallel currents." In a self-assessment written at the time of her son Claude's death, Howitt laments: "Tomorrow I intend to commence my regular avocations. Poor dear Claude! at this very moment I see the unfinished translation lying before me, which was broken off by his death."[6] It seems impossible for Howitt, in medias res or in retrospect, to sort out a happy relationship between literary and maternal work.

Within their historical and literary contexts, in other words,

Cholmondeley's two autobiographies may need simply to be read as a private reassessment, not as a historical trend or generic trajectory. By the end of the century, both Brontëan and Eliotian models offered possibilities for women writers to assess their domestic and professional experiences in autobiography. Like other examples of Victorian life writing, these models became part of a rich, complicated literary field that allowed for different versions of the self, alternative paradigms for imagining personal and professional experience.

The contours of this field emerge from Margaret Oliphant's articles on autobiography—taken as an oeuvre rather than as separate pieces. When Oliphant read and reviewed the memoirs of her contemporaries and of the men and women whose accounts had shaped the English autobiographical tradition, she engaged, albeit with deeper critical analysis and greater historical range, in a process common among Victorian women. As Joanne Shattock has demonstrated, Victorian women read, analyzed, and wrote about the lives of their contemporaries,[7] and they responded in their own life writing through emulation, imitation, or, quite often, difference.

The impulse to know the details of other women's lives—and to use them for one's own purposes—goes back at least as far as Mrs. Elwood's *Memoirs of the Literary Ladies of England* (1843), no doubt further. Anne Elwood began her research for a "Biography of Literary Females" because she had a "partiality to the literary performances of her sex" but found it difficult "to obtain information concerning the lives and characters of those individuals in whose productions she took an interest."[8] Although she modestly refrains from saying so, Elwood began her research because she hoped to join the ranks of those illustrious women authors.

By the 1890s, when Oliphant and Cholmondeley wrote their autobiographies, the knowledge and availability of women's lives—whether written by the women themselves, by family members, or by professional biographers—had increased dramatically. In 1852 Arabella Stuart had lamented the virtual absence of "female biography" on the shelves of libraries. By 1899, as Oliphant's *Autobiography* shows, women's life writing had become a self-conscious literary tradition, one that made writers aware of the ideological implications of the shape in which a life was presented.

When Oliphant reviewed *The Life of Harriet Beecher Stowe* for *Black-*

wood's Magazine in 1890, she registered her ideological awareness, even if she simplified the history of this autobiographical tradition. In Oliphant's review, Stowe's conception of a literary life, hopefully combining familial and professional work, becomes a thing of the past, a model common for women of Stowe's (and Oliphant's own) generation but no longer operative. "The whirligig of time turns round again," a key line in the review, suggests that literary history is cyclical or perhaps, given the downward motion of the whirligig, even declining or decadent. For Oliphant, the Corinne of the 1890s represents a version of the authorial self that has appeared before—and one that will fade out of fashion again.

Yet the autobiographical examples available to women in the final decade of the nineteenth century reveal a far more complicated literary field than Oliphant's 1890 review admits, not one simply subject to the ups and downs, the ins and outs of history. As her multiple articles on autobiography from the 1870s to 1890s prove, the publication of past and contemporary accounts included diverse forms of life writing—the domestic memoir and the professional life; the personal confession and the public record; the literary, artistic, scholarly, and professional life in many forms and with different emphases. Their range and variety made both men and women autobiographers conversant with multiple approaches to conceptualizing and writing a life history. Indeed, Oliphant drew on her historical knowledge of English domestic memoirs as she composed her own *Autobiography*.

If Oliphant believed that the "whirligig of time turns round again" and that autobiographical fashions repeat themselves, she also allowed for the possibility that, in the turnings of literary history, "literary biography"—which for her meant what we today designate auto/biography—might "perhaps become a little more interesting."[9] To her hopeful prediction we might add that the greater interest emerged, at least in part, from the less formulaic, more generically diverse life writing that the editors, critics, and writers of Victorian autobiography had made possible.

Notes

Preface

1. Epstein, "Recognizing the Life-Course," in *Recognizing Biography,* 138–71.
2. Carlisle, *John Stuart Mill and the Writing of Character,* 242–45.

Chapter I. On the Victorian "Origins" of Women's Autobiography

1. Heilbrun's book is not, strictly speaking, a historical study, but it assumes the histori-
   cal development of a women's tradition in its discussion of certain modern texts as
   "revolutionary" (Adrienne Rich's autobiographical works) or as a "turning point"
   (May Sarton's *Journal of a Solitude*) or as otherwise exemplifying progress in the genre.
   Collections that attempt at least in part to identify a women's tradition include
   Jelinek, *Women's Autobiography;* Stanton, *Female Autograph;* Benstock, *Private Self;*
   Brodzki and Schenck, *Life/Lines;* and Broughton and Anderson, *Women's Lives/
   Women's Times.* The last collection, perhaps because it is most recent (1997), perhaps
   because several contributors are historical or materialist-feminist critics, is less concerned with a women's tradition than with questions of intertextuality, including one
   that motivates my study: "What is gained from intertextual study—from juxtaposing
   pairs or groups of 'selves' from the same historical moment, or from setting men's
   autobiographies in the context of women's?" (xiv).
2. Jelinek, *Tradition of Women's Autobiography,* 8. Cf. Susan Stanford Friedman's conclusion to "Women's Autobiographical Selves: Theory and Practice," in Benstock, *Private Self,* 55–56: "Women's autobiography comes alive as a literary tradition of self-
   creation when we approach its texts from a psycho-political perspective based on the
   lives of women. . . . Individualistic [male] paradigms do not take into account the
   central role collective consciousness of self plays in the lives of women and mi-
   norities."
3. The exclusion of women's autobiographies from major theoretical studies is well
   documented in Jelinek, *Tradition of Women's Autobiography,* 1–8; Smith, *Poetics of
   Women's Autobiography,* 3–19; and Friedman, "Women's Autobiographical Selves,"
   34–44. About this exclusion, Smith asserts: "The poetics of autobiography, as the
   history of autobiography, remains by and large an androcentric enterprise. Despite
   the critical ferment brought about by feminist critiques of the academy, of disciplinary methodologies, of the canon, the majority of autobiography critics still persist in
   either erasing women's story, relegating it to the margins of critical discourse, or,
   when they treat women's autobiographies seriously, uncritically conflating the dy-
   namics of male and female selfhood and textuality" (15).

4. Shirley Neuman makes a related point in "Autobiography: From Different Poetics to a Poetics of Differences," in Kadar, *Essays on Life Writing*, 213–30, when she argues that neither traditional critics who use the concept of "self" nor more recent theorists who speak of "subjectivities" or "subject positions" have formulated a poetics of women's autobiography flexible enough to account for the variety of women's texts: "Whether a 'self' is an 'empty self' and a 'masquerade' as [Alicia Dojovne] Ortiz claims, a plentitude of selves, or a multilayered subject is a question with which the poetics of autobiography has not yet come to terms" (222).

5. Gagnier, *Subjectivities*, 3–30; Marcus, *Auto/biographical Discourses*, 11–55.

6. Folkenflik surveys the history of the term *autobiography* in his introduction to *Culture of Autobiography*, 1–20; he points out that the reviewer in *The Monthly Repository* chooses the term "self-biography" because "*autobiography* would have seemed pedantic." See also Buckley's discussion of the terminology in its cultural context in *Turning Key*, 18–19.

7. Cavendish, *True Relation;* Fanshawe, *Memoirs;* Hayes, *Legacy;* Warwick, *Autobiography;* Thornton, *Autobiography;* Halkett, *Autobiography.* Except for Cavendish's *True Relation*, first published in the seventeenth century, and Hayes's *Legacy*, published in the eighteenth, these texts are all "Victorian," and my citations come from them. There is a modern edition of *The Memoirs of Anne, Lady Halkett and Ann, Lady Fanshawe*, ed. John Loftis (Oxford: Clarendon, 1979). Excerpts from Alice Thornton's autobiography and Margaret Cavendish's *True Relation* are included in Graham et al., *Her Own Life*.

8. The tradition of turning to auto/biography for self-analysis and self-understanding is as ancient as Plutarch's *Parallel Lives of the Greeks and Romans* and as popular as Bunyan's *Grace Abounding to the Chief of Sinners*, both of which English readers have recurrently consulted to analyze their own lives. The Victorians read Plutarch to discover "the perils and pitfalls of public life"; they read Bunyan to understand their spiritual perils and, like him, they composed memoirs and autobiographies to provide models for their successors. On the Victorians' reading of Plutarch, see Rose, *Parallel Lives*, 5–6; on their reading of Bunyan and other spiritual autobiographers, see Landow, *Victorian Types, Victorian Shadows*, 11–12, 21.

9. Mason, "Other Voice," 210. Not all critics take the same position on the relevance of Rousseau's exploratory mode. On women writers' use of the autobiographical "I" as a means of self-discovery, see Frye, *Living Stories, Telling Lives*, esp. chaps. 3 and 6. Although Frye does not explicitly associate this mode with Rousseau, she suggestively shows how contemporary women novelists use a subversive "I" to write novels about the "recognition of self in process" (149).

10. Delany, *British Autobiography in the Seventeenth Century*, 5; Estelle C. Jelinek, "Women's Autobiography and the Male Tradition," in Jelinek, *Women's Autobiography*, 5; de Man, "Autobiography as De-facement," 920.

11. I use the form *auto/biography* throughout this book to designate texts that combine both modes or collections that assume no fundamental difference between modes and thus include both biographies and autobiographies.

12. Evans and Evans, *Friends' Library*, 1:1–2. Besides the rationale provided by the prospectus, it is likely that the Evans brothers shared the concern of many nineteenth-century Friends that Quakerism was losing its spiritual center and needed models to restore its members to a purer form of faith; see, e.g., the anonymous pamphlet *The*

Quakers, or Friends: Their Rise and Decline (London: Sampson Low, 1859). In his *Journal of the Life and Religious Services of William Evans, a Minister of the Gospel in the Society of Friends* (Philadelphia: Caxton, 1870), 164, William Evans also mentions the "large number of members . . . growing up in the Society, who must be unable to procure the approved writings of Friends" as another motive for the collection.

13. Because the influence of Augustine's *Confessions* on the tradition of English spiritual autobiography was negligible (or at least indirect) until the nineteenth century, I refer to a "Bunyanesque" tradition. This label, meant to acknowledge the crucial influence of *The Pilgrim's Progress* as well as *Grace Abounding to the Chief of Sinners*, still neglects the early contributions of women writers to the formation of the English tradition.

14. See Elizabeth Stirredge, *The Life and Christian Testimony of That Faithful Servant of the Lord, Elizabeth Stirredge*, in Evans and Evans, *Friends' Library*, 2:187–212; and Thomas Wilson, *A Brief Account of the Life and Travels of Thomas Wilson*, ibid., 319–33. Stirredge's account was written in the 1690s, first published in 1711, and reissued throughout the eighteenth century.

15. Vann, *Social Development of English Quakerism*, 1–46; Brinton usefully summarizes the major episodes of Quaker conversion in *Quaker Journals*.

16. For the episodes summarized in this paragraph, see Elizabeth Ashbridge, *Some Account of the Life of Elizabeth Ashbridge*, in Evans and Evans, *Friends' Library*, 4:11; Joseph Pike, *Some Account of the Life of Joseph Pike*, ibid., 2:358; Alice Hayes, *A Short Account of Alice Hayes, a Minister of the Gospel*, ibid., 2:73–74; *Memoirs of the Life and Convincement of Benjamin Bangs*, ibid., 4:224–25; and Wilson, *Brief Account*, ibid., 2:330. Quaker women may have been somewhat different from other women in giving accounts of their traveling and public preaching, but not from Quaker men. My point is that *religious* subjectivity more than gender shapes their accounts.

17. Erickson, " 'Perfect Love,' " 83.

18. Hayes, *Short Account*, 2:71; cf. Mal. 3:2–3 and Ezek. 22:17–22.

19. "Prospectus," in Evans and Evans, *Friends' Library*, 1:1–2.

20. See Mary Eagleton's discussion of this critical position, now fairly rare, in *Feminist Literary Theory*, 200–201, as well as Moers, *Literary Women*, 209–10, for a passage that exemplifies this sort of criticism in early feminist scholarship.

21. See, e.g., Cynthia S. Pomerleau's statement that "for seventeenth-century English women, much more than men, love acted as a defining force," in "The Emergence of Women's Autobiography in England," in Jelinek, *Women's Autobiography*, 25. On "relational" modes of self-understanding, see Chodorow, *Reproduction of Mothering*, and Gilligan, *In a Different Voice*. The models proposed by these two fine cultural studies, highly influential on feminist criticism, are problematic when applied to seventeenth- and eighteenth-century accounts. Chodorow and Gilligan themselves recognize the historical limits in their discussions of methodology.

22. Stirredge, *Life and Testimony*, 2:193; Jane Hoskens, *The Life of That Faithful Servant of Christ*, in Evans and Evans, *Friends' Library*, 1:471. The practice of including "testimonies" (character references) holds for all autobiographers, male and female alike.

23. Pennington, *Some Account*, 10–13, 68–70; Pike, *Some Account*, 2:351–56. The first half of Pennington's account is a spiritual record left to her daughter, Gulielma Maria Springett, which focuses on the mother's history before marriage and with her first husband; the second half, a family memoir intended for her grandson, focuses on the paternal heritage. One knows only after reading both halves that Mary Pennington

had two children—one daughter, one son. (In some sources her name is spelled "Penington.")

24. *Memoirs of the Life and Convincement of That Worthy Friend Benjamin Bangs* (London: Luke Hinde, 1757), 48.

25. The revision in Evans and Evans, *Friends' Library*, 4:227, reads: "Here I imparted my mind to her, which, although we had often met together before in our journeys, I never so much as mentioned to her; though my spirit was united in a Divine fellowship with her." The original "Word of Courtship" disappears in this version.

26. Quoted by Lloyd in his discussion of Quaker marriage in *Quaker Social History,* 48–65.

27. Pennington, *Some Account,* 48–50; Pike, *Some Account,* 2:371.

28. This title appears in the initial eighteenth-century publication of Hayes's autobiography (London: T. S. Raylton & L. Hinde, 1749), in the first American edition (New York: Samuel Wood, 1807), and in a nineteenth-century edition (London: Darton & Harvey, 1836). The *Friends' Library* edition, which I cite, uses the simpler title *A Short Account of Alice Hayes.*

29. See Evans and Evans, *Friends' Library,* 2:68 (Hayes); 2:351 (Pike); 2:415 (Oxley). This rationale for autobiography as a spiritual legacy is formulaic, but not universal in Nonconformist traditions. The first known published autobiography to use it, *A Legacy for Saints; Being Several Experiences of the Dealings of God with Anna Trapnel* (1654), recounts the experiences of a believer in the doctrine of "free grace."

30. Hayes, *Short Account,* 2:75, 78. When Hayes first attended Quaker meetings, Smith became a cruel husband, locking up her clothes to prevent her attendance and threatening to desert her and the children unless she renounced the Friends.

31. Stirredge, *Life and Testimony,* 2:190, 192. The editorial materials surrounding Stirredge's account help to clarify the question of her motherhood. The "testimonies" mention her late husband but no children; the biographical notice attached by the Hemel Hempstead Friends, however, is signed by a James Stirredge, presumably her son.

32. The last judgment requires qualification, as it has been used to argue against the spiritual autobiography as a legitimate or "full" autobiographical form—as in Olney's chapter "Autobiography Simplex," in *Metaphors of Self,* 151–81. In fact, any autobiography that adopts a consistent hermeneutic focuses (and thus limits) its writer's self-presentation, and we should no more credit a modern writer's "Freudian" or "Marxist" reading of his past than discredit a seventeenth-century writer's "biblical" self-interpretation. All hermeneutics illumine and blind.

33. Stirredge, *Life and Convincement,* 2:194–97.

34. Ibid., 2:199. The autobiography here echoes Isa. 65:4. As Stirredge knew well, Story had led the battle against George Fox's more rigorous plans for church governance; thus, by denying others the right he had claimed in argument against Fox, he was compromising his position. On the issue of individual freedom vs. group authority in early Quakerism, see Lloyd, *Quaker Social History,* 17–31.

35. *Journal of the Life of that Worthy Elder and Faithful Servant of Jesus Christ, William Edmundson,* in Evans and Evans, *Friends' Library,* 2:115–16; Wilson, *Brief Account,* 2:325.

36. *Memoir of Sarah Morris,* in Evans and Evans, *Friends' Library,* 6:479; *Sketches of the Life and Religious Experiences of Jane Pearson,* ibid., 4:451–53; Ashbridge, *Life,* ibid., 4:14.

In the shift from the seventeenth to eighteenth century, Deborah Bell's autobiography, *A Short Journal of the Labours and Travels in the Work of the Ministry,* represents a transitional text (ibid., 5:1–23). Unlike Stirredge, Bell lived after the Act of Toleration and so did not shape her account as a battle of conscience against external authority. Unlike later autobiographers, however, she did not treat the "women's speech" issue as primarily an internal struggle. Bell addressed the issue by reproducing a letter written to a Baptist woman to defend Quaker practice, thus making the Baptists (who condemned women's preaching) function as prohibitors of self-expression.

37. Hayes, *Short Account,* 2:74–75.

38. Armstrong, *Desire and Domestic Fiction.*

39. Miller, *Fiction and Repetition,* 1–21 and passim.

40. In addition to Quaker publications, there were many autobiographies by Methodist, Baptist, Congregational, and Evangelical women in print during the nineteenth century, many republications of older documents, and some new specimens of spiritual autobiography.

41. I discuss women's loss of this tradition in *Victorian Autobiography,* 120–55.

42. The term "family history" or "family memoir" is preferred by such historians as Natalie Zemon Davis for early modern accounts (see "Gender and Genre: Women as Historical Writers, 1400–1820," in Labalme, *Beyond Their Sex,* 153–82). I use "domestic memoir" for Victorian accounts because it reflects the emphasis on private, domestic life reported by these writers and the corollary deemphasis of public history.

43. The earliest secular autobiography by a woman may be Lady Margaret Cunninghame's *Pairt of the Life* (1827). This fragmentary document seems to have been written in 1607 or 1608, when Lady Margaret took legal action against her husband for failure to maintain her and their children. It may be a court deposition, and thus lacks many of the characteristic features of the domestic memoir, e.g., a full family chronology, an account of family achievements, and a sense of itself as a record for posterity.

44. Thornton, *Autobiography,* v.

45. Halkett, *Autobiography,* i; Fanshawe, *Memoirs,* viii; Warwick, *Autobiography,* xi; Hutchinson, *Memoirs,* xxiv.

46. Mary Beth Rose, "Gender, Genre, and History: Seventeenth-Century English Women and the Art of Autobiography," in Rose, *Women in the Middle Ages,* 245, 273. Although Rose initially states that she is "not attempting to establish the extent to which women may be credited with influencing the development of secular autobiography" (247), throughout her essay and especially at its close she refers to women's "contributions" to the genre.

47. Oliphant, "Autobiographies, No. I," 2.

48. I discuss this trend in "Gender and Autobiographical Form: The Case of the Spiritual Autobiography," in Olney, *Studies in Autobiography,* 211–22. Except for Quaker women and some black American preachers, nineteenth-century women tended to eschew public accounts and turned instead to private spiritual diaries. On the African-American tradition, see Andrews, *Sisters of the Spirit.*

49. See Matthews, *British Autobiographies,* s.v. "Religion." It should be noted that most of the nineteenth-century women's accounts listed in Matthews's bibliography as spiritual autobiographies are private diaries to which biographical accounts have been added.

50. See Matthews, *British Autobiographies,* s.v. "Diplomats' and consuls' wives" and "Pol-

iticians' wives." As in the seventeenth century, such nineteenth-century accounts tended to be written by women of the upper classes.

51. See ibid, s.v. "Domestic and family life" and "Housewives." Women wrote two-thirds of the memoirs listed under these headings.

52. Delany, *British Autobiography in the Seventeenth Century,* 5, describes women's autobiographies in these terms, but similar descriptions have been given by such critics as Pomerleau ("Emergence of Women's Autobiography," 22) to characterize the sensibility of all women's autobiography.

53. The quest for tradition underlies Elaine Showalter's account of nineteenth-century women's fiction in *A Literature of Their Own.* A parallel quest occurs among writers of autobiography, but it is complicated by strong predilections for masculine modes and competing senses of what a women's tradition is or should be.

54. Thornton refers to "the first book of my life" (174), to a "first booke of my widdowed condition" (154), to a "2nd booke" (184), and to "my booke of meditations" (142). Her editor simply arranged the entries in chronological order, omitting repetitious material and deleting many of her meditations or thanksgivings for God's mercy. From what remains intact, I suspect that the original documents resemble a spiritual diary kept by one of Cromwell's female relatives and preserved in the British Library as Add. 5858, ff. 213–21. After a brief account of childhood, this unknown autobiographer makes dated entries, each followed by a prayer or meditation.

55. Presumably Lady Cunninghame thought it appropriate to appeal to her errant husband in the language of Scripture, although one rhetorical consequence is a vagueness about her plight and her specific demands. Whatever her intention, the religious discourse seems to have had little effect on his behavior.

56. Chodorow, *Reproduction of Mothering,* 166–69, 173–77. See also Gilligan, *In a Different Voice,* and Belenky et al., *Women's Ways of Knowing.*

57. Cavendish, *Lives of William Cavendishe . . . and of His Wife,* 258, 263. This edition reprints the *True Relation* edited by Sir Egerton Brydges in 1814, who wrote the critical comments quoted above.

58. Cavendish, *True Relation,* 262–63.

59. Fanshawe, *Memoirs,* viii–ix.

60. Hutchinson, *Memoirs,* xxvi–xxvii, xxiii, xxviii.

61. Between January 1881 and April 1883 Oliphant published seven anonymous review essays on autobiography, including one on Margaret Cavendish and another comparing Lucy Hutchinson and Alice Thornton (see *Blackwood's Edinburgh Magazine* 129 [May 1881]: 617–39, and 132 [May 1882]: 74–101). Oliphant composed her own autobiography sporadically between February 1885 and January 1895.

62. [McTaggart], *Memoirs of a Gentlewoman;* Lisle, *Long, Long Ago;* Porter, *Years That Are Told;* [Gregg], *Leaflets from My Life;* Bathgate, *Aunt Janet's Legacy to Her Nieces.* For other examples, see Matthews, s.v. "Domestic and family life" and "Housewives."

63. The term "emplotment" comes from Hayden White's *Historical Imagination in Nineteenth-Century Europe,* 7–29. White distinguishes between interpretations by "emplotment" and those by "formal argument" or "ideological implication" (i.e., arguments about "the nature of historical knowledge" or implications "that can be drawn from the study of past events for the understanding of present ones").

64. Rose, "Gender, Genre, and History," in her *Women in the Middle Ages and Renaissance,* 270. Rose also notes that Halkett's account depicts "a self-definition through separa-

tion and conflict [that] is characteristically masculine rather than feminine," a point that accounts, I think, for its relatively successful narrative construction.

65. These phrases come from the titles of two influential works of the 1970s, Olney's *Metaphors of Self* and Patricia Meyer Spacks's "Selves in Hiding," in Jelinek, *Women's Autobiography*, 112–32.

66. Coleridge, *Memoirs and Letters*, 1 : 1.

67. Nussbaum discusses this form in her chapter "Heteroclites: The Scandalous Memoirs," in *Autobiographical Subject*, 178–200.

68. I take these categories and names from the "Advertisement" that prefaces Hunt and Clarke's *Autobiography: A Collection of the Most Instructive and Amusing Lives Ever Published, Written by the Parties Themselves*, 1:n.p. In 1829 the series was taken over by the publishers Whittaker, Treacher, & Arnot, who seem to have been more interested in translating and publishing contemporary accounts (as vols. 27–34 show). The series ceased publication in 1833.

69. Paulson, *Popular and Polite Art*, 117 and passim.

70. According to the editor of the Hunt and Clarke series, "It is evident that, when disposed to be sincere, no man can do so much justice to the springs and motives of his own character and actions as himself; and when even otherwise, by showing what he wishes to appear, he generally discovers what he really is." See "Advertisement," 1:n.p.

71. The titillation we feel, whether as male readers seducing the young woman or as female readers resisting seduction, is a necessary prerequisite to the autobiographer's portrayal of herself as victim. Because we have implicated ourselves in Mary Robinson's fall, we cannot resist the appeal for pity—or forgiveness.

72. Robinson, *Memoirs*, 34. The autobiography was originally published as *Memoirs of the Late Mrs. Robinson, Written by Herself, with Some Posthumous Pieces*, in 1801. Citations are to the 1826 Hunt and Clarke edition.

73. On Robinson's relations with Sheridan, see Steen, *Lost One*, 94–95.

74. Robinson was an obsessive chronicler of fashion, particularly her own. We learn that she is pregnant, e.g., when she details her sartorial preparation for a public concert, for which she spent "at least some hours in decorating my person . . . because my shape at that period required some arrangement, owing to the visible increase of my domestic solicitudes" (45). For other descriptions of dress, see *Memoirs*, 30, 35, 43, 52, 71, 76, 122.

75. Maria, her daughter, gives the date as 1787, but the chronological sequence makes it clear that they arrived back in England at the beginning of 1788.

76. Charke, *Life*, 34, 48, 71, 76–77. All citations are to the 1827 Hunt and Clarke edition, except where I note otherwise. Whatever the causes of the disaffection from her father, when Charke sues by letter for his "blessing and pardon," she concedes her failure in "those unhappy miscarriages which . . . justly deprived me of a father's fondness" (72–73).

77. Spacks, *Imagining a Self*, 57–91; for a different explanation of why women autobiographers (especially working-class women) turn to this literary plot, see Swindells, *Victorian Writing and Working Women*, 137–53, who argues that when issues not normally public (such as women's sexuality) are "kept from articulation," such "literary" plots emerge.

78. Charke, *Narrative of the Life of Mrs. Charlotte Charke* (1755), 276–77. The autobiog-

raphy was first issued in eight installments during March and April 1755 and then in a bound volume that sold for two shillings and sixpence.

79. "Dedication," in Charke, *Narrative of the Life* (1755), viii–ix.
80. Twentieth-century editions have continued the distortions of the Hunt and Clarke version. In 1929 Constable & Company reissued *A Narrative of the Life of Mrs. Charlotte Charke* in their Miscellany of Original and Selected Publications of Literature, again with a preface that focused on the author's pathetic demise; the next year an identical American edition appeared (New York: Richard R. Smith, 1930). Only a facsimile edition, ed. Leonard R. N. Ashley (Gainesville, Fla.: Scholars' Facsimiles and Reprints, 1969), avoids judging Charke and gives a reliable, appreciative introduction to her work.
81. Ironically, it was Henry Fielding who launched Charke's career as a male actress when he asked her to substitute for Richard Yates in *Pasquin*. Fielding's ambivalent response to transvestism has been brilliantly discussed by Terry Castle in "Matters Not Fit to Be Mentioned," 602–22, rpt. in Castle, *The Female Thermometer: Eighteenth-Century Culture and the Invention of the Uncanny* (New York: Oxford University Press, 1995), 67–81. To Castle's suggestion that Charke's life influenced the composition of Fielding's *Female Husband,* one might add that Charke created her most successful male role (MacHeath) in 1744–45, the year before Fielding published his account of Mary (Charles) Hamilton. One might also speculate that Fielding's ambivalent tone in that work reflects his own mixture of guilt and pleasure in the *lusus naturae* he had created in his protégée Charke (or perhaps only encouraged: we do not know if Charke had previously taken to male clothes).
82. In "Desperate Measures," 863, Erin Mackie argues that "it is improbable that Charke was a transvestite in the contemporary [twentieth-century] sense of that term," which "denotes a compulsive fetishistic practice engaged in by men for erotic pleasure." Given Charke's refusal to reveal her motives for dressing *en cavalier,* we cannot know whether or not they included "fetishistic practice." Seventeenth- and eighteenth-century usage is less specific about motivation than Mackie acknowledges; as Lynne Friedl notes in "'Passing Women,'" 251, "the *Oxford English Dictionary* dates the word 'transvestite' back to 1652, when it referred to women who dressed as men."
83. "Vagabondism" may signal transvestism or, more generally, sexual deviance. In *The Female Husband* Fielding's Jane Hamilton is arrested and tried for "vagrancy"; in the nineteenth century, the antiquarian John Ashton retold stories of male impersonators in a collection called *Eighteenth Century Waifs.*
84. Mason, "Other Voice," 210.
85. In Charke's *Life* and in other accounts of eighteenth-century male impersonators (e.g., Davies, *Life and Adventures*), the picaresque novel is a primary influence. Charke's narrative moves rapidly from one crisis to another (cf. the episodic structure of the picaresque), and while she becomes wiser in the ways of the world, she does not trace a moral development in her account (cf. the ambiguous moral stance of the picaro).
86. Munro, *Lives of Girls and Women,* 147.
87. Friedl, "'Passing Women,'" 241.
88. Senior, *Life and Times of Colley Cibber.*
89. Quoted in Barker, *Mr. Cibber of Drury Lane,* 225. Barker does not suggest that Charlotte's assumption of this role caused the rift.

90. Neuman, "Autobiography," 222.
91. Charke's literary admirers tend to be modern rather than Victorian; see, e.g., Maureen Duffy's reworking of Charke's *Narrative of the Life* in her novel *The Microcosm* (London: Hutchinson, 1966).

Chapter II. The Polemics of Piety

1. For an excellent statement of this position, see Mary Jean Corbett's "Literary Domesticity and Women Writers' Subjectivities," in her *Representing Femininity*, 83–106. See also Davidoff and Hall, *Family Fortunes*, esp. chap. 3, " 'The Nursery of Virtue': Domestic Ideology and the Middle Class," which treats Sarah Ellis and Harriet Martineau as inheritors of the domestic tradition of William Cowper and Hannah More.
2. In *Harriet Martineau: The Poetics of Moralism* Hunter places Martineau within a tradition of nineteenth-century didactic literature by women, in which Tonna also belongs.
3. Tonna, *Personal Recollections*, 1, 3. All quotations are from the fourth edition. The autobiography was first published in 1841; in later editions it was continued "to the close of her life, 1847."
4. In this link, Tonna follows the lead of such late eighteenth-century writers as Cowper and More, who, as Davidoff and Hall argue in *Family Fortunes*, 162–79, saw proper domestic relations as central to religious life.
5. On the importance of reading not only the Bible but other accounts of conversion, see my discussion of Bunyan's *Grace Abounding to the Chief of Sinners* and Thomas Scott's *Force of Truth* in Peterson, *Victorian Autobiography*, 1–28.
6. Corbett, *Representing Femininity*, 29, n. 13.
7. Roger Sharrock discusses this feature of spiritual autobiography in the introduction to his edition of Bunyan's *Grace Abounding to the Chief of Sinners*.
8. Corbett, *Representing Femininity*, 15; this version of the argument follows closely Nancy Armstrong's approach in *Desire and Domestic Fiction*. In *The Private Lives of Victorian Women*, Sanders emphasizes the adoption of a religious perspective and rhetoric as a means of overcoming personal frustration, emotional turmoil, and intellectual boredom; see also Sanders, " 'Absolutely an act of duty,' " 54–70.
9. Answers to these questions seem irrecoverable. The only known sources of biographical data are the *Personal Recollections* and Tonna's occasional comments in the *Christian Lady's Magazine*, both of which give her own representations of events.
10. In her *Autobiography* Besant attacks the equation of an earthly and heavenly father, as well as the cultural alignment of her clergyman-husband with divine authority. See esp. the chapters "Marriage" and "The Storm of Doubt," 65–130, as well as T. L. Broughton's thoughtful analysis, "Women's Autobiography: The Self at Stake?" in Neuman, *Autobiography and Questions of Gender*, 76–94.
11. Corbett calls it "quite maddening" in *Representing Femininity*, 74; in " 'The Heroine of Some Strange Romance,' " 141–53, Elizabeth Kowalski sees neuroses in this as in other repressions.
12. Tonna explains her style in these terms: "My little books and tracts became popular; because, after some struggle against a plan so humbling to literary pride, I was able to adopt the suggestion of a wise Christian brother, and form a style of such homely simplicity, that if, on reading a manuscript to a child of five years old, I found there

was a single sentence or word above his comprehension, it was instantly corrected to suit that lowly standard" (179).

13. The Old Testament explains the free-will offering as a "tribute" given "as the Lord thy God hath blessed thee" (Deut. 16:10, KJV) in contrast to the required tithe or the burnt offering.

14. See Corbett, *Representing Femininity*, 77–79. Tennyson writes in *In Memoriam*, sec. 33:

> *Leave thou thy sister when she prays,*
> > *Her early Heaven, her happy views;*
> > *Nor thou with shadowed hint confuse*
> *A life that leads melodious days.*
> *Her faith through form is pure as thine,*
> > *Her hands are quicker unto good:*
> > *Oh, sacred be the flesh and blood*
> *To which she links a truth divine!*

15. Davis, "Anglican Evangelicalism," 30–31.

16. Just as she refuses to repeat the gossip about her own life, so Tonna fails to specify what the "domestic treachery" afflicting Hannah More was, saying only that it caused More to be displaced from her house and garden, "a perfect bower from slips and seeds of her own planting" (226). In fact, the "treachery" was that More's servants cheated her out of money and goods. The situation became so scandalous that several of More's friends had to intervene by removing More to another home and firing the servants, as Hopkins explains in *Hannah More and Her Circle*, 247–49. Tonna's second account of More (261–62) again mentions a calumny, "a most infamous lie" (262), but again without specification. The function of this second account is to show her brother's reaction to More—"he was perfectly charmed with her"—and thus to dispense with prejudices against Evangelicals as dour, humorless people.

17. More, *Works*, 1:313.

18. Ibid., 1:364.

19. Martineau, "Female Writers on Practical Divinity," 593–96, 746–50. The first part discusses More, the second More, Anna Laetitia Barbauld, and the late Elizabeth Smith, translator of the Book of Job.

20. Pichanick, *Harriet Martineau*, 17.

21. Martineau, "Female Writers on Practical Divinity," 593.

22. Lant Carpenter, *Principles of Education: Intellectual, Moral, and Physical* (London: Longman, Hurst, Rees, Orne & Brown, 1820), 41–42.

23. Although Martineau does not name More specifically in the third article, her discussion of women's education and intellectual capacities responds directly to More's *Strictures on the Modern System of Female Education*. Martineau began her first article by discussing More's *Practical Piety*, saying that she would address "other authors of the same class" in her second (596). In the interim, however, she read and was impressed by More's *Essay on the Character and Practical Writings of St. Paul*, so she again treated More, along with Barbauld and Smith. For the third article she seems to have read More's *Strictures* and possibly *Hints for Forming the Character of a Young Princess*, but since her response was more critical than approving, Martineau presents her analysis "On Female Education" without naming names.

24. Letter to Lord Brougham, 10 October 1832, in Martineau, *Selected Letters*, 32. An unpublished letter to Richard Horne, dated 4 June 1844, reinforces this self-conceived

uniqueness as a woman writer; Martineau refers to her work as "a new case" and to her earnings of £5,000–6,000 as surpassing "the rarest thing in the world for a woman to earn £1000" (Wolff Collection, Harry Ransom Library, University of Texas). In both letters Martineau is thinking not of literary precedents but of professional and political achievement.

25. For a brief discussion of the "cheap repository tract" in relation to the "social-problem novel," see Kovacevic and Kanner, "Blue Book into Novel," 152–73.

26. Hunter's *Harriet Martineau* treats the early writing within a feminine tradition of didactic literature. Evidence supporting this approach includes Martineau's private resolution, written in 1829, "to become a forcible and elegant writer on moral and religious subjects, so as to be useful to refined as well as unenlightened minds" (included in the "Memorials" added by Maria Weston Chapman, editor of the *Autobiography*, 3:166–68; rpt. in Yates, *Harriet Martineau on Women*, 33–35). The *Autobiography* extends the range of Martineau's work beyond that mentioned in the private resolution, as well as her perspective on her relations with other literary figures.

27. Davidoff and Hall, *Family Fortunes*, chap. 3, which treats Sarah Ellis and Harriet Martineau as inheritors of the domestic tradition of Cowper and More. In her chapter "Literary Domesticity and Women Writers' Subjectivities," Corbett discusses Martineau, following Sidonie Smith in *A Poetics of Women's Autobiography*, 123–49, as a female autobiographer who, despite her defiance of feminine conventions, "continues to measure herself against the normative middle-class standard of women's sphere" (*Representing Femininity*, 89). My argument is that Martineau uses the common currency of domesticity to achieve different social, political, and literary ends.

28. Martineau describes cultural life in Norwich in her biographical essay on Amelia Opie, another Norwich author; see Martineau, *Biographical Sketches*, 329–36. See also Marjorie Allthorpe-Guyton's "Artistic and Literary Life of Nineteenth Century Norwich," in *Norwich in the Nineteenth Century*, ed. Christopher Barringer (Norwich: Gliddon Books, 1984), 1–46, which discusses the Norwich School of painters, as well as local writers, musicians, architects, and antiquarians.

29. In *Place Matters*, 1–20, Morgan argues that women travel writers' voices change from "familiar constructions" to different "selves" as they move from home to Southeast Asia. I believe that geographical location matters for Victorian women autobiographers as much as for travel writers.

30. Tonna, *Mesmerism*, 6–7.

31. Letter of 3 August 1846, in Martineau, *Letters to Fanny Wedgwood*, 91–92.

32. Martineau began her autobiography first in 1831, once again in the early 1840s in Tynemouth, where she went to recuperate from what she believed was a cancerous tumor. Although there is no evidence of direct influence, Martineau may have read Tonna's *Personal Recollections* during her Tynemouth recuperation, as her comments to Fanny Wedgwood during this period suggest.

33. The doctrine that denies the concept of a triune God and the divinity of Christ.

34. The M.P. was probably one of the Gurneys, a Quaker family active in politics and later supportive of Martineau's *Illustrations of Political Economy*. The Leigh Smiths, a Unitarian family, also represented Norwich during this period.

35. Martineau's description of Norwich literary life (*Autobiography*, 1:297–303) is critical, however, of its provincialism.

36. Ruth A. Symes's study of another Unitarian woman's autobiography, "The Educative

'I' in Nineteenth-Century Women's Autobiographies: Catharine Cappe of York (1822)," in Swindells, *Uses of Autobiography,* 128–36, leads me to suggest that Martineau's interest in "the growth of a human mind" reflects a general Unitarian interest in associationist psychology and its application in early childhood development.

37. See Kowalski, "'Heroine of Some Strange Romance,'" 141–53, for a fascinating reading of Tonna's adolescent behavior as alternately "self-aggrandizing" and "self-destructive or masochistic."

38. Catherine Marsh, quoted in Davidoff and Hall, *Family Fortunes,* 89. The quotation comes from the preface to the Marsh sisters' biography of their father, William: *The Life of the Rev. William Marsh, D.D.* (New York: R. Carter, 1867).

39. For an early instance in which parental authority interferes with social and moral growth, see Martineau's discussion of the "taking down" system, *Autobiography,* 1 : 19–21.

40. Davidoff and Hall, *Family Fortunes,* 186.

41. Martineau, trans., *Positive Philosophy of Auguste Comte,* 1 : 3.

42. More, *Works,* 1 : 367.

43. Period III, secs. i and iii, treat her theological crisis; Period III, secs. ii and iv, her first attempt at professional authorship.

44. Martineau, *Household Education,* 238.

45. "Miss Martineau's Monthly Novels," *Quarterly Review* 49 (April 1833): 151. The review, often attributed to John Wilson Croker, was written by George Poulett Scrope. Elsewhere Martineau expresses admiration for Edgeworth's literary achievement, as well as deep pity for the limitations she endured. In a letter to Fanny Wedgwood dated 23 June 1867, Martineau writes of "the exquisite beauty of M. E.'s spirit and temper,—the thorough generosity of her whole long domestic life,—the exemption from the worst and most provoking faults of literary women,—and yet—the dreary worldliness and lowness in which she was held down, in spite of all possible capacity for aspiration, and of a temperament made up of enthusiasm! It is one of the most pathetic spectacles that ever came before me,—her life as it was in comparison with what it should have been." See Martineau, *Letters to Fanny Wedgwood,* 286.

46. Hannah More, *Strictures on the Modern System of Female Education,* in *Works,* 1 : 365. In "On Female Education," 77–81, Martineau refers to—and refutes—the claim that "the vanity so universally ascribed to the sex is apt to be inflated by any degree of proficiency of knowledge, and that women therefore become forgetful of the subordinate station assigned them by law, natural and divine."

47. Martineau, "On Female Education," 78.

48. Letter to Henry Reeve, 6 February 1859, in Martineau, *Selected Letters,* 169.

49. Beecher, *Treatise on Domestic Economy,* 27. Although it is uncertain whether Martineau knew this treatise, she had met Beecher, the sister of Harriet Beecher Stowe, in Cincinnati in 1835 during her tour of America. Beecher reacted negatively to Martineau's depiction of American women in *Society in America,* later inserting a footnote in the *Treatise,* 30–31, to chastise Martineau for her false and negative views. For Martineau's relations with American feminists, see Yates, *Harriet Martineau on Women,* 127–60; for a discussion of the American tour as a formative moment in Martineau's feminism, see Pichanick, *Harriet Martineau,* 92–99; on Martineau's views on domestic education, see Linda H. Peterson, "Harriet Martineau's *Household Education:* Revising the Feminine Tradition," in Scott and Fletcher, *Culture and Education in Victorian England,* 183–94.

50. Martineau, *Household Education,* 198–99. As my example suggests, the work she assigns falls into predictable gender categories, perhaps because she believes that specialization in labor is the most efficient system for managing a house as well as a factory.

51. See Martineau, *Household Education,* chaps. 8–9.

52. In this sense Martineau follows the tradition of Hannah More, embodied in *Coelebs in Search of a Wife,* where both the hero and his future wife, Lucilla Stanley, show their propensity for domestic life. In *Coelebs,* domesticity is aligned with country (vs. city) life rather than gender. Consider the advice Coelebs's father gives: "I know your domestic propensities; and I know, therefore, that the whole colour of your future life will be, in a particular manner, determined by the turn of mind of the woman you may marry. Were you to live in the busy haunts of men; were you of any profession, or likely to be engaged in public life, . . . your happiness would not so immediately, so exclusively depend on the individual society of a woman, as that of a country gentleman must do" (9).

53. Pichanick, *Harriet Martineau,* 97.

54. Martineau, *Society in America,* 1:153.

55. Martineau, "On Female Education," 80.

56. Martineau, *Household Education,* 159.

57. Ibid., chaps. 8–9.

58. Letter of 11 October 1836[?], quoted in Pichanick, *Harriet Martineau,* 113.

59. Pichanick argues this point persuasively in *Harriet Martineau,* 110–14, pointing out that the living arrangements in London with her mother and elderly aunt were extremely taxing on Martineau's nerves.

60. Charles Dickens, *David Copperfield* (Oxford: Oxford University Press, 1981), chap. 53. Mary Poovey discusses the contradictions within this Victorian myth in "*David Copperfield* and the Professional Writer," in *Uneven Developments,* 101: "not only is the Copperfields' domestic security a function of David's material success as a writer, not only does his success as a writer (as he describes it) depend on the selflessness Agnes's example inspires, but the representation of the domestic sphere as immune to the alienation of work is produced by the very writing with which it is compared."

61. It is important to note also that the publication and sale of *Eastern Life* represents the simultaneous climax of her spiritual and professional narrative. To George Jacob Holyoake she wrote that "the most important part [of the *Autobiography*] was the true account of my conscious transition from the Xn faith to my present philosophy" (quoted in Pichanick, *Harriet Martineau,* 201). That transition was complete with her research and composition of *Eastern Life,* the book that also paid off the mortgage and allowed her to write, during the next decade, as "a gentleman of the press."

62. By "nonheterosexual" I do not mean that Martineau established a lesbian or protolesbian community of women, only that she created a domestic life independent of heterosexual marriage.

63. Poovey, *Uneven Developments,* 115.

Chapter III. *"The Feelings and Claims of Little People"*

1. Quoted by Harriet Martineau in her *Autobiography,* 2:324. As Shelagh Hunter suggests in *Harriet Martineau: The Poetics of Moralism, Household Education* (1849) might be

seen as a dry run for the *Autobiography* (1855) in that it recounts many of Martineau's childhood experiences, sometimes with the sex of the exemplary child altered.

2. Martineau, *Autobiography*, 2:324.

3. Martineau titled her life history an "autobiography," the first instance I know in which a woman writer chose this generic label. The first edition of Jane Eyre is subtitled *An Autobiography*, an early use of the term in fiction.

4. David, *Rule Britannia*, 85. David calls Jane "The Governess of Empire."

5. *Daily News*, 3 February 1853, in Allott, *Critical Heritage*, 172–73. Virginia Woolf makes a similar point in "*Jane Eyre* and *Wuthering Heights*" when she suggests that "the drawbacks of being Jane Eyre are not far to seek. Always to be a governess and always to be in love is a serious limitation in a world which is full, after all, of people who are neither one nor the other" (included in Barrett, *Women and Writing*, 128).

6. "Death of Currer Bell," rpt. in Wise and Symington, *The Brontës*, 4:181.

7. Ibid., 4:42.

8. Moglen, *Charlotte Brontë*, 225.

9. Millgate, "Jane Eyre's Progress," xxi–xxix, emphasizes the influence of Bunyan's *Pilgrim's Progress;* Beaty, "*Jane Eyre* and Genre," 619–54, later revised for *Misreading Jane Eyre*, discusses the providentialist element common in governess novels prior to *Jane Eyre;* Vargish, *Providential Aesthetic in Victorian Fiction*, emphasizes the centrality of the novel's religious structure; and Qualls, *Secular Pilgrims of Victorian Fiction*, traces the influence of Bunyan's *Pilgrim's Progress* and Carlyle's *Sartor Resartus*.

10. Gilbert and Gubar, *Madwoman in the Attic*, 336–39; see also Karen E. Rowe's " 'Fairyborn and human-bred': Jane Eyre's Education in Romance," in Abel, Hirsch, and Langland, *Voyage In*, 169–89.

11. Hardy, *Appropriate Form*, 68; Merrett, "Conduct of Spiritual Autobiography in *Jane Eyre*," 2, 9; Dale, "Charlotte Brontë's 'Tale Half-Told,' " 108–29. These readings are consonant with new feminist approaches to *Jane Eyre* that, like Bette London's "Pleasure of Submission," 195–213, question the revolutionary effect of the novel and point to its repressive elements.

12. Brontë's "secularization"—or what I prefer to call "domestication"—of spiritual autobiography is what makes *Jane Eyre* so significant in the Victorian tradition of women's autobiography and the cultural work of domestic literature. With Victorian women increasingly shut out from the hermeneutic tradition of spiritual autobiography—with its theological issues becoming more complex, its interpretive techniques more professional and systematic, its writers more exclusively male—an alternative form of spiritual autobiography became almost a necessity. Women needed a form that recognized and accounted for spiritual concerns in their sphere, and *Jane Eyre* adapts spiritual autobiography to domestic life in a way unprecedented in Victorian literature. Indeed, the novel gives a lesson in how to make spiritual autobiography a viable form—even if it proposes a way that women writers such as Martineau could not finally approve.

13. Throughout this chapter I cite the text of *Jane Eyre*, ed. Richard J. Dunn (New York: Norton, 1987).

14. As Landow explains in *Victorian Types, Victorian Shadows*, Victorian religious practice encouraged individuals to apply biblical models to their lives in order to interpret their experiences, a practice known today as "correlative typology." The Reverend Henry Melvill, chaplain to Queen Victoria and canon of St. Paul's, told his congre-

gation, for instance, that the history of Israel was "a figurative history, sketching, as in parable, much that befalls the Christian Church in general, and its members in particular"; it was, he suggested, a material prophecy that would "find its accomplishment in the experiences of true disciples of Christ in every nation and age." When Jane finds an Exodus pattern in her experiences at Thornfield, in other words, she is finding what a good Victorian Christian might expect to find. See, e.g., Melvill's sermon "Honey from the Rock," in *Lectures on Practical Subjects* (New York: Stanford & Swords, 1853), 30–31.

15. See Hardy, *Appropriate Form*, 68; as Barry Qualls argues in *Secular Pilgrims of Victorian Fiction*, 55, however, Jane's "questions to the dying Helen Burns—'Where is God? What is God?'—bring no answer that is comprehensible to her."

16. Richard J. Dunn quotes contemporary sources for Helen's beliefs, including stories from the juvenile magazine *The Children's Friend*, in his edition of *Jane Eyre*, 403–6.

17. [Elizabeth Rigby], in *Quarterly Review* 84 (December 1848), rpt. in Allott, *The Brontës*, 109. With less vituperation, the reviewer for the *Christian Remembrancer*, April 1848, also complained that the novel "seldom invoked [Christianity] but for the purpose of showing that all Christian profession is bigotry and all Christianity is hypocrisy" (rpt. ibid., 88–92).

18. Burnett, *Annals of Labour;* see also Burnett, Mayall, and Vincent, *Autobiography of the Working Class.*

19. [Rigby], 109–10; [Margaret Oliphant], "Modern Novelists," 558.

20. Gilbert and Gubar, *Madwoman in the Attic,* 339. Commenting on Jane's departure for Thornfield, Qualls notes: "The first phase of Jane Eyre's journey is thus complete; she now enters upon the stage of larger temptations at Thornfield" (*Secular Pilgrims of Victorian Fiction,* 56).

21. While I concur with Beaty's reading of the governess tale and the gothic as "dialogic genres," I depart from his treatment of "Love" as "the transgeneric topic" (*Misreading "Jane Eyre,"* 77–100). As I argue below, romantic love is minimized in the autobiographical genre that Jane resists in vol. 3: the female missionary memoir.

22. "Moral gothic" is Gilbert and Gubar's term in *Madwoman in the Attic,* 337; "secular pilgrim" comes from the title of Quall's book.

23. As Robert A. Heilman pointed out years ago, the addition of gothic elements to the domestic novel gives Brontë access to a language of passion unavailable to Austen and her contemporaries. See "Charlotte Brontë's 'New' Gothic," in Rathburn and Steinman, *From Jane Austen to Joseph Conrad,* 118–32.

24. In *Coelebs in Search of a Wife,* More satirizes women enthusiasts who treat every personal experience in religious terms as much as she criticizes women who fail to take religion seriously.

25. *Caroline Mordaunt; or, The Governess,* in *Works of Mrs. Sherwood,* vol. 13. Beaty discusses the importance of *Caroline Mordaunt* in the tradition of the governess novel ("*Jane Eyre* and Genre," 632–40).

26. See Qualls, *Secular Pilgrims of Victorian Fiction,* 43–84, for a detailed, if differently nuanced, account of this transformation.

27. Mark Rutherford [William White Hale], *Catharine Furze* (1893) and *Clara Hopgood* (1896).

28. As Piggin's dates suggest in *Making Evangelical Missionaries,* clergymen went to India even before the official ban was lifted, often as chaplains to British troops stationed in

the East. Despite the fact that many clergymen took their wives to India and several groups (including the Church Missionary Society of the Church of England) sent women teachers, Piggin discusses only male missionaries officially deputized by Protestant organizations.

29. I have concentrated on these three women because of the unusually large number of memoirs published about them. In some histories of women's missionary work, Hannah Marshman, the wife of the Reverend Joshua Marshman, is credited as the first woman to undertake educational work in India (as in Chatterjee's *Hannah Marshman: The First Woman Missionary in India*), but because the memoirs written by her daughter were unpublished in the nineteenth century, I say little about her life. Another important female missionary was Harriet Newell, who sailed for India at the same time as Judson and Boardman but died within months of her arrival.

30. In a lecture at the Yale Center for British Art, 4 October 1997, "Godly Adventures for Boys and Girls: Missionary Heroism, Romance, and Domesticity in Victoria's England," Mary Ellen Gibson suggested that Brontë encountered missionary tales in her reading of the Methodist magazines brought to Haworth by her aunt. There were in fact many sources of information about missions in the periodical press, beginning with Sydney Smith's attack on Indian missions in *Edinburgh Review* 12 (April 1808): 151–81 and Robert Southey's counterdefense, "Periodical Accounts, Relative to the Baptist Missionary Society," *Quarterly Review* 1 (February 1809): 193–226. Given the Reverend Patrick Brontë's ties with Evangelical circles at Cambridge, including the famous Indian missionary Henry Martyn, it is possible that Brontë learned of missions from her father; see Gibson's forthcoming article in *Victorian Literature and Culture,* "Henry Martyn and England's Christian Empire: Rereading *Jane Eyre* through Missionary Biography," for a discussion of the widespread influence of the *Memoir of Henry Martyn;* see Piggin, *Making Evangelical Missionaries,* 18–20, for a discussion of the important early influence of Cambridge-educated chaplains in India.

31. Wilson, *Memoir of Mrs Margaret Wilson,* includes several chapters about the Bombay School for girls. The minutes of the Society for Promoting Female Education in China, India and the East (later called the Female Education Society) include numerous notes of women approved for service in Calcutta and elsewhere in India—e.g., on 4 May 1835, the appointment of Miss Wakefield "as Assistant to Mrs Wilson at Calcutta" and, in the same year, "a suitable applicant to be stationed at Gorrickspur." The minutes of the Female Education Society, a branch of the Church Missionary Society, are an important source for documenting the remarkable work of female educators, married and unmarried, during the 1830s and 1840s. See "Missions to Women," in *Church Missionary Society Archive,* sec. II, pt. 1.

32. Ann Judson, "Address to the Females of America" and her "Address to Females in America, relative to the situation of Females in the East," rpt. in Knowles, *Memoir of Mrs. Ann Judson,* 313–24.

33. See Stuart, *Lives of Mrs. Ann H. Judson and Mrs. Sarah B[oardman] Judson,* 300. The primary difference between Mrs. Boardman's school and others in Burma was that, while Mrs. Boardman was allowed to continue religious instruction, British schools were officially prohibited from teaching the Christian religion on the grounds that it disrupted relations with—and created rebellions of—the native inhabitants.

34. Minute 8, 29 July 1834, *Church Missionary Society Archive.*

35. Judson, "Address . . . relative to the Situation of Females in the East," 321, and Mar-

garet Wilson's "Review of the Life of Mrs. Judson," reprinted as an appendix to Wilson, *Memoirs of Margaret Wilson*, 612–13. For a similar but more rhetorically restrained discussion, see Wilson, *Memoirs of Margaret Wilson*, 231–35.

36. Judson, "Address . . . relative to the Situation of Females in the East," 321.

37. Wilson, *Memoirs of Margaret Wilson*, 613. Leslie A. Fleming points out, in "A New Humanity: American Missionaries' Ideals for Women in North India, 1870–1930," in Chadhuri and Strobel, *Western Women and Imperialism*, 191–206, that the "low status" of Indian women remained a primary concern of American missionaries throughout the nineteenth and twentieth centuries. See also Barbara N. Ramusack's discussion in the same collection, "Cultural Missionaries, Maternal Imperialists, Feminist Allies: British Women Activists in India, 1865–1945," 119–36.

38. Davin, "British Women Missionaries in Nineteenth-Century China," 257–71; Donovan, "Women as Foreign Missionaries in the Episcopal Church, 1830–1920," 16–39; and Donovan, "Women and Mission," 297–305. For a nineteenth-century example, see "Dr. Mary McGeorge of India," in Pitman, *Missionary Heroines of Eastern Lands*, 93, which states: "How great and many were the difficulties and prejudices that had to be overcome by any women who longed to enter the noble profession of medicine."

39. Wilson, *Memoirs of Margaret Wilson*, 611.

40. Stuart, preface to *Lives of Mrs. Ann H. Judson and Mrs. Sarah B. Judson*, iii. The other Mrs. Judsons were subsequent wives of Adorinam Judson, the first male missionary to Burma. Pitman's preface to *Lady Missionaries in Foreign Lands*, v–x, makes similar arguments about the importance of "free intercourse of the educated mothers and women of Europe . . . with the mothers and women of India."

41. Beasley, *Pagodas and Prisons*, 1.

42. See *OED*, entries 5b, 3, and 4.

43. The first title is affixed to Duff's many pamphlets on missions in India; the second derives from Paton's biography, *Alexander Duff: Pioneer of Missionary Education*. Paton credits Duff with formulating the practice of educating first, evangelizing second, which was adopted by the Church of Scotland's missionaries in India.

44. Duff, *Vindication of the Church of Scotland's India Mission*, v, vii. Duff's reasoning depends on his view of Hindu society as caste-based; in effect, he argues for a trickledown effect, by which women and members of the lower classes would receive the benefits of education as high-caste Brahmins became better educated in Christian beliefs and mores. Women missionaries of the 1830s and 1840s had much less interest in this gender- and class-based approach and tended to work directly with other women and members of lower castes. Viswanathan discusses Duff's blueprint for Christian education in India in *Masks of Conquest*, chaps. 2–3. Her analysis concentrates on the role of literary study in Indian education and includes nothing on women's education, no doubt because Duff thought it relatively unimportant.

45. Stuart, *Lives of Mrs. Ann H. Judson and Mrs. Sarah B. Judson*, iii–iv.

46. David, *Rule Britannia*, 84–85.

47. Stuart, *Lives of Mrs. Ann H. Judson and Mrs. Sarah B. Judson*, iii; Wilson, *Memoir of Margaret Wilson*, 611.

48. Stuart, *Lives of Mrs. Ann H. Judson and Mrs. Sarah B. Judson*, 242.

49. Quoted in Hill, *Reminiscences*, 98, 65.

50. Quoted ibid., 65. Missionary memoirs debate who is to be credited as the first woman

missionary. American Nonconformist publications stake the claim for Ann Judson and Harriet Newell, who sailed for India in 1812. British publications often name Hannah Marshman, who went out with her husband in 1799.

51. Quoted in Michie, *Flesh Made Word,* 36. Jameson made this statement in 1846. Michie points out that early and mid-Victorian novels avoid depicting the work of their "leisure class heroines" while they reveal the hard physical labor of working-class women.

52. Suleri discusses Parlby's *Wanderings,* as well as *An Englishwoman in India: The Memoirs of Harriet Tytler, 1828–1858* (Oxford: Oxford University Press, 1986), in *Rhetoric of English India,* 75–110.

53. *The Life of Mrs. Sherwood, Chiefly Autobiographical,* edited by her daughter Sophia Kelly, is not a missionary memoir but the account of the wife of a military officer stationed in India, later a famous Evangelical writer. Sherwood discusses the efforts at education undertaken by British women in Calcutta, including the school established for British officers' children and half-castes, as well as her translations of *Pilgrim's Progress* and a simple "Church Catechism" for native children.

54. Stuart, *Lives of Mrs. Ann H. Judson and Mrs. Sarah B. Judson,* 289–90.

55. E. R. Pitman's language in "Mrs. Ann Hasseltine Judson of Burmah, First Lady Missionary to the Heathen," in Pitman, *Lady Missionaries in Foreign Lands,* 38, 51, which condenses the earlier *Memoir of Ann H. Judson* by Knowles.

56. J. Macdonald, *Statement of Reasons for accepting a Call to go to India as a Missionary,* quoted in Piggin, *Making Evangelical Missionaries,* 19. Ann Hasseltine Judson responded similarly after reading the *Life of David Brainerd,* another influential missionary biography.

57. In addition to the *Memoir of the Life of the Henry Martyn* (1814), it is possible that Brontë had in mind one of the most important missionary memoirs of the 1830s in her depiction of St. John: *The Memoirs of Reginald Heber, by his Widow* (1830). The exemplary life of Heber, a popular poet and hymn writer, and his sudden death soon after he had accepted the bishopric of Calcutta became the basis of several popular biographies; unlike Martyn, Heber had a wife who was willing to accompany him to India and later to edit his papers and compose his memoir.

58. Adrienne Rich, "The Temptations of a Motherless Woman," and Helene Moglen, *Charlotte Brontë,* both included in Dunn's edition of *Jane Eyre,* 473, 487; Gilbert and Gubar, *Madwoman in the Attic,* 365–66.

59. David does not frame her discussion in terms of subjection to patriarchy vs. some sort of feminist freedom. Rather, she argues that "Jane suffers on the road to achieving a Victorian female subjectivity that is defined, in part, by a gendered service to empire" (*Rule Britannia,* 78).

60. Stuart enumerates these qualities in her preface to *Lives of Mrs. Ann H. Judson and Mrs. Sarah B. Judson,* iii.

61. Wilson, *Memoir of Mrs. Margaret Wilson,* 33.

62. Ibid., 90–91.

63. Quoted in Stuart, *Lives of Mrs. Ann H. Judson and Mrs. Sarah B. Judson,* 194–95.

64. The Reverend Boardman's final letters suggest that his love for his wife and family was intense and sincere: "In thinking on the probability of dying soon, two or three things occasion considerable unwillingness to meet the solemn event. One is, the sore affliction I know it will occasion to my dear family, especially my fond, too fond wife. Her heart will be well-high riven" (quoted ibid., 267).

65. As Moglen has argued, "Jane, like Charlotte Brontë herself, must *be* loved in order to know herself lovable; . . . her deprivation of love has been too great and lasted too long" (*Charlotte Brontë,* 151). Using the memoir of a female missionary to Sierra Leone, Deirdre David critiques the "desire for power" that motivated some male missionaries (*Rule Britannia,* 86).

66. In "Three Women's Texts and a Critique of Imperialism," 248–49, Spivak rereads this difference as "the distance between sexual reproduction and soul making," the former embodied in the *narrative* conclusion of the novel, the latter escaping "the closed circle" as a tangent that is "granted the important task of concluding the *text.*" She draws this distinction to display the inadequacies of early feminist readings that "see the novel as simply replacing the male protagonist with the female" without registering its imperialist project.

67. Armstrong, *Desire and Domestic Fiction,* 192. Whether this representation of "unseen desires" results, as Armstrong later argues, in "a new basis of the self, thus a new human nature," is more problematic to demonstrate.

68. Gilbert and Gubar, *Madwoman in the Attic,* 370. Gilbert incorrectly asserts that this revision of Bunyan is the "last" in *Jane Eyre.* As Carolyn Williams's essay "Closing the Book: The Intertextual End of *Jane Eyre,*" in McGann, *Victorian Connections,* and my own argument point out, the "last" revision of Bunyan applies to St. John Rivers's spiritual achievement, as Brontë gives him "the sternness of the warrior Greatheart, who guards his pilgrim convoy from the onslaught of Apollyon" (Brontë, *Jane Eyre,* 398).

69. Williams, "Closing the Book," 82. Williams is more certain than I am that this final gesture "closes with"—i.e., "engages and maintains a strong sense of struggle with"—the biblical text on which Jane's account is modeled and that the final contrast privileges Jane's "immediate, ongoing life 'here and now'" in contrast to St. John's "death on the 'Himalayan ridge.'" In my reading, the ending is ambivalent, literally "taking two directions."

70. Leonard Woods, "A Sermon Delivered on the Occasion of the Lamented Death of Mrs. Harriet Newell," in his *Memoirs of Mrs. Harriet Newell,* 213, 197.

71. Ibid., 212. Woods's sermon recognizes the need, on the one hand, to offer Newell as a model for potential missionaries and the importance, on the other, of using her life story to inspire more ordinary listeners to greater commitment and faith at home.

72. The comparisons with biblical types appear on the following pages: 370, when Jane resists St. John's final admonition; 394, when Jane remains silent about her visionary experience; and 386, when Rochester praises her ministrations to his depressed spirits.

Chapter IV. *"For My Better Self"*

1. Barrett Browning, *Aurora Leigh,* 3 : 158, 303. Further citations are given parenthetically by book and line numbers in McSweeney's edition.

2. Herbert Tucker, "*Aurora Leigh:* Epic Solutions to Novel Ends," 62.

3. Ibid., 67.

4. Letter 139, 4 February 1842, in Raymond and Sullivan, *Letters of Elizabeth Barrett Browning to Mary Russell Mitford,* 1 : 345. The letter is also included in Miller, *Elizabeth Barrett to Miss Mitford,* 106. As a subsequent letter written on 18 November 1842 attests (letter 200, 2 : 81), Barrett disputed with friends about the value of Wordsworth's poetry, in this case with Hugh Boyd, who considered the poet laureate third-

rate. Boyd, she reports, "was very angry . . IS . . . will be perhaps in spite of all—and why?—why because I wont agree with him that Wordsworth is at best, a *third rate poet.*"

5. The exception may be Caroline Bowles's *Birthday* (1836), which was considered autobiographical in the tradition of Cowper's *Task*. Barrett Browning knew and admired Bowles (later the wife of Robert Southey), as her letter in response to Richard Hengist Horne's *New Spirit of the Age* attests: "Caroline Southey should have been mentioned with some distinction. She is a womanly Cowper, with much of his sweetness, and some of his strength, and there is much in her poems to which the heart of the reader leans back in remembrance" (Stoddard, *Letters of Elizabeth Barrett Browning, Addressed to Richard Hengist Horne,* 200). I have found no evidence, however, that Barrett Browning viewed *The Birthday* as a poem about artistic development.

6. Ross, *Contours of Masculine Desire,* 229.

7. Landon, *Poetical Works,* 223. Unless I indicate otherwise, all citations of Landon's work are to F. J. Sypher's edition, which is a reprint of the volume edited and illustrated by William Bell Scott and published by George Routledge in 1873.

8. It is possible to read the opening lines of *Aurora Leigh* as autobiographically relevant to Barrett Browning's career. If, as Tricia Lootens suggests in *Lost Saints,* 122, Barrett Browning's "Vision of Poets" "celebrates Romantic genius, Pythian inspiration, and the agonies of Christian sanctity," and if the only woman poet included in this poem is Sappho, "Who died for Beauty as martyrs do" (l. 289), then we may read *Aurora Leigh* as a (partial) renunciation of that earlier vision. L.E.L.'s Eulalie is based on Sappho and on Madame de Staël's Sapphic writer Corinne—figures Barrett had admired greatly in her youth.

9. Glennis Stephenson, "Poet Construction: Mrs Hemans, L.E.L., and the Image of the Nineteenth-Century Woman Poet," in Neuman and Stephenson, *ReImagining Women,* 66. See also Landon's *Erinna:* "It was my other self that had a power; / Mine, but o'er which I had not a control. . . . / A song came gushing, like the natural tears, / To check whose current does not rest with us" (Landon, *Poetical Works,* 216).

10. Leighton, *Victorian Women Poets,* 61.

11. Robinson, *Memoirs* (1826), 132.

12. Landon left biographical materials with Laman Blanchard, her literary executor, who wrote a "sketch of the literary and personal life of L.E.L.," as he put it, "in fulfilment of a pledge given to her long before she meditated leaving England" (*Life and Literary Remains of L.E.L.,* v).

13. The phrases come from Ross's chapter on More and Barbauld, "The Birth of a Tradition: Making Cultural Space for Feminine Poetry," in *Contours of Masculine Desire,* 192, 202. As his chapter title implies, Ross views More and Barbauld as key figures in a single "feminine" tradition, as differentiated from a "masculine" Romantic tradition; yet the transmission from Robinson to Landon suggests that there were two feminine traditions, one less invested in woman's role as "sociomoral handmaiden."

14. E[mma] R[oberts], "Memoir of L.E.L.," in Landon, *"Zenana" and Minor Poems,* 9; Blanchard, *Life and Literary Remains of L.E.L.,* 1 : 17, 40. Roberts also refers to Landon's poetry as "her effusions" (10).

15. William Howitt, *Homes and Haunts of the Most Eminent British Poets,* 2:134.

16. Norma Clarke, "The Cause of Infant Genius," paper given at the International Conference on Women's Poetry, Birkbeck College, London University, 21 July 1995.

17. Roberts, "Memoir of L.E.L.," 16, 11.

18. Speaking specifically of Landon's *Improvisatrice,* Blanchard notes, "Thus, though it was but Sappho who sang, Sappho and L.E.L. were voted to be one, and the minstrel was identified as a martyr to ill-starred passion and blighted hope": *Life and Literary Remains of L.E.L.,* 2:41. See also Howitt's anecdote in *Homes and Haunts of the Most Eminent British Poets,* 2:132–33, about Landon's deflating of "a young sentimental man" by explaining, "with an air of merry scorn," that her poetry was "all professional, you know!"

19. Landon, preface to *"Venetian Bracelet,"* vii–viii.

20. Howitt, *Homes and Haunts of the Most Eminent British Poets,* 2:137. Howitt follows this passage with an anecdote he heard from Emma Roberts, which she apparently suppressed: that Landon, "when calumny was dealing very freely with her name," told Roberts that she had a "remedy" for her "suffering" and showed her friend "a vial of prussic acid." Howitt treats this anecdote as a real-life version of a fictional incident in Landon's novel *Ethel Churchill,* thus suggesting another link between the poetess's life and her work.

21. Letter dated 16 July 1841, in Miller, *Elizabeth Barrett to Miss Mitford,* 77–78.

22. There is also Elizabeth Barrett's commentary in her poem "L.E.L.'s Last Question," which suggests that, had L.E.L. thought more of Him "who drew / All life from dust, and for all tasted death," her poetry might have achieved a greater, more long-lasting significance. This sense of the poetess's focus on things domestic and mundane to the omission of higher, spiritual matters continues in *Aurora Leigh.*

23. Kathleen Blake traces the parallels to Wordsworth's *Prelude* in "Elizabeth Barrett Browning and Wordsworth," 387–98, and argues that the primary difference lies in Barrett Browning's emphasis on love. My point, a slightly different one, is that Barrett Browning uses parallels with Wordsworth to distinguish Aurora from the Romantic female poetess.

24. Aurora takes the lark as her counterpart in bk. II:744–45, "The little lark reached higher with his song / Than I with crying," and in bk. III:151–52: "The music soars within the little lark, / And the lark soars." These passages recall most notably bk. VII:18–31 of *The Prelude,* in which Wordsworth allies himself with a "choir of redbreasts" at winter's end, and bk. XIV:381–89, in which he figures his autobiographical poem as "this Song, which like a lark / I have protracted, in the unwearied heavens / Singing."

25. Blanchard, *Life and Literary Remains of L.E.L.,* 1:13. Biographers also noted that her reviewing for the *Literary Gazette* required wide and thoughtful reading.

26. "Prefatory Notice," in Hemans, *Poetical Works,* 22.

27. Rundle, "'Inscription of these volumes,'" 247.

28. Leighton, *Victorian Women Poets,* 51, suggests that in this detail Barrett Browning "may well be remembering the life of LEL." I would add that the geographical shift from the parish of Brompton to the adjacent Kensington follows a historical shift of respectable Victorian authors and artists in a westward direction. Bohemians moved southward to Chelsea.

29. Blanchard, *Life and Literary Remains of L.E.L.,* 1:79. This description also appears in Elwood, *Memoirs of the Literary Ladies of England,* 2:319, and Howitt, *Homes and Haunts of the Most Eminent British Poets,* 2:130. It continues: "—with a simple white bed, at the foot of which was a small, old, oblong-shaped sort of dressing-table, quite covered with a common worn writing-desk heaped with papers, while some strewed the ground, the table being too small for aught besides the desk; a little high-backed

cane-chair which gave you any idea rather than that of comfort—a few books scattered about completed the author's paraphernalia."

30. See, for example, Emma Roberts's comment that "the history and literature of all ages and all countries were familiar to her, . . . the extent of her learning, and the depth of her research, manifesting themselves in publications which do not bear her name" ("Memoir of L.E.L.," 17).

31. Blanchard, *Life and Literary Remains of L.E.L.,* 1 : 32–33.

32. Barrett Browning may also be defending the "Cockney School," a derogatory label she thought ill chosen. To Mary Russell Mitford she complained, "And, what *is* the cockney school? . . . Is it not their locality which gave the name—& still less resonably [*sic*] than the Lakes gave another? And are any of us the worse for living in London, if we dont roll in the dust of the streets?" (letter 737, 6 March 1840, in Kelley and Hudson, *Brownings' Correspondence,* vol. 4).

33. Howitt, *Homes and Haunts of the Most Eminent British Poets,* 2 : 137; Blanchard, *Life and Literary Remains of L.E.L.,* 1 : 52.

34. Landon, *Poetical Works,* 226. Cf. Hannah More's use of the myth of Atalanta in *Strictures on the Modern System of Female Education* (in *Works,* 1 : 367) to argue that women writers cannot sustain their careers as men can.

35. On this score, Angela Leighton incorrectly suggests that Aurora's father is more important than Romney to her poetic development: "It is not the realisation that she has loved and lost Romney, but that she has lost her father, which tests and educates her imagination," Leighton argues in *Elizabeth Barrett Browning,* 136. Romney is important because he becomes the patriarchal mouthpiece, arguing the traditional challenges to women's abilities and for Aurora's "proper" place in the domestic sphere. Her father is not put in this position because Barrett Browning wants Aurora to claim her paternal inheritance—the learning, the intellectual contribution—without undue complication.

36. Landon, *Poetical Works,* 229. The Englishman listens to a long monologue in which Eulalie laments the ill effects of fame and praises the virtues of "the loveliness of home" and "support and shelter from man's heart" (226). When the monologue ends, he abruptly states, "I soon left Italy; it is well worth / A year of wandering, were it but to feel / How much our England does outweigh the world" (230). One could read this hiatus simply as an acknowledgment that poetic genius is unsuited to domestic life. Landon seems to have intended, however, a stronger link between the continuing work of the poetess and the approval—including love—of her male audience.

37. Cora Kaplan, in her ground-breaking study of the sources of *Aurora Leigh,* calls it the "most vulgar" alteration of the Corinne myth ("Introduction" to *"Aurora Leigh" and Other Poems,* 17). Dorothy Mermin writes more ambivalently: "Perhaps the oddest thing about *Aurora Leigh,* after all, is the triumphantly happy ending—happy for the heroine at any rate, if not for her disempowered and humiliated lover" (*Elizabeth Barrett Browning,* 217). In "*Aurora Leigh:* Epic Solutions to Novel Ends," Herbert F. Tucker explains, to my mind convincingly, the ending as the combination of novelistic convention and epic apocalypse.

38. Browning, *Letters of Robert Browning and Elizabeth Barrett Barrett,* 1 : 232.

39. Mermin, *Elizabeth Barrett Browning,* 1. Later Mermin suggests that Barrett Browning's "real rival was L.E.L., not Homer or Byron or even Mrs. Hemans, whom she consid-

ered too ladylike and deficient in passion to be seriously reckoned with" (32). If Mermin is correct, as I think she may be, then the density of allusions to Landon's work in *Aurora Leigh* points to that rivalry.

40. The term "Self-biography" comes from Coleridge's notebooks, 4 January 1804, cited in the apparatus of Wordworth, *Prelude, 1799, 1805, 1850*, 529. The 1850 title page of the poem reads: *The Prelude, or Growth of a Poet's Mind, An Autobiographical Poem*. Throughout this chapter I cite the 1850 edition.

41. "On a Portrait of Wordsworth by B. R. Haydon," in *Poetical Works of Elizabeth Barrett Browning*, 98.

42. Blake, "Elizabeth Barrett Browning and Wordsworth," 390.

43. On the problematic substitution of maternal nature for real mothers, see Steinmetz, "Images of 'Mother-Want' in Elizabeth Barrett Browning's *Aurora Leigh*," 351–67.

44. On the importance of *Corinne* for Barrett Browning and other nineteenth-century women writers, see Moers, *Literary Women*, 173–310, and Cora Kaplan, "Introduction" to *"Aurora Leigh" and Other Poems*, 16–23. To Hugh Stuart Boyd, Elizabeth Barrett wrote on 9 June 1832 that she had been reading *Corinne* "for the third time, & admired it more than ever" (letter 453 in Kelley and Hudson, *Brownings' Correspondence*, 3:25, which includes the phrase "immortal book").

45. Staël-Holstein, *Germany*, 1:224–25. The chapter in which this quotation occurs is titled "Of the Judgment formed by the English on the subject of German Literature."

46. Letter of 8 November 1842, in Miller, *Elizabeth Barrett to Miss Mitford*, 141.

47. Miller, *Fiction and Repetition*, 9.

48. Friedrich Schiller, "On Simple and Sentimental Poetry," in Bate, *Criticism*, 408–9.

49. That this advance is conceived in terms of social class rather than progressive civilizations reminds us of the recurring problem Barrett Browning faces in treating working-class characters and issues, a problem discussed by Kaplan, "Introduction" to *"Aurora Leigh" and Other Poems*, 35–36.

50. These lines and phrases come from the fuller account of the Maid of Buttermere in the 1805 *Prelude*, ed. Wordsworth, Abrams, and Gill, 7:342–46, 325, 323. Like Barrett Browning's account of Marian Erle, Wordsworth's of Mary Robinson wavers between the language of melodrama, traditionally associated with lower-class characters, and the more "universal" language of *The Prelude*, with which Wordsworth narrates his own life. This failure to convert Mary Robinson's story from stage drama to auto/biography reveals his difficulty with both class and gender differences.

51. Kramer, "Gender and Sexuality in *The Prelude*," 626.

52. See ibid., 625–30, as well as Onorato, *Character of the Poet*.

53. Barrett Browning follows Wordsworth in imagining the fallen but pure mother as "dead" to the world. At the end of *Aurora Leigh*, when Romney proposes to marry Marian and adopt her child, Marian insists that "since we've parted I have passed the grave" (9:282) and that she will not "get up from my grave, / And wear my chin-cloth for a wedding-veil" (9:392–93). Barrett Browning emphasizes the life of the child, who, fathered by God, not man, represents the future redemption of humankind.

54. The melodrama was performed at Sadler's Wells in April–June 1803, and Mary Lamb wrote Coleridge and Wordsworth about it in July 1803. It is unclear whether Wordsworth actually saw the play.

55. In "Lamb, Lloyd, London," 169–87, Newlyn argues that the 1805 version of *The*

Prelude includes not just traditional negative judgments of the city but almost Lamb-like moments of recognizing its vitality and imaginative potential. Her argument re-lies, however, on passages in the 1805 version that were expurgated from the 1850 published edition, which was the text Barrett Browning read. Less optimistically, in "Gender and Sexuality in *The Prelude*," 622, Kramer suggests that Wordsworth rele-gates London to the "realm of fancy, the imagination's poor relation, the mundane, indiscriminate, and capricious manipulation of images."

56. This is Marcus's formulation in *Auto/biographical Discourses*, 37. She amplifies Jacobus's reading in *Romanticism, Writing and Sexual Difference*, 230–36.

57. See letter 200, 18 November 1842, in Raymond and Sullivan, *Letters of Elizabeth Bar-rett Browning to Mary Russell Mitford*, 2:81.

58. In an essay on Mary and William Howitt in Horne's *New Spirit of the Age*, 177–98, Mary is credited with having "the true ballad spirit" and the couple (who published jointly) with "the irresistible tendency of one to describe natural scenery, and the legendary propensities of the other" (185). As we know from comments to Mitford, however, Barrett believed that Mary Howitt's represented a literary career gone bad, that Howitt had failed to consolidate her powers and, with *The Seven Temptations*, declined as a poet. To Robert Browning she suggests that the Howitts' journalism, including their editorship of the *People's Journal*, led Mary to publish "pure nonsense," "pretty, washy, very meritorious" stuff (*Letters of Robert Browning and Elizabeth Barrett Barrett, 1845–1846*, 2:124).

59. The fullest discussion of bk. V as *ars poetica* appears in Holly A. Laird's "*Aurora Leigh*: An Epical Ars Poetica," in Jones, *Writing the Woman Artist*, 355–70. Laird emphasizes Barrett Browning's "twofold" vision of heroism in life and art, its articulation and embodiment in *Aurora Leigh*.

60. Landon's *Improvisatrice* begins: "I am a daughter of that land, / Where the poet's lip and the painter's hand / Are most divine,—where the earth and sky / Are picture both and poetry— / I am of Florence" (ll. 1–5). Eulalie, the poetess of *A History of the Lyre*, is, like Staël's Corinne, from Rome. On Italy as a mythic source of women's poetry, see Sweet, "Bowl of Liberty," one part of which was presented at the Con-ference on Eighteenth- and Nineteenth-Century British Women Writers, University of South Carolina, March 1996.

61. The titles of bks. XII and XIII are "Imagination and Taste, How Impaired and Re-stored."

62. Mermin, *Elizabeth Barrett Browning*, 190. Mermin does not believe, however, that Aurora and Romney achieve the "complicated reciprocity" depicted in the *Sonnets from the Portuguese*. In this judgment we differ, in that I believe Barrett Browning signals the reciprocity through the dialogic form in which most scenes involving Aurora and Romney occur.

63. Romney alludes to the traditional interpretation of the Song of Songs as an emblem of Christ and his church when he speaks of "the love of wedded souls" as "that mys-tery's counterpart, . . . Of such mystic substance, Sharon gave a name to" (9:882–86). In Protestant hermeneutics, the Song of Songs represents "(1) a vivid unfolding of Solomon's love for a Shulamite girl, (2) a figurative revelation of God's love for His covenant people, Israel, and (3) an allegory of Christ's love for His heavenly bride, the Church" (as explained in *The New Scofield Reference Bible* [New York: Oxford University Press, 1967], 705). Barrett Browning in effect adds a fourth level of inter-

pretation that includes public forms of human love, including the fraternal, neighborly, and civic.

64. Deirdre David, for whom this passage signifies "the appropriation of Aurora's art and sexuality by male power," is partially correct in suggesting that the biblical emblem indicates that "all political and social action will originate in and be sweetened from their marriage," but as the passage actually states, for Aurora, such action *originates* in "God's love" (9:880)—perhaps not a satisfying distinction for a modern feminist but crucial to Barrett Browning's insistence that divine, not earthly, models inform her poetry and politics (see her chapter "Woman's Art as Servant of Patriarchy," in *Intellectual Women and Victorian Patriarchy*, 152–53).

65. Riess, "Laetitia Landon and the Dawn of English Post-Romanticism," 815. Like Stuart Curran ("Romantic Poetry: The I Altered," in Mellor, *Romanticism and Feminism*, 185–207), I would distinguish these early volumes from Landon's later poems of the 1830s, especially *The Zenana: An Eastern Tale* (1839), which "focus on exile and failure" and which recognize the limited sphere in which the poetess operates.

66. Ross, *Contours of Masculine Desire*, 204.

67. Ibid., 259. In defining the poet's vocation, Barrett Browning participates in a long tradition, from Milton through Cowper to Wordsworth, about the value of poetic labor; on this tradition, see Goodman, "'Wasted Labor'?" 415–46, as well as Liu, "The Economy of Lyric," in *Wordsworth*, 311–58, and Clifford Siskin, "Wordsworth's Prescriptions: Romanticism and Professional Power," in Ruoff, *Romantics and Us*, 303–21.

68. Moers, *Literary Women*, 59. David's harsher view of *Aurora's* politics—"In this poem we hear a woman's voice speaking patriarchal discourse—boldly, passionately, and without rancour"—stems from a reaction against celebratory feminist readings that hear in the poem "women's language" but also, I think, from a neglect of the politics of genre. When David ironically concludes that Barrett Browning "was a good deal more political and a good deal more intellectual than literary history has imagined" (*Intellectual Women and Victorian Patriarchy*, 157–58), she implies a political innocence about the poet's work that the self-conscious manipulation of genres belies.

69. Tucker, "*Aurora Leigh*," 80.

70. On Hemans, see Ross, *Contours of Masculine Desire*, 251. Even Landon chose to observe the convention of letting a friend write a biography rather than compose an autobiography herself. Blanchard begins his introduction to the *Life and Literary Remains of L.E.L.* with an explanation that "long before she meditated leaving England," she left him "with some materials for a slight sketch of her life," and that the rest of the information "has been supplied by the anxious care of her family" (v–vi).

Chapter V. Family Business

1. Coghill, "Mrs. Oliphant," 277; Mermin, *Godiva's Ride*, 92; Robert Aguirre, "Writing Subjects: Ideology and Self-Representation in Victorian Autobiography" (Ph.D. diss., Harvard University, 1990); Helms, "'A little try at the autobiography,'" 76.

2. Oliphant, *Autobiography and Letters*, 81, 75. Throughout this chapter, unless I note otherwise, I quote the original 1899 edition of the text, edited by Annie Coghill, which includes the family letters on which some of my argument is based. Elisabeth Jay has published a new edition of the autobiography, based on the manuscript in the

National Library of Scotland, which does not include letters but reinstates some passages excised by Coghill: see Jay, *Autobiography of Margaret Oliphant.*

3. Mermin, *Godiva's Ride,* 87.

4. Corbett, *Representing Femininity,* 106. Despite this conclusion, Corbett seems less convinced than other critics about the inevitability of a dysphoric life for nineteenth-century women writers; "what I find interesting," she notes, "is how deeply Oliphant believes that the two alternatives—'a fine novel' or 'fine boys'—are mutually exclusive" (105), and she offers Barrett Browning's *Aurora Leigh* as a model of their mutual compatibility.

5. Oliphant's version combines the narrative perspective of the Victorian domestic memoir, with mother as central historian, and the older, aristocratic memoir that traces the history of family achievements. The terminology for these memoirs varies from critic to critic, in part because of changes from their origins in the seventeenth century to their uses in the nineteenth. When the historian Natalie Zemon Davis writes about such memoirs, she calls them "family histories"; when literary critics discuss them, they tend to use the term "domestic memoirs." This difference reflects disciplinary assumptions, as well as a shift within the generic tradition from more public family chronicles to more intimate accounts of domestic life.

6. The second volume of Howitt's *Homes and Haunts,* which begins with George Crabbe and James Hogg and ends with Waller Bryan Procter and Tennyson, incorporates Howitt's personal memories of the poets. Women writers also wrote this sort of literary memoir, among Victorians most notably Mrs. Newton Crosland, *Landmarks of a Literary Life, 1820–1892.*

7. Oliphant, "Harriet Martineau," 472–98.

8. Ibid., 481. In Martineau's narrative, her eldest brother makes the distinction, thus bestowing his masculine blessing on his sister's career as a professional writer.

9. These phrases come from Oliphant's reviews of the memoirs of Mary Somerville, George Grote, and Sara Coleridge in "New Books," April 1874, 446, and September 1873, 378, 371, 368–69.

10. Oliphant, "Old Saloon," March 1890, 410. This column reviews *The Life of Harriet Beecher Stowe* (London: Sampson Low, 1889).

11. Marcus's important survey of nineteenth-century criticism in *Auto/biographical Discourses,* 11–55, reveals that nineteenth-century critics tended to treat autobiographical genres in terms of historical progress or evolution—as in Edith Simcox's use of Comtean terminology (Monumental, Positive, Metaphysical) in the *North British Review,* January 1870. Oliphant is the only critic I have found who begins with the generic distinction between public *res gestae* and private domestic memoirs.

12. Oliphant, "Autobiographies. No. I," 1–2, and "Autobiographies. No. VI," 80.

13. In the article on Margaret Cavendish, Duchess of Newcastle, moreover, Oliphant articulated the autobiographical function of such memoirs, recognizing Cavendish both as an autobiographer and as a "family historian" and terming her biography of the duke "a second autobiography." See Oliphant, "Autobiographies. No. III," 638.

14. Oliphant, "Autobiographies. No. VI," 81.

15. Oliphant, "New Books," April 1874, 13. Oliphant recalls Mrs. Somerville saying that, "so far from feeling old, she was not always quite certain (up in the seventies) whether she was quite grown up."

16. Carlisle, "Specular Reflections," in *John Stuart Mill and the Writing of Character,* esp. 242–43.

17. This phrase, taken from Oliphant's comparison of herself with George Eliot and George Sand (not Charlotte Brontë), forms the basis of critical assessment in such studies as Robert and Vineta Colby's *Equivocal Virtue.*

18. Joanne Shattock, "Victorian Women as Writers and Readers of (Auto)biography," in Newey and Shaw, *Mortal Pages,* 146.

19. Somerville, *Personal Recollections,* 1–2.

20. Annie Coghill, Oliphant's cousin and editor, confirms that Oliphant wrote "to please her last surviving son," and that after his death and near her own she "bade us deal with this autobiography as we thought best"; see her preface to Oliphant, *Autobiography and Letters,* xxi.

21. Howitt, *Mary Howitt: An Autobiography.* The account was serialized, in a shorter version and in slightly different order, in *Good Words,* 26–27 (1885–86), as "Reminiscences of My Life" and "Reminiscences of My Later Life."

22. Howitt's daughter Margaret assembled the book version of the *Autobiography,* expanding the "Reminiscences" at the suggestion of the editors of *Good Words* and writing to old friends for additional letters. See letter of 13 July 1888, Briggs Collection 22, University of Nottingham Library.

23. Oliphant, "Two Ladies," 206.

24. The article also includes a third point against the ideology of the younger generation. When Oliphant observes that neither Jameson nor Kemble "found any obstacles worth speaking of between them and the professions which they respectively chose" (207), she refutes the position that blames the "male sect" (206) for women's lack of professional work. For Oliphant it is the combination of genius (or at least talent) and the need to support a family (that "strongest stimulus") that leads to professional achievement. It goes without saying that this argument relates to professional middle-class women, not to all classes; but these were the women most likely to occupy the ideological position Oliphant rejects.

25. Oliphant, "Two Ladies," 210, 219–20.

26. Ibid., 220. It is tempting to read Oliphant's account of daughterly work in the artist classes as a variant on the patterns of female labor outlined by Joan Scott and Louise Tilly in "Women's Work and the Family in Nineteenth-Century Europe," 36–64. Scott and Tilly explain that daughters and mothers in working-class families went to work occasionally or sporadically to supplement the family income and that this pattern in families of the urban working class is a carry-over from earlier agricultural, preindustrial practices. While this pattern seems somewhat relevant to artisanal families, especially dynasties of painters that engaged all family members in the business, the cases Oliphant discusses do not represent rural to urban movement or working- to middle-class mobility. These are bourgeois families in which the daughter works only in *extraordinary* circumstances; the labor of working-class daughters, as Scott and Tilly describe it, was *ordinary* in that it commonly occurred. See also Sally Alexander's complementary study, "Women's Work in Nineteenth-Century London: A Study of the Years 1820–60," in Alexander, *Becoming a Woman,* 3–55, which gives details of married women who worked alongside their husbands in such trades as shopkeeping, innkeeping, and cobbling.

27. See Jay, *Autobiography of Margaret Oliphant,* 1–2.

28. Oliphant's insistence on a continuous sense of self should make us rethink a tendency in autobiography studies to emphasize the discontinuities within the female self and

to theorize women's autobiography in terms of its hiatuses. While it is possible to point out discontinuities and incoherences, as Gilmore does in *Autobiographics,* it is also important to observe historical and individual differences that women autobiographers register.

29. Cherry, *Painting Women,* 20.
30. Howitt, "Reminiscences of My Life," 661.
31. Margaret and Frank Oliphant were married on 4 May 1852. *Katie Stewart* appeared in serialized form in *Blackwood's Edinburgh Magazine* in 1852, in the July through December numbers.
32. Oliphant, "Dedication," *Katie Stewart,* n.p.
33. See letters of 13 August 1852 (Margaret Oliphant to Blackwood) and 8 October 1852 (Frank Oliphant to Blackwood) in the National Library of Scotland, which discuss the possibility of Frank's undertaking the work of illustration.
34. I am grateful to Professor Vaughan for discussing this early nineteenth-century practice with me and thus helping to clarify the Oliphants' working arrangements.
35. Oliphant, "Old Saloon," November 1889, 718. Oliphant's *Autobiography* recalls this historical moment in the running head on p. 45, "Halcyon Days at an End"—a phrase that refers to the discovery of her husband's tuberculosis but also, I think, to the end of that calm merging of domestic and professional life.
36. Benson, *Memories and Friends,* 79.
37. Merryn Williams, "The Black Holes in the *Autobiography,*" paper delivered at the Margaret Oliphant Centenary Conference, Westminster College, Oxford, 13 September 1997.
38. Anonymous, "In Maga's Library," *Blackwood's Edinburgh Magazine* 156 (December 1894): 873.
39. Jay, *Autobiography of Margaret Oliphant,* xv.
40. Elisabeth Jay has kindly pointed out to me that Oliphant never entirely abandoned the notion of the writer-artist family as a dynastic mix: Oliphant trained her nieces to fulfill the artistic role.
41. Oliphant, "New Books," September 1873, 369.
42. Oliphant, "Two Ladies," 217. Oliphant was largely responsible for this biographical union in that she added, after Geddie Macpherson died while the *Memoirs* were in manuscript, a brief preface to the *Memoirs of the Life of Anna Jameson* and saw the volume through the press. Macpherson also illustrated some of Oliphant's work, including the novel *Madonna Mary* (1867).
43. Oliphant, "Old Saloon," November 1889, 717. After years of work translating and transcribing documents, Margaret produced a biography of the German Nazarene painter Overbeck, *Friedrich Overbeck, Sein Leben und Schaffen* (1886), her only independent achievement.
44. She rejects this verdict in the manuscript of her autobiography, where she labels the reproach against Scott "foolish" and goes on say that "it would be vain to explain him to such a mind, which is of a different species" (57), thus identifying herself with Scott as a fellow artist of the same professional class.
45. The passage is restored in Jay, *Autobiography of Margaret Oliphant,* 55–57.
46. Oliphant, "Old Saloon," November 1889, 718.
47. Oliphant, "Old Saloon," March 1890, 409.
48. Ibid., 410. The review of Stowe's life and work includes an extended discussion of

mid-century domestic ideology and the historical shifts in self-conceptions of women writers.

49. Jay, *Autobiography of Margaret Oliphant,* xiv.

50. Oliphant, "New Books," September 1873, 376–77, 375.

51. Trollope, *Autobiography,* 1.

52. The Colbys recognized this effect in *Equivocal Virtue.* I discuss the "del Sarto pattern" in greater detail in "Audience and the Autobiographer's Art," in Landow, *Approaches to Victorian Autobiography,* 158–74.

53. Despite this analysis of the limitations of domestic ideology, the tensions Oliphant registers are less between mother and writer, as has so often been argued, than between two different sets of expectations: on the one hand, that the woman writer work to support her family and, on the other, that she strive to produce great books. Oliphant's 1890 review of *The Life of Harriet Beecher Stowe* shows that she continued to puzzle over the ability of some women writers to embrace domesticity *and* to produce lasting work. Reminiscing about *Uncle Tom's Cabin,* she writes: "It had no literary excellence to speak of," but "it had, which is much higher and more prevailing, a certain flash of genius which lit up, not only a human subject, but a whole country" (408). That "higher and more prevailing" element was what eluded Oliphant.

54. See Howitt, *Autobiography,* 1:237, 278–80, and 2:181, for passages in which Mary recalls the collaborations with her young daughter and her encouragement of her daughter's artistic career; Anna Mary Howitt's "Sisters in Art" was published in *Illustrated Exhibitor and Magazine of Art* 2 (1852): 214–26, 238–40, 262–63, 286–88, 317–19, 334–36, 347–48, 362–64.

55. Howitt, *Autobiography,* 2:86.

56. Oliphant, "Old Saloon," November 1889, 718. Oliphant's lament directs itself not at the gendered distinction but at the loss of the literary workplace and marketplace that she and the Howitts had known.

57. Oliphant's article "Anthony Trollope" is a retrospect of Trollope's career more than an account of his *Autobiography* per se. When Oliphant comments that "a short life, a limited period of activity, are much the best for art; and a long period of labour, occupied by an active mind and fertile faculties, tell against, and not for, the writer" (143), she anticipates the explanation she will offer for the inverse relation between her "industry" and her loss of reputation. When she writes that "it is a foregone conclusion that the man who does little is likely to do that little better than the man who does much" (143), she generalizes what she will say more specifically in the *Autobiography* when she compares her career with that of a lesser writer, Dinah Mulock Craik.

58. Ibid., 144.

Chapter VI. Mary Cholmondeley's Bifurcated Autobiography

1. For a classic definition of autobiography, see Shumaker, *English Autobiography,* 106, who calls it a professedly truthful record of a life, composed as a single work and told from a consistent temporal point of view. For a useful analysis of nineteenth- and twentieth-century definitions of autobiography as a genre, see Marcus, *Auto/biographical Discourses,* esp. the "Introduction," 1–10, and "The Law of Genre," 229–72.

2. See "Autobiography and Fiction," 709–10.

3. Quoted by Lubbock in *Mary Cholmondeley*, 91. As her literary executor, Lubbock had access to Cholmondeley's journals, "three locked volumes" (71), which have since disappeared.

4. Letter to Rhoda Broughton, 30 October 1899, Delves-Broughton Collection, Cheshire Public Record Office, Chester. Broughton, a popular novelist, was a close family friend and mentor to Mary and her artist-sister, Victoria. Mary's letter, which responds to Broughton's praise of *Red Pottage,* answers questions about the autobiographical elements of the novel but also distinguishes between moments in the protagonist's experience that reflect Mary's own and those that do not—e.g., "I think the character is entirely opposed to mine, but of course I have put my own feelings exactly about 'writing.'"

5. "Novels of the Week," *Spectator* 83 (28 October 1899): 613; Colby, "'Devoted Amateur,'" 214, cites the second review without naming the periodical. Cholmondeley recounts the negative reactions, including the claim that she had been jilted, in the preface to *Lowest Rung,* 17–18.

6. Lubbock, *Mary Cholmondeley*, 24.

7. Ibid., 48–49.

8. Colby identifies these Eliotian concerns in "'Devoted Amateur,'" 223–25, and Elaine Showalter returns to them in the context of the New Woman novel in her editorial preface to *Red Pottage,* viii–ix. Using an Iserian model of reading in "Aliens in the Garden," 101–19, Rainwater and Scheick stress Cholmondeley's creation of an active reader, but they do not explicitly associate this concern with Eliot's influence or aesthetics. In addition to Eliotian themes in *Red Pottage,* Cholmondeley borrowed other plots and scenes from Eliot's novels, most notably in *Sir Charles Danvers:* from *The Mill on the Floss,* the singing of duets becomes part of the rivalry between Ruth's two lovers; from *Middlemarch,* Dorothea's scheme for model cottages is reproduced in Ruth's plan for improvements on Dare's estate; again from *Middlemarch,* Dorothea's all-night struggle with her conscience is repeated in Ruth's struggle between her pledge to Dare and her love for Sir Charles.

9. Cross, *George Eliot's Life,* 1 : 19–23.

10. "Prefatory Notice" to Hemans, *Poetical Works,* 12–13; Martineau, *Autobiography,* 1 : 42.

11. "Prefatory Notice" to Hemans, *Poetical Works,* 13–14; Martineau, *Autobiography,* 1 : 26.

12. In *Real Life of Mary Ann Evans,* 38, Rosemarie Bodenheimer suggests that in the early letters Eliot "contrives . . . an extraordinary representation of a passionate intellect at work." This impression is even more striking in Cross's *Life* than in the modern *George Eliot Letters* edited by Gordon Haight because Cross did not use the familial correspondence with Eliot's aunt and uncle Samuel and Elizabeth Evans and hence many domestic details were omitted.

13. Haight, *George Eliot,* 10. In *Real Life of Mary Ann Evans,* 23–46, Bodenheimer points out that correspondences between young women were common in the nineteenth century, but she also notes the intellectual ambition and complex rhetorical negotiation of Eliot's letters, even in comparison with Charlotte Brontë's.

14. Oliphant, *Autobiography and Letters,* 5.

15. In *Female Friendships and Communities,* 7–27, Pauline Nestor discusses nineteenth-

century debates over female friendships and points out the contradictions in Eliot's letters to her Coventry friends in the alternation between expressions of deep affection and reservations about the limits of same-sex attachments: "somehow my male friends always eclipse the female," Eliot confided to Sara Hennell, the woman she had once addressed as her "dearly beloved spouse" (147–48). These contradictions are less obvious in Cross's *Life,* which omits and excises some of the more passionate letters to Hennell.

16. Emerson, "Friendship," in *Selected Writings,* 206–20. Emerson's notion of friendship as requiring "that rare mean between likeness and unlikeness" (216) and dropping of "even those undermost garments of dissimulation, courtesy, and second thought" (212) seems an obvious influence on Cholmondeley.

17. Quoted in Cholmondeley, *Under One Roof,* 93.

18. Cholmondeley, *Red Pottage,* 29. As Nestor points out in her chapter "Women Beware Women," esp. 12–16, a debate raged during the 1860s and 1870s about whether women were capable of sustaining same-sex friendships or whether such friendships were merely preparatory for marriage and motherhood. Cholmondeley was a bit too young to have read the periodicals in which these debates flourished, but she may have registered their aftereffects in her reading of *George Eliot's Life.*

19. In chap. 2 of *Real Life of Mary Anne Evans,* Bodenheimer points out that correspondence between young women was encouraged but always with "strictures on stylistic vanity, frivolity, gossip, and violations of privacy" (29)—and, of course, with the assumption that marriage would provide a natural end to such correspondence.

20. In *Suppressed Sister,* Amy K. Levin points out that Eliot's fictional sisters are largely "superfluous" or "competitive"; "the disloyalty among sisters dramatically sets off the social isolation of her unconventional heroines" (79).

21. Ardis, *New Women, New Novels,* 339.

22. See Lubbock, *Mary Cholmondeley,* 83, which quotes Cholmondeley's journal from August 1886, when Bentley accepted *The Danvers Jewels:* "And this is the story which I forced myself to write when I was in the depths last winter. I hated doing it. I hated the hour when it came round, when I knew I must go upstairs and write. . . . I look back with a sort of grim smile at the darkness and depression out of which this brightness and humour came."

23. Victoria Cholmondeley is best remembered for the Arts and Crafts furniture she exhibited and sold. Mary Cholmondeley also dedicated a novel, *Diana Tempest* (1893), to Hester, using an epigraph from Tennyson's *In Memoriam:* "He put our lives so far apart / We cannot hear each other speak."

24. We know how highly Cholmondeley valued Broughton's literary friendship from the correspondence preserved in the Delves-Broughton archive, Cheshire Public Record Office, Chester. In a letter dated 30 October 1889, just after *Red Pottage* was published, Mary wrote to thank her friend and mentor for her praise: "How I wish I could have more readers like you, but alas! I know very well that I must not expect in others the sympathy and kindly feeling which you have brought to bear upon 'Red Pottage'. Thank you many *many* times. I value your letter much, and am proud of it." Broughton's letter to Cholmondeley has not been preserved.

25. Howitt, "Sisters in Art," 2:334.

26. Ardis, *New Women, New Novels,* 343–44.

27. This parallel with Hester Gresley's life was frequently noted. According to contem-

porary accounts of Cholmondeley's life, while growing up Mary "spent part of every year in London with her grandmother, Mrs. Legard, . . . a beautiful and witty woman [who] had known all the distinguished men of her day." See "Literary Chat," 709, as well as the preface to the 1900 edition of *Diana Tempest*, v–ix, which devotes a paragraph to Mrs. Legard's social and intellectual influence.

28. Oliphant, *Autobiography and Letters*, 5.
29. Eliot, *Middlemarch*, chap. 73, p. 793.
30. *Spectator* 83 (28 October 1899): 613.
31. Eliot, *Middlemarch*, chap. 58, p. 644; chap. 64, p. 699; and chap. 65, p. 718.
32. For a fascinating analysis of the family conflict Eliot provoked by refusing to attend church services, see Bodenheimer, "Mary Anne Evans's Holy War," in *Real Life of Mary Ann Evans*, 57–84.
33. Quoted in Lubbock, *Mary Cholmondeley*, 92.
34. Cholmondeley, *Red Pottage*, 258. An allegory of Love from Hester Gresley's new novel is included in Cholmondeley's later novel *Moth and Rust* (1902), where the agony of earthly love is transformed in a vision of divine Love.
35. As Bodenheimer notes in *Real Life of Mary Ann Evans*, 202, Eliot and Lewes began referring to her books as children just at the moment she assumed responsibility as stepmother to Lewes's sons.
36. Showalter, *Literature of Their Own*, 108.
37. Letter to Rhoda Broughton dated 21 November 1917, Delves-Broughton Collection, Cheshire Public Record Office, Chester.
38. Lubbock, *Mary Cholmondeley*, 25.
39. As a nontitled branch of an aristocratic family in Cheshire and Shropshire, the Cholmondeleys were socially better born and financially better off than the Brontës. As Cholmondeley explains, however, they were often financially hard-pressed because of their large family and their father's generosity to parishioners and needy relatives.
40. Elizabeth Gaskell's *Life of Charlotte Brontë* was first published in 1857 by Smith, Elder, the publisher of Charlotte's novels.
41. In a compelling analysis of Gaskell's *Life*, Deirdre d'Albertis characterizes the central myth of the text as that "of martyred feminine creativity, . . . of the lonely woman artist as a heroic genius set apart by aesthetic integrity, intellectual detachment, and physical dis-ease" ("'Bookmaking out of the Remains of the Dead,'" 1). This characterization is apt for the conclusion of the biography but less so, I believe, for the first volume, in which Charlotte is shown as part of a close-knit, intellectually and literarily expansive group of sisters.
42. This "Biographical Notice" appears in Gaskell's *Life of Charlotte Brontë*, 285; in the 1857 edition, it was the opening page of vol. 1, chap. 14.
43. Cholmondeley's letters during World War I to Rhoda Broughton dwell repeatedly on the dangers to male relatives and friends serving in the war and to herself and Victoria under threat of bombing. Significantly, a footnote in *Under One Roof* commemorates her nephew Reginald, who "became an expert airman in the Royal Flying Corps . . . and fell [in March 1915] at Neuve Chapelle" (48).
44. The novels, of course, commemorate not Anne or Hester but the older sisters, Emily Brontë and Diana Cholmondeley.
45. Cholmondeley's comment that she gave up on the idea of "a memoir for private

circulation" because "Who would read it?" begs the question. Who was likely to read *Under One Roof?* What she implies is that her fame as an author would attract readers beyond family and friends, but as the sales of the memoir reveal, there was little public interest.

46. Cholmondeley, *Prisoners Fast Bound in Misery and Iron,* 171.

47. See d'Albertis, "'Bookmaking out of the Remains of the Dead,'" 16, who here quotes the final paragraph of Charlotte Brontë's "Biographical Notice of Ellis and Acton Bell," published in 1850 in a new edition of *Wuthering Heights* and *Agnes Grey.*

48. This title derives from the original table of contents, reprinted on p. 46 of the Penguin edition.

49. In a letter dated 30 October 1899, Delves-Broughton Collection, Cheshire Public Record Office, Chester, Cholmondeley writes in response to Broughton's praise of *Red Pottage:* "I suppose there is a good deal of me in Hester, tho' I had hardly realized it."

50. The phrase comes from Hughes and Lund's discussion of Gaskell's portrayal of Charlotte Brontë in *Engendered Lives.*

51. Letter to Rhoda Broughton, 14 February 1918, Delves-Broughton Collection, Cheshire Public Record Office, Chester. Other letters to Broughton express her continuing interest in the reputation of her books, her concern with literary craft, and her pressing need for the money that writing added to the family funds.

52. Letter dated 5 February 1917, Macmillan archive, Add. Ms. 55628/9, British Library. Stella Benson's first novel was *I Pose* (1915); her second, *This Is the End* (1917).

53. *Stella* is the Latin word for *star.* The names Esther and Hester come from the Hebrew *'ester,* which also means *star.* Mary Cholmondeley mentions this naming of her niece for an aunt, but does not explain the shift from the Hebrew to the Latin form of the name.

Afterword

1. Angela Leighton characterizes the work of Michael Field with this phrase in *Victorian Women Poets,* 203. Yet as she goes on to suggest in discussing the critical response to Michael Field, "Certainly the idea of 'collaboration' seems to have threatened some notional sanctity of authorship"—as Browning's "ruffled distress" at their dual authorship and Walter Besant's negative article "On Literary Collaboration," published in *The New Review* (1892), reveal.

2. Margaret Llewelyn Davies, ed., *Life as We Have Known It: By Co-operative Working Women* (1931; New York: Norton, 1975). Gagnier discusses this collaborative model of autobiography in *Subjectivities,* 37–45, 59–62.

3. Besant, "On Literary Collaboration," 204. At the end of the article, Besant advises the "young literary workman" to find "a girl, intelligent, sympathetic, and quick; a girl who will lend him her ear, listen to his plot, and discuss his characters." In this ideal version of collaboration, Besant specifies that "she should be a girl of quick imagination, who does not, or cannot write—there are still, happily, many such girls" (209).

4. Gubar, "Birth of the Artist as Heroine," 19–59. Gubar argues that in general the tradition moves "from the Victorian anxiety of female authorship, which infects the woman artist with the fear that she is a monstrous contradiction in terms, . . . toward

a celebration of female artistry that blurs the distinction between life and art so as to privilege neither one" (26).

5. Gaskell, *Life of Charlotte Brontë,* 334.

6. Howitt, *Mary Howitt: An Autobiography,* 2:17.

7. Joanne Shattock, "Victorian Women as Writers and Readers of (Auto)biography," in Newey and Shaw, *Mortal Pages, Literary Lives,* 140–52.

8. Elwood, *Memoirs of the Literary Ladies of England,* v.

9. Oliphant, "Old Saloon," March 1890, 410.

Selected Bibliography

Abel, Elizabeth, Marianne Hirsch, and Elizabeth Langland, eds. *The Voyage In: Fictions of Female Development*. Hanover, N.H.: University Press of New England, 1983.

Alexander, Sally. *Becoming a Woman and Other Essays in 19th and 20th Century Feminist History*. London: Virago, 1994.

Allott, Miriam, ed. *The Brontës: The Critical Heritage*. London: Routledge & Kegan Paul, 1974.

Andrews, William L., ed. *Journeys in New Worlds: Early American Women's Narratives*. Madison: University of Wisconsin Press, 1990.

———, ed. *Sisters of the Spirit: Three Black Women's Autobiographies of the Nineteenth Century*. Bloomington: Indiana University Press, 1986.

Ardis, Ann. *New Women, New Novels: Feminism and Early Modernism*. New Brunswick: Rutgers University Press, 1990.

Armstrong, Nancy. *Desire and Domestic Fiction: A Political History of the Novel*. New York: Oxford University Press, 1987.

Ashton, John. *Eighteenth Century Waifs*. London: Hurst & Blackett, 1887.

Autobiography: A Collection of the Most Instructive and Amusing Lives Ever Published, Written by the Parties Themselves. London: Hunt & Clarke, 1826–29; Whittaker, Treacher & Arnot, 1829–33.

"Autobiography and Fiction—Mary Cholmondeley's Stories and Her Life." *Munsey's Magazine* 23 (August 1900): 709–10.

Barker, Richard Hindry. *Mr. Cibber of Drury Lane*. New York: Columbia University Press, 1939.

Barrett, Michele, ed. *Women and Writing*. London: Women's Press, 1979.

Bate, Walter Jackson, ed. *Criticism: The Major Texts*. New York: Harcourt Brace Jovanovich, 1970.

Bathgate, Janet. *Aunt Janet's Legacy to Her Nieces: Recollections of Humble Life in Yarrow in the Beginning of the Century*. Selkirk: George Lewis, 1894.

Beasley, Ina. *Pagodas and Prisons: The Life of Ann Hasseltine Judson (1789–1826)*. Fawcett Library Papers no. 5. London: LLRS, 1982.

Beaty, Jerome. "*Jane Eyre* and Genre." *Genre* 10 (1977): 619–54.

———. *Misreading "Jane Eyre": A Postmodernist Paradigm*. Columbus: Ohio State University Press, 1996.

Beecher, Catherine. *A Treatise on Domestic Economy for the Use of Young Ladies at Home and at School*. Rev. ed. Boston: Thomas H. Webb, 1842.

Belenky, Mary Field, et al. *Women's Ways of Knowing: The Development of Self, Voice, and Mind*. New York: Basic Books, 1986.

Benson, A.C. *Memories and Friends*. London: J. Murray, 1924.

Benstock, Shari, ed. *The Private Self: Theory and Practice of Women's Autobiographical Writings*. Chapel Hill: University of North Carolina Press, 1988.

Besant, Annie. *An Autobiography*. London: T. Fisher Unwin, 1893.

Besant, Walter. "On Literary Collaboration." *New Review* 6 (1892): 200–209.

Blake, Kathleen. "Elizabeth Barrett Browning and Wordsworth: The Romantic Poet as Woman." *Victorian Poetry* 24 (1986): 387–98.

Blanchard, Laman. *Life and Literary Remains of L.E.L.* London: Henry Colburn, 1841.

Bodenheimer, Rosemarie. *The Real Life of Mary Ann Evans: George Eliot, Her Letters and Fiction*. Ithaca: Cornell University Press, 1994.

Brinton, Howard T. *Quaker Journals: Varieties of Religious Experience among Friends*. Wallingford, Pa.: Pendle Hill, 1972.

Brodzki, Bella, and Celeste Schenck, eds. *Life/Lines: Theorizing Women's Autobiography*. Ithaca: Cornell University Press, 1988.

Brontë, Charlotte. *Jane Eyre*. Ed. Richard J. Dunn. New York: Norton, 1987.

Broughton, Trev Lynn, and Linda Anderson, eds. *Women's Lives/Women's Times: New Essays on Auto/biography*. Albany: State University of New York Press, 1997.

Browning, Elizabeth Barrett. *Aurora Leigh*. Ed. Kerry McSweeney. New York: Oxford University Press, 1993.

———. *The Poetical Works of Elizabeth Barrett Browning*. Cambridge ed. Boston: Houghton Mifflin, 1974.

B[rowning], R[obert] B[arrett], ed. *The Letters of Robert Browning and Elizabeth Barrett Barrett, 1845–1846*. 2 vols. London: Smith, Elder, 1899.

Buckley, Jerome Hamilton. *The Turning Key: Autobiography and the Subjective Impulse since 1800*. Cambridge: Harvard University Press, 1984.

Bunyan, John. *Grace Abounding to the Chief of Sinners*. Ed. Roger Sharrock. Oxford: Clarendon, 1962.

Burnett, John, ed. *The Annals of Labour: Autobiographies of British Working-Class People, 1820–1920*. Bloomington: Indiana University Press, 1974.

Burnett, John, David Mayall, and David Vincent, eds. *The Autobiography of the Working Class: An Annotated Bibliography*. Brighton: Harvester, 1984–89.

Carlisle, Janice. *John Stuart Mill and the Writing of Character*. Athens: University of Georgia Press, 1991.

Castle, Terry. "Matters Not Fit to Be Mentioned: Fielding's *The Female Husband*." *ELH* 49 (1982): 602–22.

Cavendish, Margaret. *The Lives of William Cavendishe, Duke of Newcastle, and of his Wife, Margaret Duchess of Newcastle. Written by the thrice noble and illustrious princess, Margaret, Duchess of Newcastle. Edited with a preface and occasional notes by Mark Antony Lower*. London: John Russell Smith, 1872.

———. *True Relation of the Birth, Breeding, and Life of Margaret Cavendish, Duchess of Newcastle. Written by Herself. With a critical preface, &c. by Sir Egerton Brydges*. Kent: Johnson & Warwick, 1814.

Chadhuri, Nupur, and Margaret Strobel, eds. *Western Women and Imperialism: Complicity and Resistance*. Bloomington: Indiana University Press, 1992.

Charke, Charlotte. *A Narrative of the Life of Mrs. Charlotte Charke (Youngest Daughter of Colley Cibber, Esq.)*. London: W. Reeve, 1755.

———. *A Narrative of the Life of Mrs. Charlotte Charke, Youngest Daughter of Colley Cibber, Esq., Written by Herself*. London: Hunt & Clarke, 1827.

Chatterjee, Sunil Kumar. *Hannah Marshman: The First Woman Missionary in India.* Calcutta: People's Little Press, 1987.

Cherry, Deborah. *Painting Women: Victorian Women Artists.* London: Routledge, 1993.

Chodorow, Nancy. *The Reproduction of Mothering: Psychoanalysis and the Sociology of Gender.* Berkeley: University of California Press, 1978.

Cholmondeley, Mary. *Diana Tempest.* New York: D. Appleton, 1900.

———. *The Lowest Rung, Together with The Hand on the Latch, St. Luke's Summer and the Understudy.* London: John Murray, 1908.

———. *Moth and Rust.* London: John Murray, 1902.

———. *Prisoners Fast Bound in Misery and Iron.* New York: Dodd, Mead, 1906.

———. *Red Pottage.* London: Edward Arnold, 1899.

———. *Under One Roof: A Family Record.* London: John Murray, 1918.

Church Missionary Society Archive. Marlborough: Adam Matthew, n.d.

Cobbe, Frances Power. *Life of Frances Power Cobbe by Herself.* Boston: Houghton Mifflin, 1894.

Cockshut, A. O. J. *The Art of Autobiography in 19th- and 20th-Century England.* New Haven: Yale University Press, 1984.

Coghill, Mrs. Harry. "Mrs. Oliphant." *Fortnightly Review* n.s. 62 (1897): 277–85.

Colby, Robert, and Vineta Colby. *The Equivocal Virtue: Margaret Oliphant and the Victorian Literary Marketplace.* Hamden, Conn.: Archon Books, 1966.

Colby, Vineta. "'Devoted Amateur': Mary Cholmondeley and *Red Pottage*." *Essays in Criticism* 20 (1970): 213–28.

Coleridge, Sara. *Memoirs and Letters of Sara Coleridge.* Ed. by her daughter. London: Henry S. King, 1873.

Corbett, Mary Jean. *Representing Femininity: Middle-Class Subjectivity in Victorian and Edwardian Women's Autobiographies.* New York: Oxford University Press, 1992.

Crosland, Mrs. Newton [Camilla Toulmin]. *Landmarks of a Literary Life, 1820–1892.* London: Sampson Low, Marston, 1893.

Cross, John Walter, ed. *George Eliot's Life as Related in Her Letters and Journals.* Edinburgh: William Blackwood, 1885.

Cunninghame, Margaret. *A Pairt of the Life of Lady Margaret Cunninghame, Daughter of the Earl of Glencairn, that she had with her first husband, the Master of Evandale.* Edinburgh: James Ballantyne, 1827.

d'Albertis, Deirdre. "'Bookmaking out of the Remains of the Dead': Elizabeth Gaskell's *The Life of Charlotte Brontë*." *Victorian Studies* 39 (1995): 1–31.

———. "The Domestic Drone: Margaret Oliphant and a Political History of the Novel." *Studies in English Literature* 37 (1997): 805–29.

Dale, Peter Allen. "Charlotte Brontë's 'Tale Half-Told': The Disruption of Narrative Structure in *Jane Eyre*." *Modern Language Quarterly* 47 (1986): 108–29.

Danahay, Martin A. *A Community of One: Masculine Autobiography and Autonomy in Nineteenth-Century Britain.* Albany: State University of New York Press, 1993.

David, Deirdre. *Intellectual Women and Victorian Patriarchy.* Ithaca: Cornell University Press, 1987.

———. *Rule Britannia: Women, Empire, and Victorian Writing.* Ithaca: Cornell University Press, 1995.

Davidoff, Leonore, and Catherine Hall. *Family Fortunes: Men and Women of the English Middle Class, 1780–1850.* Chicago: University of Chicago Press, 1987.

Davies, Mrs. Christian. *The Life and Adventures of Mrs. Christian Davies, commonly call'd Mother Ross*. London: R. Montagu, 1740.

Davin, Delia. "British Women Missionaries in Nineteenth-Century China." *Women's History Review* 1 (1992): 257–71.

Davis, Robin Reed. "Anglican Evangelicalism and the Feminine Literary Tradition." Ph.D. diss., Duke University, 1982.

Delany, Paul. *British Autobiography in the Seventeenth Century*. New York: Columbia University Press, 1969.

de Man, Paul. "Autobiography as De-facement." *Modern Language Notes* 94 (1979): 919–30.

Donovan, Mary Sudman. "Women and Mission: Toward a More Inclusive Historiography." *Historical Magazine of the Protestant Episcopal Church* 53 (1984): 297–305.

———. "Women as Foreign Missionaries in the Episcopal Church, 1830–1920." *Anglican and Episcopal History* 61 (1992): 16–39.

Duff, Alexander. *A Vindication of the Church of Scotland's India Mission: being the substance of an address delivered before the General Assembly of the Church on Wednesday, May 24, 1837*. Edinburgh: John Johnstone, 1837.

Eagleton, Mary. *Feminist Literary Theory: A Reader*. Oxford: Basil Blackwell, 1986.

Eliot, George. *Middlemarch*. Ed. Gordon Haight. 1871–72; Harmondsworth: Penguin, 1965.

Elwood, Mrs. [Anne Katharine]. *Memoirs of the Literary Ladies of England, from the Commencement of the Last Century*. 2 vols. London: Henry Colburn, 1843.

Emerson, Ralph Waldo. *Selected Writings of Emerson*. Ed. Donald McQuade. New York: Modern Library, 1981.

Epstein, William H. *Recognizing Biography*. Philadelphia: University of Pennsylvania Press, 1987.

Erickson, Joyce Quiring. "'Perfect Love': Achieving Sanctification as a Pattern of Desire in the Life Writings of Early Methodist Women." *Prose Studies* 20 (1997): 72–89.

Evans, William, and Thomas Evans, eds. *The Friends' Library*. 14 vols. Philadelphia: Joseph Rakestraw, 1837–50.

Fanshawe, Ann. *Memoirs of Lady Fanshawe*. Ed. E. Harris Nicolas. London: Henry Colburn, 1829.

Fleishman, Avrom. *Figures of Autobiography: The Language of Self-Writing in Victorian and Modern England*. Berkeley: University of California Press, 1983.

Folkenflik, Robert, ed. *The Culture of Autobiography: Constructions of Self-Representation*. Stanford: Stanford University Press, 1993.

Friedl, Lynne. "'Passing Women': A Study of Gender Boundaries in the Eighteenth Century." In *Sexual Underworlds of the Enlightenment,* ed. G. S. Rousseau and Roy Porter, 234–60. Chapel Hill: University of North Carolina Press, 1988.

Frye, Joanne S. *Living Stories, Telling Lives: Women and the Novel in Contemporary Experience*. Ann Arbor: University of Michigan Press, 1986.

Gagnier, Regenia. *Subjectivities: A History of Self-Representation in Britain, 1832–1920*. New York: Oxford University Press, 1991.

Gaskell, Elizabeth. *The Life of Charlotte Brontë*. 1857; Harmondsworth: Penguin, 1975.

Gibson, Mary Ellen. "Henry Martyn and England's Christian Empire: Rereading *Jane Eyre* through Missionary Biography." *Victorian Literature and Culture,* forthcoming.

———. "The Seraglio or Suttee: Brontë's *Jane Eyre*." *Postscript* 4 (1987): 1–9.

Gilbert, Sandra, and Susan Gubar. *The Madwoman in the Attic: The Woman Writer and the Nineteenth-Century Literary Imagination.* New Haven: Yale University Press, 1979.

Gilligan, Carol. *In a Different Voice: Psychological Theory and Women's Development.* Cambridge: Harvard University Press, 1982.

Gilmore, Leigh. *Autobiographics: A Feminist Theory of Women's Self-Representation.* Ithaca: Cornell University Press, 1994.

Goodman, Kevis. "'Wasted Labor'? Milton's Eve, the Poet's Work, and the Challenge of Sympathy." *ELH* 64 (1997): 415–46.

Graham, Elspeth, Hilary Hinds, Elaine Hobby, and Helen Wilcox, eds. *Her Own Life: Autobiographical Writings by Seventeenth-Century Englishwomen.* London: Routledge, 1989.

[Gregg, Mary Kirby.] *Leaflets from My Life: A Narrative Autobiography.* London: Simpkin, 1887.

Gubar, Susan. "The Birth of the Artist as Heroine: (Re)production, the *Künstlerroman* Tradition, and the Fiction of Katherine Mansfield." In *The Representation of Women in Fiction,* ed. Carolyn G. Heilbrun and Margaret R. Higonnet. Baltimore: Johns Hopkins University Press, 1983.

Haight, Gordon. *George Eliot: A Biography.* Oxford: Oxford University Press, 1968.

———, ed. *The George Eliot Letters.* 9 vols. New Haven: Yale University Press, 1954–74.

Halkett, Anne, Lady. *The Autobiography of Anne Lady Halkett.* Ed. John Gough Nichols. Westminster: Camden Society, 1875.

Hall, S. C. *A Book of Memories of Great Men and Women of the Age, from Personal Acquaintance.* London: Virtue, 1871.

Hardy, Barbara. *The Appropriate Form: An Essay on the Novel.* London: Athlone, 1964.

Harrison, Jane Ellen. *Reminiscences of a Student's Life.* London: Hogarth, 1925.

Hayes, Alice. *A Legacy, or Widow's Mite, Left by Alice Hayes.* London: Darton & Harvey, 1836.

Heber, Reginald. *The Memoirs of Reginald Heber, by His Widow.* London: John Murray, 1830.

Heilbrun, Carolyn G. *Writing a Woman's Life.* New York: Norton, 1988.

Helms, Gabriele. "'A little try at the autobiography': Conflict and Contradiction in Margaret Oliphant's Writing." *Prose Studies* 19 (1996): 76–92.

Hemans, Felicia. *The Poetical Works of Mrs. Felicia Hemans.* Ed. W. M. Rossetti. London: E. Moxon, [1873].

Hill, M[arilla] M[arks] Hutchins. *Reminiscences: A Brief History of the Free Baptist India Mission.* Boston: Free Baptist Woman's Missionary Society, 1885.

Hopkins, Mary Alden. *Hannah More and Her Circle.* New York: Longmans, Green, 1947.

Horne, R. H., ed. *A New Spirit of the Age.* 2d ed. London: Smith, Elder, 1844.

Howitt, Anna Mary. "The Sisters in Art." *Illustrated Exhibitor and Magazine of Art* 2 (1852): 214–26, 238–40, 262–63, 286–88, 317–19, 334–36, 347–48, 362–64.

Howitt, Mary. *Mary Howitt: An Autobiography.* Edited by her daughter Margaret Howitt. 2 vols. Boston: Houghton Mifflin, 1889.

———. "Reminiscences of My Later Life." *Good Words* 27 (1886): 52–59, 172–79, 330–37, 394–402, 592–601.

———. "Reminiscences of My Life." *Good Words* 26 (1885): 383–90, 423–29, 494–502, 565–73, 660–67.

Howitt, William. *Homes and Haunts of the Most Eminent British Poets.* 2 vols. London: Richard Bentley, 1847.

Hughes, Linda, and Michael Lund. *Victorian Publishing and Mrs. Gaskell's Work.* Charlottesville: University Press of Virginia, 1999.

Hunter, Shelagh. *Harriet Martineau: The Poetics of Moralism.* Brookfield, Vt.: Scolar Press, 1995.

Hutchinson, Lucy. *Memoirs of the Life of Colonel Hutchinson . . . to which is prefixed the Life of Mrs. Hutchinson, Written by Herself.* Ed. Rev. Julius Hutchinson. 3d ed. London: Longman, Hurst, Rees, & Orme, 1810.

Jacobus, Mary. *Romanticism, Writing and Sexual Difference: Essays on "The Prelude."* Oxford: Oxford University Press, 1985.

Jameson, Anna. *Memoirs of the Life of Anna Jameson.* Ed. Geraldine Macpherson. London: Longmans, Green, 1878.

Jay, Elisabeth. *Mrs Oliphant: A Fiction to Herself, A Literary Life.* Oxford: Clarendon, 1995.

———, ed. *The Autobiography of Margaret Oliphant: The Complete Text.* Oxford: Oxford University Press, 1990.

Jelinek, Estelle C. *The Tradition of Women's Autobiography: From Antiquity to the Present.* Boston: Twayne, 1986.

———, ed. *Women's Autobiography: Essays in Criticism.* Bloomington: Indiana University Press, 1980.

Jones, Suzanne W., ed. *Writing the Woman Artist: Essays on Poetics, Politics, and Portraiture.* Philadelphia: University of Pennsylvania Press, 1991.

Kadar, Marlene, ed. *Essays on Life Writing: From Genre to Critical Practice.* Toronto: University of Toronto Press, 1992.

Kaplan, Cora, ed. *"Aurora Leigh" and Other Poems.* London: Women's Press, 1978.

Kelley, Philip, and Ronald Hudson, eds. *The Brownings' Correspondence.* 14 vols. Winfield, Kans.: Wedgestone Press, 1984–98.

Kelly, Sophia, ed. *The Life of Mrs. Sherwood, Chiefly Autobiographical.* London: Darton, 1854.

Kemble, Frances Ann [Fanny]. *Records of a Girlhood.* New York: Henry Holt, 1879.

Kennedy, Deborah. "Hemans, Wordsworth, and the 'Literary Lady.'" *Victorian Poetry* 35 (1997): 267–85.

Knowles, James D. *Memoir of Mrs. Ann Judson.* 3d ed. Boston: Lincoln & Edmands, 1829.

Kovacevic, Ivanka, and S. Barbara Kanner. "Blue Book into Novel: The Forgotten Industrial Fiction of Charlotte Elizabeth Tonna." *Nineteenth-Century Fiction* 25 (1970): 152–73.

Kowalski, Elizabeth. "'The Heroine of Some Strange Romance': The *Personal Recollections* of Charlotte Elizabeth Tonna." *Tulsa Studies in Women's Literature* 1 (1982): 141–53.

Kramer, Lawrence. "Gender and Sexuality in *The Prelude:* The Question of Book VII." *ELH* 54 (1987): 619–37.

Labalme, Patricia H., ed. *Beyond Their Sex: Learned Women of the European Past.* New York: New York University Press, 1980.

Landon, Letitia. *Poetical Works of Letitia Elizabeth Landon, "L.E.L."* Ed. F. J. Sypher. Delmar, N.Y.: Scholars' Facsimiles and Reprints, 1990.

———. *"The Venetian Bracelet," "The Lost Pleiad," "A History of the Lyre," and Other Poems.* Boston: Cottons & Barnard, 1830.

———. *"The Zenana" and Minor Poems of L.E.L., with a Memoir by Emma Roberts.* London: Fisher, 1839.

Landow, George P. *Victorian Types, Victorian Shadows: Biblical Typology in Victorian Literature, Art and Thought.* London: Routledge & Kegan Paul, 1980.

———, ed. *Approaches to Victorian Autobiography.* Athens: Ohio University Press, 1979.

Leighton, Angela. *Elizabeth Barrett Browning.* Brighton: Harvester, 1986.

———. *Victorian Women Poets: Writing against the Heart.* Charlottesville: University Press of Virginia, 1992.

Levin, Amy K. *The Suppressed Sister: A Relationship in Novels by Nineteenth- and Twentieth-Century British Women.* Lewisburg: Bucknell University Press, 1992.

Lisle, Mary. *Long, Long Ago: An Autobiography.* London: J. & C. Mozley, 1856.

Liu, Alan. *Wordsworth: The Sense of History.* Stanford: Stanford University Press, 1989.

Lloyd, Arnold. *Quaker Social History, 1669–1738.* London: Longmans, Green, 1950.

London, Bette. "The Pleasure of Submission: *Jane Eyre* and the Production of the Text." *ELH* 58 (1991): 195–213.

Lootens, Tricia. *Lost Saints: Silence, Gender, and Victorian Literary Canonization.* Charlottesville: University Press of Virginia, 1996.

Lubbock, Percy. *Mary Cholmondeley: A Sketch from Memory.* London: Jonathan Cape, 1928.

McGann, Jerome, ed. *Victorian Connections.* Charlottesville: University Press of Virginia, 1989.

Machann, Clinton. *The Genre of Autobiography in Victorian Literature.* Ann Arbor: University of Michigan Press, 1994.

Mackie, Erin. "Desperate Measures: The Narratives of the Life of Mrs. Charlotte Charke." *ELH* 58 (1991): 841–65.

[McTaggart, Ann.] *Memoirs of a Gentlewoman of the Old School, by a Lady.* London: Hurst, Chance, 1830.

Marcus, Laura. *Auto/biographical Discourses: Theory, Criticism, Practice.* Manchester: Manchester University Press, 1994.

Martineau, Harriet. *Autobiography.* Ed. Maria Weston Chapman. London: Smith, Elder, 1877.

———. *Biographical Sketches.* London: Macmillan, 1869.

———. "Female Writers on Practical Divinity." *Monthly Repository* 17 (1822): 593–96, 746–50.

———. *Harriet Martineau's Letters to Fanny Wedgwood.* Ed. Elisabeth Sanders Arbuckle. Stanford: Stanford University Press, 1983.

———. *Household Education.* London: Edward Moxon, 1849.

———. "On Female Education." *Monthly Repository* 18 (1823): 77–81.

———. *Selected Letters.* Ed. Valerie Sanders. Oxford: Clarendon, 1990.

———. *Society in America.* London: Sanders & Otley, 1837.

———, trans. *The Positive Philosophy of Auguste Comte.* London: John Chapman, 1853.

Martyn, Henry. *Journals and Letters of the Rev. Henry Martyn.* Ed. S. Wilberforce. New York: M. W. Dodd, 1851.

Mason, Mary G. "The Other Voice: Autobiographies of Women Writers." In *Autobiography: Essays Theoretical and Critical,* ed. James Olney, 207–35. Princeton: Princeton University Press, 1980.

Matthews, William. *British Autobiographies: An Annotated Bibliography of British Autobiographies Published or Written before 1951.* 1955; Hamden, Conn.: Archon Books, 1968.

Mellor, Anne K., ed. *Romanticism and Feminism.* Bloomington: Indiana University Press, 1988.

Mermin, Dorothy. *Elizabeth Barrett Browning: The Origins of a New Poetry.* Chicago: University of Chicago Press, 1989.

————. *Godiva's Ride: Women of Letters in England, 1830–1880.* Bloomington: Indiana University Press, 1993.

Merrett, Robert James. "The Conduct of Spiritual Autobiography in *Jane Eyre.*" *Renascence: Essays on Values in Literature* 37 (1984): 2–15.

Michie, Helena. *The Flesh Made Word: Female Figures and Women's Bodies.* New York: Oxford University Press, 1987.

Miller, Betty, ed. *Elizabeth Barrett to Miss Mitford.* London: John Murray, 1954.

Miller, J. Hillis. *Fiction and Repetition: Seven English Novels.* Cambridge: Harvard University Press, 1982.

Millgate, Jane. "Jane Eyre's Progress." *English Studies* 50 (1969): xxi–xxix.

Moers, Ellen. *Literary Women: The Great Writers.* New York: Oxford University Press, 1963.

Moglen, Helene. *Charlotte Brontë: The Self Conceived.* New York: Norton, 1976.

More, Hannah. *Coelebs in Search of a Wife, comprehending Observations on Domestic Habits and Manners, Religion and Morals.* London: J. Chidley, 1837.

————. *The Works of Hannah More.* New York: Harper, 1854.

Morgan, Susan. *Place Matters: Gendered Geography in Victorian Women's Travel Books about Southeast Asia.* New Brunswick: Rutgers University Press, 1996.

Munro, Alice. *Lives of Girls and Women.* New York: New American Library, 1971.

Nestor, Pauline. *Female Friendships and Communities: Charlotte Brontë, George Eliot, Elizabeth Gaskell.* Oxford: Clarendon, 1985.

Neuman, Shirley, ed. *Autobiography and Questions of Gender.* London: Frank Cass, 1991.

Neuman, Shirley, and Glennis Stephenson, eds. *ReImagining Women: Representations of Women in Culture.* Toronto: University of Toronto Press, 1993.

Newey, Vincent, and Philip Shaw, eds. *Mortal Pages, Literary Lives: Studies in Nineteenth-Century Autobiography.* Aldershot: Scolar Press, 1996.

Newlyn, Lucy. "Lamb, Lloyd, London: A Perspective on Book Seven of *The Prelude.*" *Charles Lamb Bulletin* n.s. 47–48 (July–October 1984): 169–87.

Nussbaum, Felicity A. *The Autobiographical Subject: Gender and Ideology in Eighteenth-Century England.* Baltimore: Johns Hopkins University Press, 1989.

Oliphant, Margaret. "Anthony Trollope." *Good Words* 24 (1883): 142–44.

————. "Autobiographies, No. I.—Benvenuto Cellini." *Blackwood's Edinburgh Magazine* 129 (January 1881): 1–30.

————. "Autobiographies, No. II.—Lord Herbert of Cherbury." *Blackwood's Edinburgh Magazine* 129 (March 1881): 385–410.

————. "Autobiographies: No. III.—Margaret, Duchess of Newcastle." *Blackwood's Edinburgh Magazine* 129 (May 1881): 617–39.

————. "Autobiographies: No. IV.—Edward Gibbon." *Blackwood's Edinburgh Magazine* 130 (August 1881): 229–47.

————. "Autobiographies: No. V.—Carlo Goldoni." *Blackwood's Edinburgh Magazine* 130 (October 1881): 516–41.

————. "Autobiographies: No. VI—In the Time of the Commonwealth: Lucy Hutchinson–Alice Thornton." *Blackwood's Edinburgh Magazine* 132 (July 1882): 79–101.

————. *Autobiography and Letters of Mrs Margaret Oliphant.* Ed. Mrs Harry Coghill. 1899; Leicester: Leicester University Press, 1974.

————. *The Autobiography of Margaret Oliphant: The Complete Text.* Ed. Elisabeth Jay. Oxford: Oxford University Press, 1990.

———. "Harriet Martineau." *Blackwood's Edinburgh Magazine* 121 (April 1877): 472–96.

———. *Katie Stewart: A True Story.* Edinburgh and London: William Blackwood, 1853.

———. "Modern Novelists—Great and Small." *Blackwood's Edinburgh Magazine* 57 (May 1855): 554–68.

———. "New Books." *Blackwood's Edinburgh Magazine* 114 (September 1873): 368–90.

———. "New Books." *Blackwood's Edinburgh Magazine* 115 (April 1874): 443–51.

———. "The Old Saloon." *Blackwood's Edinburgh Magazine* 146 (November 1889): 696–723.

———. "The Old Saloon." *Blackwood's Edinburgh Magazine* 147 (March 1890): 408–28.

———. "Two Ladies." *Blackwood's Edinburgh Magazine* 125 (February 1879): 206–24.

———. *Victorian Age of English Literature.* New York: Tait, 1892.

Olney, James. *Metaphors of Self: The Meaning of Autobiography.* Princeton: Princeton University Press, 1972.

———, ed. *Autobiography: Essays Theoretical and Critical.* Princeton: Princeton University Press, 1980.

———, ed. *Studies in Autobiography.* New York: Oxford University Press, 1987.

Onorato, Richard. *The Character of the Poet: Wordsworth in "The Prelude."* Princeton: Princeton University Press, 1971.

Parlby, Mrs. Fanny Parks. *Wanderings of a Pilgrim, in Search of the Picturesque.* London: P. Richardson, 1850.

Paton, William. *Alexander Duff: Pioneer of Missionary Education.* New York: George H. Doran, n.d.

Paulson, Ronald. *Popular and Polite Art in the Age of Hogarth and Fielding.* Notre Dame: University of Notre Dame Press, 1979.

Pennington, Mary. *Some Account of Circumstances in the Life of Mary Pennington.* London: Harvey & Darton, 1821.

Peterson, Linda H. *Victorian Autobiography: The Tradition of Self-Interpretation.* New Haven: Yale University Press, 1986.

Piggin, Stuart. *Making Evangelical Missionaries, 1789–1858: The Social Background, Motives and Training of British Protestant Missionaries to India.* N.p.: Sutton Courtenay Press, 1984.

Pichanick, Valerie Kossew. *Harriet Martineau: The Woman and Her Work, 1802–76.* Ann Arbor: University of Michigan Press, 1980.

Pitman, E[mma] R[aymond]. *Lady Missionaries in Foreign Lands.* 2d ed. London: S. W. Partridge, n.d.

Pitman, Emma Raymond. *Missionary Heroines of Eastern Lands.* London: Pickering & Inglis, n.d.

Poovey, Mary. *Uneven Developments: The Ideological Work of Gender in Mid-Victorian England.* Chicago: University of Chicago Press, 1988.

Porter, Rose. *The Years That Are Told.* London: Ward, Lock, 1870.

Qualls, Barry V. *The Secular Pilgrims of Victorian Fiction: The Novel as Book of Life.* Cambridge: Cambridge University Press, 1982.

Rainwater, Catherine, and William J. Scheick. "Aliens in the Garden: The Re-vision of Mary Cholmondeley's *Red Pottage*." *Philological Quarterly* 71 (1992): 101–19.

Rathburn, Robert, and Martin Steinman, Jr., eds. *From Jane Austen to Joseph Conrad.* Minneapolis: University of Minnesota Press, 1958.

Raymond, Meredith B., and Mary Rose Sullivan, eds. *The Letters of Elizabeth Barrett Browning to Mary Russell Mitford*. Waco, Tex.: Armstrong Browning Library, 1983.

Riess, Daniel. "Laetitia Landon and the Dawn of English Post-Romanticism." *Studies in English Literature* 36 (1996): 807–27.

R[oberts], E[mma]. "Memoir of L.E.L." In *"The Zenana" and Minor Poems of L.E.L., with a Memoir by Emma Roberts*. 2 vols. London: Fisher, 1839.

Roberts, Emma. *Scenes and Characteristics of Hindostan*. London: Fisher, n.d.

Robinson, Mary. *Memoirs of the Late Mrs. Robinson, Written by Herself. From the Edition Edited by Her Daughter*. London: Hunt & Clarke, 1826.

———. *Memoirs of the Late Mrs. Robinson, Written by Herself. With Some Posthumous Pieces. Edited by her daughter, Miss Mary Elizabeth Robinson*. London: Wilks & Taylor for R. Phillips, 1801.

Rose, Mary Beth, ed. *Women in the Middle Ages and the Renaissance*. Syracuse: Syracuse University Press, 1986.

Rose, Phyllis. *Parallel Lives: Five Victorian Marriages*. New York: Knopf, 1983.

Ross, Marlon B. *The Contours of Masculine Desire: Romanticism and the Rise of Women's Poetry*. New York: Oxford University Press, 1989.

Rundle, Vivienne. "'The inscription of these volumes': The Prefatory Writings of Elizabeth Barrett Browning." *Victorian Poetry* 34 (1996): 247–78.

Ruoff, Gene, ed. *The Romantics and Us: Essays on Literature and Culture*. New Brunswick: Rutgers University Press, 1990.

Rutherford, Mark [William White Hale]. *Catharine Furze*. London: T. Fisher Unwin, 1893.

———. *Clara Hopgood*. London: T. Fisher Unwin, 1896.

Sanders, Valerie. "'Absolutely an act of duty': Choice of Profession by Victorian Women." *Prose Studies* 9 (1986): 54–70.

———. *The Private Lives of Victorian Women: Autobiography in Nineteenth-Century England*. London: Harvester Wheatsheaf, 1989.

Sargent, John. *Memoir of the Rev. Henry Martyn, B.D.* 4th American ed. Hartford: G. Goodwin, 1822.

Sattin, Anthony, ed. *An Englishwoman in India: The Memoirs of Harriet Tytler, 1828–1858*. Oxford: Oxford University Press, 1986.

Scott, Joan W., and Louise A. Tilly. "Women's Work and the Family in Nineteenth-Century Europe." *Comparative Studies in Society and History* 17 (1975): 36–64.

Scott, Patrick, and Pauline Fletcher, eds. *Culture and Education in Victorian England*. Lewisburg: Bucknell University Press, 1990.

Senior, F. Dorothy. *The Life and Times of Colley Cibber*. New York: Rae D. Henkle, 1925.

[Shand, A. Innes.] "In 'Maga's' Library." *Blackwood's Edinburgh Magazine* 156 (December 1894): 854–77.

Sherwood, Mary Martha. *The Works of Mrs. Sherwood*. New York: Harper, 1835.

Showalter, Elaine. *A Literature of Their Own: British Women Novelists from Bronte to Lessing*. Princeton: Princeton University Press, 1977.

———, ed. *Red Pottage*. By Mary Cholmondeley. London: Penguin-Virago, 1985.

Shumaker, Wayne C. *English Autobiography: Its Emergence, Materials, and Forms*. Berkeley: University of California Press, 1954.

Smith, Sidonie. *A Poetics of Women's Autobiography: Marginality and the Fictions of Self-Representation*. Bloomington: Indiana University Press, 1987.

Somerville, Mary. *Personal Recollections, from Early Life to Old Age, of Mary Somerville with Selections from Her Correspondence.* Ed. Martha Somerville. Boston: Roberts,1876.

Spacks, Patricia Meyer. *Imagining a Self: Autobiography and Novel in Eighteenth-Century England.* Cambridge: Harvard University Press, 1976.

Spivak, Gayatri Chakravorty. "Three Women's Texts and a Critique of Imperialism." *Critical Inquiry* 12 (1985): 243–61.

Staël-Holstein, Baroness. *Germany.* 2 vols. London: John Murray, 1813.

Stanley, Liz. *The Auto/biographical I: The Theory and Practice of Feminist Auto/biography.* Manchester: Manchester University Press, 1992.

Stanton, Domna C., ed. *The Female Autograph: Theory and Practice of Autobiography from the Tenth to the Twentieth Century.* Chicago: University of Chicago Press, 1987.

Steen, Marguerite. *The Lost One: A Biography of Mary (Perdita) Robinson.* London: Methuen, 1937.

Steinmetz, Virginia V. "Images of 'Mother-Want' in Elizabeth Barrett Browning's *Aurora Leigh.*" *Victorian Poetry* 21 (1983): 351–67.

Stoddard, Richard Henry, ed. *Letters of Elizabeth Barrett Browning, Addressed to Richard Hengist Horne.* New York: James Miller, 1877.

Stuart, Arabella W. *The Lives of Mrs. Ann H. Judson and Mrs. Sarah B. Judson with a Biographical Sketch of Mrs. Emily C. Judson.* Auburn: Derby & Miller, 1852.

Suleri, Sara. *The Rhetoric of English India.* Chicago: University of Chicago Press, 1992.

Sweet, Nanora. "The Bowl of Liberty: Felicia Hemans and the Romantic Imagination." Ph.D. diss., University of Michigan, 1993.

Swindells, Julia. *Victorian Writing and Working Women.* Minneapolis: University of Minnesota Press, 1985.

———, ed. *The Uses of Autobiography.* London: Taylor & Francis, 1995.

Thornton, Alice. *The Autobiography of Mrs. Alice Thornton of East Newton, Co. York.* Ed. Charles Jackson. London: Surtees Society, 1875.

[Tonna], Charlotte Elizabeth. *Mesmerism: A Letter to Miss Martineau.* Philadelphia: William S. Martien, 1847.

———. *Personal Recollections.* 4th ed. London: Seeleys, 1854.

Trapnel, Anna. *A Legacy for Saints; Being Several Experiences of the Dealings of God with Anna Trapnel, in and after Her Conversion.* London: T. Brewster, 1654.

Trollope, Anthony. *Anthony Trollope: An Illustrated Autobiography.* Ed. Joanna Trollope. London: Alan Sutton, 1987.

Tucker, Herbert F. "*Aurora Leigh:* Epic Solutions to Novel Ends." In *Famous Last Words: Changes in Gender and Narrative Closure,* ed. Alison Booth. Charlottesville: University Press of Virginia, 1993.

Vann, Richard T. *The Social Development of English Quakerism, 1655–1755.* Cambridge: Harvard University Press, 1969.

Vargish, Thomas. *The Providential Aesthetic in Victorian Fiction.* Charlottesville: University Press of Virginia, 1985.

Viswanathan, Gauri. *Masks of Conquest: Literary Study and British Rule in India.* New York: Columbia University Press, 1989.

Warwick, Mary, Countess. *Autobiography of Mary Countess of Warwick.* Ed. T. Crofton Croker. London: Percy Society, 1848.

White, Hayden. *The Historical Imagination in Nineteenth-Century Europe.* Baltimore: Johns Hopkins University Press, 1973.

Wilson, John, ed. *A Memoir of Mrs Margaret Wilson, of the Scottish Mission, Bombay, Including Extracts from Her Letters and Journals.* Edinburgh: John Johnstone, 1838.

Wise, Thomas James, and John Alexander Symington, eds. *The Brontës: Their Lives, Friendships and Correspondences.* Oxford: Shakespeare Head, 1933.

Woods, Leonard, ed. *Memoirs of Mrs. Harriet Newell.* 2d ed. London: Booth, 1816.

Wordsworth, William. *The Prelude, 1799, 1805, 1850.* Ed. Jonathan Wordsworth, M. H. Abrams, and Stephen Gill. New York: Norton, 1979.

Yates, Gayle Graham, ed. *Harriet Martineau on Women.* New Brunswick: Rutgers University Press, 1985.

Index

Index

Brodzki, Bella, 203 n. 1
Brontë, Anne, 191–92, 193–94
Brontë, Charlotte, 16, 26, 80–82,
    169, 187–88, 190, 200. Works:
    Jane Eyre, 28, 80–108, 216 nn. 5–
    13; *Shirley,* 194; *Villette,* 81. *See
    also* Gaskell, Elizabeth, *Life of
    Charlotte Brontë*
Brontë, Emily, 191–92, 193
Brontë, Patrick, 218 n. 30
Brougham, Lord (Henry Peter), 55,
    71, 212 n. 24
Broughton, Rhoda, 174, 182, 188,
    196, 232 n. 4, 233 n. 24, 234
    n. 43, 235 nn. 49, 51
Broughton, Trev Lynn, 203 n. 1,
    211 n. 10
Brown, Ford Madox, 142
Browning, Elizabeth Barrett, 109–
    10, 117, 223 n. 22, 224 n. 32, 226
    nn. 58–59. Works: *Aurora Leigh,*
    109–10, 120–45, 178–79; *The
    Battle of Marathon,* 136; *A Drama
    of Exile,* 136; *Prometheus Bound,*
    136
Browning, Robert, 235 n. 1
Brydges, Sir Edgerton, 24
Buckley, Jerome Hamilton, 204 n. 6
Bulwer-Lytton, Edward, 71, 122–23
Bunyan, John, 6, 105, 221 n. 68.
    Works: *Grace Abounding,* 204 n. 8,
    205 n. 13, 211 n. 5; *Pilgrim's Prog-
    ress,* 91, 107–8, 205 n. 13
Burnett, John, 87
Burns, James Dawson, *Autobiography
    of a Beggar Boy,* 87

Carlisle, Janice, x, 151
Carlyle, Jane, 168
Carpenter, Lant, 54–55, 65, 212
    n. 22
Castle, Terry, 210 n. 81
Cavendish, Margaret, Duchess of
    Newcastle, 3, 4, 16, 18, 23,
    24, 228 n. 13
Cellini, Benvenuto, 28, 150
Chapman, Maria Weston, 75, 79,
    213 n. 26

Charke, Charlotte, 28–29, 48, 209
    nn. 76, 78, 210 nn. 79–85; *A
    Narrative of the Life,* 34–42
Chatterjee, Sunil Kumar, 218 n. 29
Cherry, Deborah, 157
childhood and children, 10–11, 27,
    44–45, 57–59, 60–63, 65–66,
    84–86, 127–31, 146–49, 165–
    66, 168–69, 177, 190–91, 200–
    201
Chodorow, Nancy, 22, 205 n. 21,
    208 n. 56
Cholmondeley, Hester, 189–98, 234
    nn. 44–45
Cholmondeley, Mary, 199–200,
    201, 234 n. 27. Works: *Danvers
    Jewels,* 181–82, 233 n. 22; *Diana
    Tempest,* 181, 194; *Moth and Rust,*
    234 n. 34; *Prisoners Fast Bound,*
    195; *Red Pottage,* 170, 173–74,
    176–87; *Sir Charles Danvers,* 181;
    Under One Roof, 173–74, 187–98,
    199
Cholmondeley, Victoria, 181, 233
    n. 23
Chorley, Jane, 157
chroniques scandaleuses, ix, 4, 27–41,
    44, 47, 53, 116. *See also* profes-
    sional artist's memoir
Cibber, Colley, 28, 35, 40–41
Clarke, Norma, 117
Cobbe, Frances Power, 16, 26, 98
Cobbett, William, 68
Cockney School, 224 n. 32
Coghill, Annie, 146, 162–64, 227
    n. 2, 229 n. 20
Colby, Robert, 229 n. 17, 231 n. 52
Colby, Vineta, 176, 229 n. 17, 231
    n. 52, 232 nn. 5, 8
Coleridge, Samuel, 115, 129, 135,
    225 nn. 40, 54
Coleridge, Sara, *Memoir and Letters,*
    27, 149, 151, 169
Comte, Auguste, 59–60, 64–67,
    143; *Positive Philosophy,* 55, 64
Corbett, Mary Jean, 45, 47, 51, 55,
    147, 211 nn. 1, 11, 213 n. 27, 228
    n. 4

Victorian Literature and Culture Series